Contesting Tears

ALSO BY STANLEY CAVELL

Must We Mean What We Say? (1969; reprinted 1976)

The World Viewed (1971; enlarged edition 1979)

The Senses of Walden (1972; expanded edition 1981)

The Claim of Reason (1979)

Pursuits of Happiness (1981)

Themes Out of School (1984)

Disowning Knowledge (1987)

In Quest of the Ordinary (1988)

This New Yet Unapproachable America (1989)

Conditions Handsome and Unhandsome (1990)

A Pitch of Philosophy (1994)

Philosophical Passages (1995)

STANLEY
CAVELL

CONTESTING
TEARS The Hollywood Melodrama of the Unknown Woman

THE
UNIVERSITY
OF CHICAGO
PRESS

Chicago
and
London

Stanley Cavell is the Walter M. Cabot Professor of Aesthetics and the General Theory of Value at Harvard University. He was awarded a MacArthur Fellowship in 1992.

Chapters 1, 2, 3, and 4 appeared earlier as shown below:

Chapter 1 is from *Languages of the Unsayable,* by Sanford Budick and Wolfgang Isler. Copyright © 1989 by Columbia University Press. Reprinted with permission of the publisher.

Chapter 2 is from Stanley Cavell, "Psychoanalysis and Drama," from Joseph Smith and William Kerrigan, eds., *Images in Our Souls.* © 1987. Reprinted by permission of The John Hopkins University Press.

Chapters 3 and 4 appeared in *Critical Inquiry* 16, no. 2 (Winter 1990). © 1990 by The University of Chicago. All rights reserved.

The cover photo and photos in Chapter 3 are from the film *Now, Voyager.* © 1942 Turner Entertainment Co. All rights reserved.

The University of Chicago Press, Chicago 60637
The University of Chicago Press, Ltd., London
© 1996 by The University of Chicago
All rights reserved. Published 1996
Printed in the United States of America
05 04 03 02 01 00 99 98 97 96   1 2 3 4 5
ISBN: 0-226-09814-1 (cloth)
        0-226-09816-8 (paper)

Library of Congress Cataloging-in-Publication Data

Cavell, Stanley, 1926–
    Contesting tears : the Hollywood melodrama of the unknown
    woman / Stanley Cavell.
        p.   cm.
    Filmography: p.
    Includes bibliographical references and index.
    1. Motion pictures for women.   2. Women in motion pictures.
    3. Melodrama in motion pictures.   4. Marriage in motion pictures.
    I. Title.
    PN1995.9.W6C38   1996
    791.43'652042—dc20   96-23834
                                                              CIP

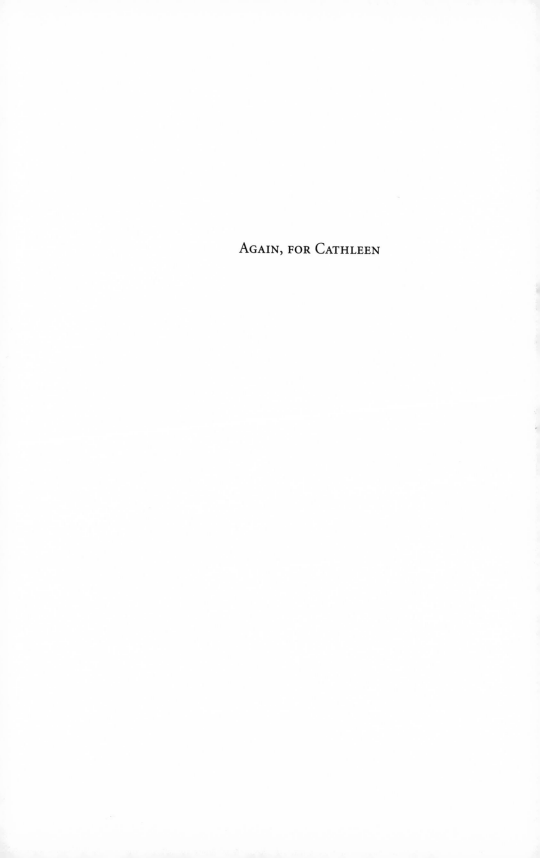

AGAIN, FOR CATHLEEN

To my way of thinking the creation of film

was as if meant for philosophy—meant to reorient

everything philosophy has said about reality and its representa-

tion, about art and imitation, about greatness

and conventionality, about judgment and pleasure,

about skepticism and transcendence, about

language and expression.

Contents

A Note on the Captions

In Chapter 3 and in the frontispiece to Chapter 4, italic captions accompanying the frame-enlargements represent dialogue from *Now, Voyager*. Otherwise, captions are in roman typeface and are sentences repeated from the respective chapters in which the illustrated moments are discussed.

Preface

The material that goes into the study of what I call the Hollywood melodrama of the unknown woman was first sketched through in a course on the aesthetics of film offered under the auspices of General Education at Harvard in the spring of 1984. The earliest public occasion on which I began presenting selections and expansions of the material was in November 1984, at a conference in New York sponsored by the Columbia Psychoanalytic Center, where under the title "Two Cheers for Romance" I broached some thoughts about *Now, Voyager*. The following October I used readings of certain sequences from *Letter from an Unknown Woman* to frame my Edith Weigert Lecture, sponsored by the Forum on Psychiatry and the Humanities at the Washington School of Psychiatry. In the spring of 1986, in Jerusalem, I gave what I still like to call a reading (a term I use in part to suggest that the next time I speak about the subject it will probably go differently) of *Gaslight*. Why I came to feel, after finding occasion a few years later to take further my thoughts about *Stella Dallas*, that I had thereupon gathered sufficient evidence to make a book that argues the case for proposing the genre of melodrama in question, it is a task of the ensuing Introduction to test and account for.

This way of accounting for the passage of time leading to the present publication is meant to emphasize primarily two features of its writing: (1) My dependence on responding to what I call "occasions" for speaking about film, and films, is in part a function of my not being a professional film scholar, so not teaching regularly or systematically courses in the study of film, even though the present publication brings the quantity of my writing about film to three and a half books—including *The World Viewed* (1971), *Pursuits of Happiness* (1981), and about half of the essays (including one on television) in *Themes out of School* (1984). (2) My thinking about film has throughout the quarter of a century in which I have been publishing about it been bound up with my thinking about most of whatever else I have been thinking about in what may be called philosophy or literature—unpredictably inspired by such things and inspiring them. So I sometimes see the trio of books *Must We Mean What We Say?* (1969), *The World Viewed* (1971), and *The Senses of Walden* (1972) as the threefold beginning of my work over the past four decades; and I sometimes see the issuing of *Pursuits of Happiness* as an expression of the relief in completing the study of skepticism and tragedy in *The Claim of Reason* (1979); etc.

Such work necessarily contests disciplinary boundaries, sometimes by behaving as if they did not exist, sometimes by asking undivided attention to them. This has, I believe, helped somewhat to stall the hearing I have hoped the work would find. But winds of change change, and I am now, happily, less often queried in terms that wonder why a philosopher is interested in film. That has been a particularly puzzling question for me, since to my way of thinking the creation of film was as if meant for philosophy— meant to reorient everything philosophy has said about reality and its representation, about art and imitation, about greatness and conventionality, about judgment and pleasure, about skepticism and transcendence, about language and expression.

While of course I have, where I could, cited in my text pertinent specific indebtedness to the writings of others, I am too aware of gifts that go beyond these notations to forgo the pleasure of recording, or rerecording, the importance of years of inspiring exchanges that go into this work. There are virtually from the beginning the conversations about film and philosophy with William Rothman, joined in later by Marian Keane, in and out of courses on film we worked on together at Harvard in the late 1970s and early 1980s. Nickolas Pappas and Charles Warren were, with Marian Keane, the Teaching Fellows for the General Education course I mentioned earlier, and their comments, at our weekly staff meetings, on my lectures and on the students' grasp of the material generally, characteristically entered into my subsequent preparations. And there are the memorable conversations, in and around those courses, or concerned with drafts of essays of mine that were as often as not caused by those courses, with Steven Affeldt, Norton Batkin, Nancy Bauer, James Conant, Arnold Davidson,

Timothy Gould, and Karen Hanson. From the first, and for me
formative, seminar I offered on film melodrama, in 1985, I
remember incorporating responses to comments from Nancy Bauer,
Gus Blaisdell, and Inez Hedges. Among the discussions after
various presentations of the melodramas at the Boston Museum
of Fine Arts, at Rutgers University, at the University of California
at San Diego, at the University of New Mexico, at Scripps College,
and at the University of Chicago, I know I profited from questions
posed by Ellen Draper, Miriam Hansen, Hélène Keyssar, Ira Jaffe,
Michael Roth, and the late Gerald Mast. Other decisive moments
developed in discussions about film and philosophy at the École
Normale in Paris in 1985, notably with Claude Imbert and Sandra
Laugier; and with Sanford Budick during the editing of the piece
on *Gaslight* for its original publication. The notable difference in
tone of the "Postscript" (Chapter 4 in what follows) from the other
chapters is evidently some function of the improvisatory, pressing
moment in which it was composed, a tone I rather cultivated, or
anyway encouraged in myself, as an acknowledgment of my participation in the anxieties that that text depicts. The possibility of the
improvisation, I mean its immediate background of ideas and soci-
ality, is importantly constituted by counterpoints of thoughts on
the distinctions, and collapses or conversions of the distinctions,
between activity and passivity and between saying and showing
(and seeing) as represented within and among the following
recently (then) published texts, cited in the Bibliography: James
Conant's "Must We Show What We Cannot Say?"; Arnold I. Davidson's "How to Do the History of Psychoanalysis: A Reading of
Freud's *Three Essays on the Theory of Sexuality*" and "Sex and the
Emergence of Sexuality"; Timothy Gould's "Where the Action Is:
Stanley Cavell and the Skeptic's Activity"; and Karen Hanson's
"Being Doubted, Being Assured."

Grateful acknowledgment is due the editors and publishers of
the four essays that have previously appeared in print, as cited in
the Bibliography. They are here edited mostly to regularize format
and to remove as far as feasible the repetitions that are artifacts of
the publication of installments from a continuing project. The
major change was to shift what originally appeared as the introductory paragraphs to the reading of *Gaslight* (Chapter 1) into the
Introduction to the book as a whole, which meant that that reading
seemed most naturally, though out of the chronological order in

which it was written, to fit as the initiating chapter of the sequence
of chapters, after the Introduction, on individual films.

The earliest of the chapters to achieve its present form, that on
Letter from an Unknown Woman, which appears here as Chapter 2,
was in any case not suitable for that initiating role, both because
the texture of its attention to film's resonance with psychoanalysis
is, with the exception of passages in the *Postscript,* rarely main-
tained explicitly in those remaining discussions; and because, on
rereading it for inclusion here, I realized afresh how selective my
discussion of that film had been in composing that text, I mean how
deliberately I had used it for my own purposes—in first intro-
ducing the genre of the unknown woman beyond the classroom,
and on an occasion sponsored by a school of psychiatry for its
lecture/book series in the Humanities—to note the uncanny
origins, at the turn of the nineteenth century into the twentieth, of
both the work of the field of psychoanalysis and the work of the
art of film in the sufferings of and the threats to women. I am
indebted to the editor of that series, Joseph H. Smith, for the invitation to deliver the Weigert Lecture, for his comments on my text,
and for his assembling of the fine group of psychiatrists and
philosophers who gathered for a discussion of my lecture the day
after it was delivered in Washington, many of whom would
contribute to the resultant volume *Images in Our Souls: Cavell,
Psychoanalysis, and Cinema,* edited by Joseph Smith and William
Kerrigan.

The next installment to take its present form, on *Gaslight,* was
prepared for a workshop on literature and philosophy held at the
Center for Advanced Studies at Hebrew University, organized by
Sanford Budick. Its proceedings, under the title *Languages of the
Unsayable,* was edited by Budick and Wolfgang Isler. It was not until
the summer of 1989, in conversation with Arnold Davidson, the
executive editor of *Critical Inquiry,* that I prepared my material on
Now, Voyager together with its companion *Postscript* for their
appearance together in that journal. The forbearance and efficiency
of its managing editor, James W. Williams, was indispensable in
bringing that to pass. From that time I knew that I wanted the
melodrama installments to exist together in one place, but the
remaining pieces took their time coming. In 1991 a version of
the *Stella Dallas* text was made available from the Cultural Studies

Project at MIT, the sponsor of one of the occasions on which a selection from that text was read.

I had at various moments contemplated the possibility of in cluding a substantial discussion of some related mode of film melodrama to further situate the place of the melodrama of the unknown woman within the constellation of film's genres of melo- drama. (In my Introduction I at least mention a genre in which, as in that of the unknown woman melodrama, marriage is shunned, but where, unlike the unknown woman melodrama, the shunning is accomplished by accident, misfortune, rather than by choice.) This possibility was, as a serious structural component, not completely ruled out until I spent several days at a conference at Warwick University in the early spring of 1992, with, among others, V. F. Perkins. Reading Perkins's elegant study of the Linz sequence from *Letter from an Unknown Woman* a decade ago (having earlier read his book *Film as Film*)—a sequence that does not come up in my discussion—confirmed my sense, in viewing and thinking about the film, of its depth and meticulousness. And these more recent conversations with him forcefully reminded and educated me about how much significant work had been done, by him and by others associated with the journal *Movie,* on that film and on film melodrama generally. Also present for some of those conversa- tions was Perkins's colleague Edward Gallafent, whose marvelous book on Clint Eastwood, as director and actor, appeared last year from Studio Vista, London. To achieve a serious weight of compar- ison with a related genre of film melodrama then presented itself, realistically, as a project on its own, and one probably not best meant for me.

The Introduction was distinctly improved by comments from Nancy Bauer, James Conant, and Alice Crary. But I have to accept the fact that a certain turgidness in those pages can not radically be reduced. Sometimes inspiration takes a form that further inspira- tion can neither refuse nor altogether refine.

The task of preparing the manuscript for publication (not just the labor of cutting and pasting the published essays and assem- bling them with the new, enclosing chapters, but the work of helping to smooth the required transitions and then of giving a final reading and editing to the whole) was efficiently and gracefully accomplished by Steven Affeldt, who also undertook the making of the Bibliography and the Filmography. The frame enlargements in Chapters 3 and 4 were commissioned by *Critical Inquiry* for the original publication of those texts, and are used here by arrangement with the editors of that journal. The remaining frame enlargements were prepared by, and chosen in consultation with, Marian Keane.

Brookline, Massachusetts
September 1, 1995

Contesting Tears

It is in the figure of Garbo that the idea of the
women's unknownness most purely takes on its aspects of the
desire of a man for a woman's knowledge, as if to know what she
knows may be taken as the answer to the question what a man
after all wants of a woman—and does not want after all.

Introduction

I claim that the four films principally considered in the following chapters define a genre of film, taking the claim to mean, most generally, that they recount interacting versions of a story, a story or myth, that seems to present itself as a woman's search for a story, or of the right to tell her story. In certain ways what I have to say adjoins the manifold projects now in the intellectual arena for discovering a feminine difference of subjectivity; in certain ways it takes on what in my work I conceive of as the call for philosophy, the right to its arrogation. It is a continuous issue for me on both of these ways to understand my right to intervene in them.

I call the genre the melodrama of the unknown woman, after its perhaps most illustrious member, Max Ophuls's *Letter from an Unknown Woman* (1948, with Joan Fontaine and Louis Jourdan); the other members featured here are *Gaslight* (directed by George Cukor, 1944, with Ingrid Bergman and Charles Boyer), *Now, Voyager* (Irving Rapper, 1942, with Bette Davis, Paul Henreid, and Claude Rains), and *Stella Dallas* (King Vidor, 1937, with Barbara Stanwyck and John Boles). The specific systematic connections of these films with one another are, I realize, at first hardly discernible; the impression they make, asked to be taken together, is apt to be one of arbitrariness. An important pattern within their mutual connections is given in their relation as a group to another genre of film I have studied and, in the light of the new genre of melodrama, continue also to study, to which I devoted the book called *Pursuits of Happiness*, a genre I name there the comedy of remarriage. The films I take as defining for remarriage comedy, a group of films also from the Hollywood of the 1930s and 1940s, are *It Happened One Night* (1934), *The Awful Truth* (1937), *Bringing Up*

Baby (1938), *His Girl Friday* (1940), *The Philadelphia Story* (1940), *The Lady Eve* (1941), and *Adam's Rib* (1949). Systematic connections among these comedies are much easier to see or to give credit to when they are formulated, for various reasons. They are individually more famous, or anyway more beloved (though I keep learning more about the fame of *Now, Voyager,* and almost everyone of a certain age remembers certain events from *Gaslight* and from *Stella Dallas*); and they share their particular directors and their characteristic stars (Katharine Hepburn, Irene Dunne, Cary Grant, Spencer Tracy, Barbara Stanwyck). Not the least interest, by the way, of *Gaslight* in particular, is that Cukor is also the director of two of the seven central remarriage comedies, *The Philadelphia Story* and *Adam's Rib.*

Remarriage comedies begin or climax with the threatened end of a marriage, that is to say, with the threat of divorce; the drive of the narrative is to get the original pair together *again*, whereas classical comedies—at least, so-called New Comedies—concern the overcoming of obstacles to a young pair's desire to be together in the first place and in a condition called marriage. The obvious obstacle to marriage in classical comedy is the woman's father (or some senex figure, some older man), who is prepared to bring down the sternness of the law upon his daughter if she goes against his wishes, whereas in remarriage comedy, if the woman's father is present he is always on the side of his daughter's desire. Moreover, in remarriage comedy the woman's mother is never present (with illuminating exceptions that prove the rule), and the woman of the principal pair is never herself shown to be a mother and is approaching an age at which the choice of motherhood will be forced upon her or forced away from her. A constellation of what may be called further "features" are consequences or causes of these circumstances, and a number will be alluded to here. I emphasize at the outset that in both remarriage comedy and its companion melodrama of the unknown woman, new circumstances or clauses of some continuing story are not limitable in advance of critical analysis (for example, it turns out that the woman's body is emphasized in some way in each of the comedies); and since the circumstances are not well thought of as common features (for example, most, but not all, open in a city and then significantly move to a place in the country, analogous to the Shakespearean so-called green world or golden world), it is critically essential to, so to speak, account for an absence in a particular instance, a process I call articulating a compensating circumstance (for example, *His Girl Friday* lacks a green world, but it contains, with equal definitiveness, what I describe as a black world). So it is part of the idea of a genre I am working with that both the specific relevant "features" of the genre and the general candidacy of an individual film for membership in the genre are radically open-ended.

Pervading each moment of the texture and mood of remarriage comedy is the mode of *conversation* that binds or sweeps together the principal pair. I suppose that this is the feature that comes in for the greatest conceptual development in *Pursuits of Happiness*. Conversation is given a beautiful theory in John Milton's revolutionary tract to justify divorce, making the willingness for conversation (for "a meet and happy conversation") the basis of marriage, even making conversation what I might call the *fact* of marriage; and conversation in these remarriage films is concerned with what religion, in the Book of Genesis, takes as what we might call its myth of marriage, namely the creation of the woman from the man—the story of Adam's rib. In these comedies the creation of the woman—the new creation of the woman, the creation of the new woman, the new creation of the human—takes the form of the woman's education by the man; hence a critical clause in the story these films tell and retell is the discerning of what it is about this man that fits him to be chosen by this woman to provide that authorization of her, of let us say her desire. This suggests a privileging of the male still within this atmosphere of equality. The genre scrutinizes this in the ways, even in this atmosphere, the male is declared, at his best, to retain a taint of villainy. This so to speak prepares the genre for its inner relation to melodrama. And if the melodrama of the unknown woman is "derived" from the genre of the comedy of remarriage, the pervasive feature of equal conversation must have its pervasive equivalent in the melodramas.

The mechanism of "derivation" is what I think of as the negation of the features of the comedies by the melodramas. For example, in the melodrama of unknownness the woman's father, or another older man (it may be her husband), is not on the side of her desire but on the side of law, and her mother is always present (or her search for or loss of or competition with a mother is always present), and she is always shown as a mother (or her relation to a child is explicit). With these differences in the presence and absence of parents and children goes a difference in the role of the past and of memory: in the comedies the past is open, shared, a recurring topic of fun, no doubt somewhat ambiguous; but in melodramas the past is frozen, mysterious, with topics forbidden and isolating. Again, whereas in remarriage comedy the action of the narration moves, as said, from a setting in a big city to conclude in a place outside the city, a place of perspective, in melodramas of unknownness the action returns to and concludes in the place from which it began or in which it has climaxed, a place of abandonment or transcendence.

The chief negation of these comedies by these melodramas is the negation of marriage itself—marriage in them is not necessarily reconceived and therewith provisionally affirmed, as in remarriage comedy, but rather marriage as a route to creation, to a new or an original integrity, is transcended and perhaps reconceived. (It is, I think, the idea of a negation of marriage taking the form of a negation of conversation that produced my title for the discussion of *Gaslight* "Naughty Orators," echoing *All's Well That Ends Well* [5.3.253]. This pair of Shakespeare's words invokes one of the Shakespearean puns in the region of the nothing, that between "naught" and "naughty," and arises as a character is explicitly remarking yet another turn in the Shakespearean problematic of marriage; and in *Gaslight* Paula will say, in reaction to the detective telling her that her "husband" already has a wife, "Then from the beginning there was nothing.") The route to this alternative integrity is still creation, or what I might call metamorphosis—some radical, astonishing, one may say melodramatic change of the woman, say of her identity. But this change must take place outside the process of a mode of conversation with a man (of course, since such a conversation would constitute marriage). It is as if the women of the melodramas are saying to their sisters in the comedies (they are sisters because both lines of women, as I argue elsewhere, descend from identifiable heroines in Shakespeare and in Ibsen): "You may call yourselves lucky to have found a man with whom you can overcome the humiliation of marriage by marriage itself. For us, with our talents and tastes, there is no further or happy education to be found there; our integrity and metamorphosis happens elsewhere, in the abandoning of that *shared* wit and intelligence and exclusive appreciation." This elsewhere is a function of something within the melodrama genre that I will call the world of women.

That there should be this alternative route to integrity and possibility is hardly surprising, since it is the one taken in characteristic films of the women who represent the highest reaches of glamourous independence registered in the idea of a star—classically, the figures of Greta Garbo and of Marlene Dietrich, that of Bette Davis at her best, and I suppose those of Barbara Stanwyck and of Ingrid Bergman. The persistence of this feature of metamorphosis indicates the cause of these genres as among the great subjects of the medium of film, since a great property of the medium is its violent transfiguration of creatures of flesh and blood, its recreation of them, let us say, in projecting and screening them.

The films represented in the melodrama of the unknown woman are among those films known to our culture, from the time of their making until the present, as "women's films" or "tearjerkers." And even in recent years, when they are receiving more attention, particularly from feminist theorists of film, they are characteristically, as far as I have seen, treated as works to be somewhat condescended to, specifically as ones that do not know their effect, the desire that is in them, and do not possess the means for theorizing this desire, as it were, for entering into the conversation over themselves. I can believe that this is true of many, even most, of the films Hollywood dubbed and merchandized as "woman's films" and that have designs upon our tears. My experience of the films in view in what follows here disputes any such condescension, and I regard them as full companions of the remarriage comedies from which I take them to derive, hence among the high achievements of the art of film—worthy companions in intelligence, in seriousness of artistic purpose, in moral imagination, and even in a sense in wit. They are of course less ingratiating than those comedies; but then so much of film, and so much in the rest of culture, is less ingratiating. But films like *Gaslight* and *Stella Dallas* are so often the reverse of ingratiating that it becomes painful to go on studying them. A compensating profit of instruction must be high for the experience to be justified.

This issue of condescension figures among the charges brought against my work in film a few years ago by Tania Modleski, in a letter written to the editors of *Critical Inquiry;* a sequel of charges by her will be addressed in section 4 of this Introduction. Here I pause to note a related divergence between other of my views and related views still reigning, I believe, in academically established film studies. Despite my repeated references to the idea of a genre, which bespeaks communal relations of law, contract, expectation, social determination, etc., I also refer repeatedly to the films as bearing the signature of certain individual directors. To some these will seem contradictory emphases; to me they reflect the specific economy of outer and inner, or of convention and intention, or of tradition and invention, that locates films within the constellation of works of the great arts. Perhaps a paragraph of explanation will serve to deflect needless conflict here, or to postpone needed exploration.

My use of expressions such as "Cukor is paying homage here . . ." or "Ophuls's camera, as one expects of him, searches . . ." may seem suspicious, quite as though I believed that film directors exercise as much control over the obviously communal work associated with their names as authors or painters do over their obviously individual works; and that I believed, what's more, that the control over even individually made texts is greater than an advanced intellect should allow itself to express. What I think is that the arts differ, that directors of film differ, and differ in the amount of control they intend to exercise; that intention and control remain seriously underanalyzed concepts in these contexts; that my allusions to a director's intention leave its exercise wide open to investigation—he or she may have a hand in setting up each camera angle, editing each sentence, sewing each costume, baking each frame of nonshatter glass for windows it is safe to jump through, play most of the parts, and develop each print; or he or she might extensively delegate some or all of these matters, and other people, aware of this possibility, might prepare themselves specifically to take over one or another task for a price; or the director may dispense with one or another such task or element, like costumes, or scripts, or actions that require jumping through windows, and subject remaining tasks to communal settlement; or there may be a committee or a bank that tells the director pretty much what to do in each dimension, and certain directors may refuse to have their names appear on such works, preferring to make nonshatter glass exclusively. As long as a reference to a director by name suggests differences between the films associated with that name and ones associated with other such names, the reference is, so far as I can see, intellectually grounded. It may be intellectually thin in a given instance. But that is more or less pitiable, not a matter for metaphysical alarm. And how about names associated with writers, actors, cinematographers, designers, studios? The intellectual warrant remains in each case the power in a given instance to show a difference. I wish I knew enough to invoke them all. (And the names of those in just which office are ultimately more important than those of which others? Is an answer to this question required before beginning to think about film? What is film? What is a film?)

I do not know whether it will help or hurt my case for the melodramas under consideration here as worthy companions of the best of the Hollywood comedies of the sound era as I go on to describe both the comedies and the melodramas as working out the problematic of self-reliance and conformity, or of hope and despair, as established in the founding American thinking of Emerson and of Thoreau. The comedies envision a relation of equality between human beings that we may characterize, using favorite terms of Emerson's, as a relation of rightful attraction, of expressiveness, and of joy. These are terms Emerson attributes to the work of poetry (in the essay "The Poet"), work which, moreover, he generally understands as that of metamorphosis. The relation as between human beings is not, in the comedies, perceived as one that pervades society as it stands, but it is shown to hold between a pair who are somehow exemplary of the possibilities of this society perceivable from its current stance. The melodramas envision the phase of the problematic of self-reliance that demands this expressiveness and joy first in relation to oneself. It is a claim of mine that in his essay "Self-Reliance" Emerson explicitly (but somehow unnoticeably) affiliates his guiding idea with the self-consciousness demanded in Descartes's famous *cogito ergo sum* (I think therefore I am), his pivotal answer to skepticism, to philosophical doubt concerning the existence of the world and of oneself and others in it—the thing philosophers learned to call hyperbolic doubt: I might call it doubt to excess, to the point of melodrama. Emerson's work thus undertakes nothing less in its proposal of self-reliance than a succeeding proof of human existence, as well as a demonstration of his right to offer such a proof, namely through his inheriting of philosophy—in this instance of Descartes's *Meditations*—for America.

Why the comedies and melodramas that engage this problematic of American transcendentalism's participation in skepticism concern the achievement or the transcendence of marriage—I mean why from a philosophical, call it even a metaphysical, point of view marriage is their theme—I will merely now suggest by quoting a sentence from near the end of an essay of mine of a few years ago, "Being Odd, Getting Even," that somewhat works out both Emerson's and Poe's inheritances of Descartes's philosophizing, and goes on to relate their achievement in this regard to the criticism of Cartesian skepticism developed in so-called ordinary language philosophy, particularly in Wittgenstein's *Philosophical Investigations* (a criticism whose originality is essential to the later Wittgenstein's philosophical originality as such):

> If some image of human intimacy, call it marriage, or domestication, is [or has become available as] the fictional equivalent of what the philosophers of ordinary language understand as the ordinary, call this the image of the everyday as the domestic, then it stands to reason that the threat to the ordinary that philosophy names skepticism should show up in fictions's favorite threats to forms of marriage, namely in forms of melodrama and of tragedy.

That essay links the link between Descartes's cogito proof and the proof through melodrama to an imagination of a cultural moment, in forms of romantic writing, at which the theatricalization of the self becomes the main proof of its freedom and its existence. The idea is taken further in Chapters 1 and 2, as they join together the discovery of psychoanalysis in thinking about hysteria in women (the power of insight within the power of suffering) with the invention of film and its discovery of the difference of women that film lives on.

The trial of such claims lies nowhere apart from the experience of individual films. Whose experience? Expressed how? To whom?

2

Among friends the taking of pleasure is an offer of pleasure, and the showing of pleasure at pleasure offered is the giving of pleasure. My book *Pursuits of Happiness* can be taken to pose the question whether the pair of a romantic marriage—whose ambitions of intimacy are apt, outside Eden, to trail a history of pain, of misunderstanding, and, despite the mutual respect in friendship, sometimes villainous antagonism—can become and stay friends.

That book studies a set of films whose answer is a conditional Yes. To name the genre "the comedy of remarriage" is to say that the complex of conditions it elaborates can be summarized as the willingness for remarriage. In the set of melodramas studied in the present book, the woman's answer to that possibility of friendship is an unreserved No. Since it follows for her that she thereby says No to marriage as such, as presently conceived (unless it is essentially for the benefit, or under the aegis, of a child under her protection), it follows further that these melodramas bear an internal relation to remarriage comedy.

The internality has to do with the principal women of both genres sharing an image of their lives—demanding, if it is to be shared, equality, mutual education, transfiguration, playfulness, etc.—which I find in the perspective I call Emersonian perfectionism (the topic of a recent book of mine, *Conditions Handsome and Unhandsome*). In neither instance is a marriage of irritation, silent condescension, and questionlessness found more desirable than solitude or, say, unknownness.

Each of the chapters here proposes various relations of the genre of melodrama in question with the genre of comedy in *Pursuits of Happiness,* notably articulating ways in which, as said, a feature defining the comedies is negated in the symbol-crammed melodramas. Since there is no single expected way in which to count the deviations, or provide the derivations, of the melodramas from the comedies, I let the separate chapters to follow speak for themselves on the subject, which sometimes causes more near-repetition than a straightforward account might tolerate. A perfect negation of remarriage comedy's basis in friendship is Nora's refusal, in Ibsen's *A Doll's House,* to stay one further night under the same roof with a man to whom she is not just legally bound but, despite all, remains attracted to, but from whom she shrinks from any longer receiving pleasure.

Since writing *Pursuits of Happiness* provided me with grateful bouts of pleasure—allowed me to think of it as a lucky book to write—and since part of the pleasure was the impulse to share it, it was naive of me, indeed inconsistent, not to recognize that the iron condition of this resounding pleasure is the luck of finding friendliness (some transferral of it) in the reader, apart from which the writing's proposed pleasure must be, and ought to be, shrunk from. While the respect necessary for friendship is no assurance of

alert and uninterrupted good feeling, it implies a recognition that
expressions even of villainous antagonism are not to violate certain
distinctions, say between a word and a deed, or, in terms from
Adam's Rib, between a real and a licorice pistol, or between a slap
and a slug. Has some token of this recognition become too much
to ask of strangers? Am I not in effect claiming that the price of
certain writing is a demand for friendship (if abstract) before it is
earned?—like asking for belief before establishing understanding.
But something of the sort was always true of the contract in the
serious reading of texts other than those of science (where terms
of understanding are clear, or clarifiable, in advance of a given text),
or of polemics (where interests are in general quite clear and
opposed in advance), or of religion (where you may even be asked
to believe *because* you do not understand).

It is a task of Emersonian perfectionism to provide a further
answer to the question, Why attend to a philosophical text? Its
answer has to do with its claim to deal in rejected thoughts, ones
not new but strange because all too familiar. While I of course
cannot claim this standing for my own text, I do claim something
analogous for the work of the films I discuss, whose principals are
holding out, or standing, for a world in which solitude is well lost—
knowing that the good city is not to be entered alone, that its
promise has to be accepted in person, from another already there,
but somehow there because you have presented yourself there.

A certain choice of solitude (figured in a refusal of marriage) as
the recognition that the terms of one's intelligibility are not welcome
to others—at least not as the basis for romantic investment in any
present other whom those terms nominate as eligible—is, as suggested, what the idea of unknownness comes to in my use of the
subtitle *The Hollywood Melodrama of the Unknown Woman*.
Nothing beyond this is settled about the specifics of what goes
unknown apart from the investigation of the lives figured in the
details of the films in question. Since I will in the progress of this
Introduction go on to track certain issues of knowledge that are left
mostly implicit in what I have so far written about the melodramas,
as indeed they were often left in *Pursuits of Happiness*, I should
note the objection made to me that four films seems a small
number on which to base a claim to the existence of a significant
genre of melodrama, as seven films seemed small in the case of the
defining films of remarriage comedy. My answer is roughly four-

fold: (1) that I am interested in developing the idea of a genre as well as in defining the specific genres in question (it is the idea of genre-as-medium, as opposed to the more familiar idea of genre-as-cycle—a distinction broached in my essay "The Fact of Television," which takes genre-as-cycle to characterize, for example, television series, where episodes are instances of a given set of characters and setting, and takes genre-as-medium, in contrast, to characterize groups of works in which members contest one another for membership, hence for the power to define the genre); (2) that the fruitfulness of articulating the genre of remarriage comedy lies in the specificity and the quality of the genre, the conceptual detail of what I claim is the best group of films among the comedies of the opening period of Hollywood talkies, not anything and everything that anyone may call, for example, Screwball Comedy; (3) that the theoretical richness is verified in the distinctness this genre gives to the related specific set of melodramas, hence potentially to further definable sets of related melodramas as well as related comedies; (4) that the idea of unknownness in the melodramas, matching the continuing demand of the woman in remarriage comedy to be known, reads back, or forward, into the various moments in which I have gone into the meeting of skepticism and tragedy at the point, or drive, of an avoidance of—terror of, disappointment with—acknowledgment; so that, again, a sense of the smallness of the number of related texts rather recedes, to my way of thinking, in the face of the number of related texts by which, and by the specificity in which, they are implied.

The melodrama of the unknown women presses the question of a woman's interest in knowledge that in the remarriage comedies is elaborated in a thematics of her demand for an education. The comedies hence raise the drama in her choice of a man to provide this education, a drama whose happiness turns on the condition that the man reciprocally craves the knowledge of (that is, by) this woman and in such a manner that the struggle between the sexes can play itself out without interruption (for example, by children, or by economic need), on the sublime level of difference mutually desired and comically overcome. In the melodramas the education of the woman is still at issue, but within their mood of heavy irony, since her (superior, exterior) knowledge becomes the object—as prize or as victim—of the man's fantasy, who seeks to share its secrets *(Now, Voyager)*, to be ratified by it *(Letter from an Unknown Woman)*, to escape it *(Stella Dallas)*, or to destroy it *(Gaslight)*, where each objective is (generically) reflected in the others. I am confident that it is because of my immersion in these structures that an avenue opened for me to think through Macbeth's murderous questioning of his wife's knowledge of herself (a way of putting the subject of my "Macbeth Appalled").

To extend a little further here the interaction of the two genres, I begin by noting a puzzling feature of three films I have not discussed in what follows but which I have variously announced there, or predicted, as members of the genre of the unknown woman: the von Sternberg-Marlene Dietrich *Blonde Venus* (1932), the James Whale-Irene Dunne-Paul Robeson *Show Boat* (1936), and the Mervyn Leroy-Ronald Colman-Greer Garson *Random Harvest* (1942) all bear a remarriage theme. I call this feature puzzling because it suggests not a participation in but rather a negation of the unknown woman genre, according to which marriage as such, as it stands, is repudiated as villanous, or prohibited, or irrelevant to the woman's desire. I treat this repudiation, after all, as perhaps the essential connection between the unknown woman melodramas and the remarriage comedies from which they derive. A point of discussion might then be to ask how this little subgenre of remarriage melodrama might be compensating for its, as it were, happy ending (negating the negation in the melodramas). This may indicate a way to understand its underscoring of the ineffectuality and irrelevance of the male (in *Blonde Venus* and *Show Boat*); or (in *Random Harvest*) leaving it unknown whether the man can live with his recovered memory that the woman who has been resourceful nurse to him, then faithful secretary, then brilliant hostess for him, is one and the same woman, the one with whom he had once bestirred himself to have a child; and unknown what precisely this woman was waiting for in awaiting this memory.

And what of this subgenre's apparent neglect of the fundamental feature of the films discussed in the following chapters that I formulate as the woman's search for the mother? This neglect is perhaps none too sure. In *Now, Voyager*, Charlotte Vale (Bette Davis) discovers, in her "idiosyncrasy," the mother in herself, having in a sense had no mother but instead a double father. In *Show Boat*, Magnolia (Irene Dunne) discovers her mother, or her kind (her biological mother represents little more than the upholder of law, or convention, before her permissive husband), in the "negress" Julie, played by the most famous (white) torch singer of the time, Helen Morgan. Magnolia is shown playing the olio in a black-face, song-and-dance called "Galavantin' Around," having joined the acting company to replace the hunted Julie; and when she is abandoned by her husband and applies for a job singing on her own it turns out to be a job currently held by that same, still haunted Julie. When asked what kind of songs she sings Magnolia replies, "Negro songs," and then auditions with "Can't Help Lovin' That Man of Mine." Julie hears the audition from her dressing room and leaves surreptitiously to make room for Magnolia. The double replacement of Julie by Magnolia is decisive for the character of both women and for the depth to which an account of the work of this narrative of gender and race must reach. I merely assert for the moment that the truth of this motherly withdrawal (I suppose as complex as the withdrawal in *Stella Dallas*)—I mean the fact that Julie has been a true teacher of her knowledge to Magnolia—is validated by its being Paul Robeson, no less, who after establishing himself by singing "Ol' Man River" watches Magnolia dancing and remarks, "Look at that gal shimmy." Irene Dunne's casting as Magnolia plays a role in her figuring definitively in both remarriage comedy and in the genre of melodrama in which it is the accidental prevention of marriage, not the deliberate rejection of it, that provides the drama (*Back Street; Love Affair*, and its remake as *An Affair to Remember*). Deliberate rejection is more the line of the borderer Julie.

An outstanding question about *Blonde Venus* is why the woman returns to the marriage—how Marlene Dietrich could, never more attractive and independent than here, and even for the sake of her child, credibly return to conjugal life with that ordinary, vindictive, stuffed shirt. (It is Herbert Marshall for whom she leaves Cary Grant. Imagine.) It makes sense of the events to say: she has judged the world she has seen, and she has seen much of it, to be second-rate, one whose unnecessary stinginess with happiness she can do nothing to improve. But her son has, even in such a world, a chance to do something, with a mother like her to teach him what men and women can be like. Watching Marlene Dietrich as a mother in this film is a revelation. I know some who have fixed ideas of what glamorous cabaret singers are like and what nurturance is like and

Her son has, even in [a second-rate] world, a chance to do something, with a mother like her to teach him what men and women can be like.

cannot look and see their superb, however rare, coincidence here. But where does the woman's ability to judge the world come from? In the four films under discussion here it comes from the woman's being confined or concentrated to a state of isolation so extreme as to portray and partake of madness, a state of utter incommunicability, as if before the possession of speech. In *Letter from an Unknown Woman,* it would accordingly be the inability of the woman to exercise this force of judgment that causes her apparently inadvertent and absolute destructiveness.

The idea of having the power to judge the world—as a place fit to live in, disdaining its demand to live without love—became guiding for me in thinking about opera, about what causes the diva's singing, something I try to locate in the span between the primitiveness of the orality of singing and the sophistication in the ecstacy in finding and presenting a voice. It is here that a reasonable space opens within which to glimpse the power of

Irene Dunne's casting as Magnolia [her dancing ratified by Paul Robeson, no less] plays a role in her figuring definitively in both remarriage comedy and in the genre of melodrama in which it is the accidental prevention of marriage, not the deliberate rejection of it, that provides the drama.

Garbo, the most famous figure of the unknown woman of film, or I might rather say, the figure about whom unknownness is felt most intuitively, most demandingly.

Arguably her greatest, most ample, role was that in *Camille* (1936, directed by George Cukor with Robert Taylor and Lionel Barrymore), based on the Dumas play *La Dame aux Camelias,* and on the knowledge of the other great setting of that play, Verdi's (and Piave's) *La Traviata.* Without the link to opera, *Camille* seems to deny its connection with the melodrama of the unknown woman in its apparent search for the father, as well as in the film's transcendence of irony in its final, tardy, recognitions. The opera all but forces us to recognize that the drama is concentrated in this woman's power to judge the world, announced early as her declaration of freedom from the world ("Sempre libera"), expressed in her choice of the half-world (this Dumas is credited with coining the term *demimonde*). Her seduction by the young, persistent admirer turns on his getting her to question her judgment of the world as unfit for love; her counterseduction by the young man's father turns on his returning her to her former judgment of the world (of men) as implacable, but now expanding her negation of that world, her mode of partaking of it, to include the negation of herself. Yet, as she and young Alfredo have agreed, love is mysterious, in its crossing of torture and bliss.

To accept her acceding to the father's plea, as the act of sacrifice worthy to make her acceptable to this old man and his daughter, is to take this man's view of the event as authoritative. But it is a view from which—demonically plausible as it is—I seem to see her way past. ("Demonically plausible": thus I mark, and hurry past, the obligation, if the power of this narrative is to be realized, to describe the frightening persuasiveness Verdi lends to the exchanges between old Germont and Violetta, in their sequence of duets and solos that constitute the heart of Act Two. In centralizing, or concentrating, the old force of the father, *Camille*, backed by *La Traviata*, accents the virtual absence of the woman's father in the unknown woman melodrama—a condition that intuitively fits the distinctive presence of the woman's magic father in remarriage comedy.) Following her links of conviction in freedom, in love, and in God's world as the counter to man's world, this father—in appealing to her to give up his son Alfredo to save him and his sister from ruin—appeals not to the rigor of law but to the tyranny of convention. While he imagines that his privately accepting her as a daughter will be her reward for her self-sacrifice, Violetta has already, in her words of agony at man's implacability, put aside the world of men as her judge—judged their judgment of her. This is not new; it was something her life of freedom had itself declared. What is new, with the choice to forgo love, is her judgment of her old world, hence her inability any longer to accept it as her habitat. Her new reward is that through this father she is giving children to the world, which both makes or modifies her sense of giving up Alfredo and which allows her, in the fantasy of a grateful and approving daughter, to place herself within the state of motherhood—evidently her only access to it. It does not prepare a life of happiness, but it also does not invite a death of madness. Why assume the father is of more importance in himself than this suggests? Who knows men better than she?

The musical setting of the words Violetta says to herself when she contrasts man's judgments with God's begins with a sonority that shifts from a key in major (here D-flat) to that key in minor, a banality that Verdi stages to terrifying effect. The capacity for such radical shifts of mood—a capacity I assume essential to that small class of narrative artists who are at once immeasurably great and incalculably popular (Verdi, Shakespeare, Dickens, Chaplin, how many more?)—is, in the realm of film acting, the signature of Garbo.

When one senses that Garbo's body of films have failed to do justice to her powers, it is, at a guess, to this capacity for mood shift that one is chiefly responding. It would be why the reference to opera, in her case, is distinctly pertinent. George Cukor's *Camille* can certainly seem not to be Garbo's equal—I cite the coarseness of all the other women in the film, of the cardboard father (Lionel Barrymore), of the insipid love music composed for the film when *Traviata*'s "Di quell'amor" is for some reason not found repeatable. But sometimes the flaws and scars seem not to matter. At such times I think one reads these awkward supports as expressive of the isolation registered in Garbo's temperament, in the narcissism of this temperament's evolution in response to itself, to its memories and anticipations more than to the promptings of perception, whose actual objects as it were transform themselves for her favor. The opening sequence, a priviledged minute or two of her shifting moods, traverses a series of moods as notable for their lucidity as for their range; it constitutes an entire course in film acting and contains a greater density of description and revelation than is likely to be found in a lifetime of respectable exposure and diligence.

It is in the figure of Garbo that the idea of the woman's unknownness most purely takes on its aspect of the desire of a man for a woman's knowledge, as if to know what she knows may be taken as the answer to the question what a man after all wants of a woman—and does not want after all. (If we thereupon take as an answer to the sublimer question, What does a woman want? that what she wants is to be known, or to know that her separateness is acknowledged, we may see the epistemological mismatch for which the genders have been headed: whatever will count as her being known—and I suppose this is quite undefined—it is precisely not to be satisfied by her having at once to tell and not to tell what she knows. At best this changes the subject.)

An idea of the man's ambivalent desire to know is worked at most consecutively, in what follows, in Chapter 4, "Postscript," where knowledge is understood as what can be told, and where wanting and not wanting for something to be told is understood, in reading a passage of Freud's, as an ambivalence toward a woman's voice. This idea fits, in various ways, the situations of Othello, Macbeth, and Antony, as well as the men of *Now, Voyager*, of *Gaslight*, and of *Letter from an Unknown Woman*. Wanting to know another's existence by knowing what the other knows is evidently a route for knowing whether your own existence is known, say acknowledgable (a way of being assured, as Karen Hanson puts the matter in her "Being Doubted, Being Assured"). This route is proposed as a specific phase of skepticism's travails (as traced in my *Claim of Reason*, for example, p. 104); hence questions of knowledge are not to be taken innocently but as motivated by their specific conditions including, in the cases of the knowledge of oneself and others, derived images of what would constitute knowing and being known.

In remarriage comedy the issue of unknownness takes on, as said, the aspect of the woman's desire to know something, to be educated, where this seems to mean to know that her desire is acceptable and what its satisfaction would look like. (The problematic is broached at its most hilarious or delirious, in the films in question, in the set of interrogations and responses that Jean [Barbara Stanwyck] in *The Lady Eve* proposes as the task of finding one's ideal, rattling the paradox that anything worthy of being held on to as an ideal is impossible to arrive at and hence is unworthy to be held on to.) To prove the radical unacceptability of the woman's desire is precisely the task of the horror story the husband tells his wife in *Gaslight* to drive her mad. In *It Happened One Night*, the puzzle of the woman's desire is elaborated by a systematic symbology of foods, that is, by the recognition of human desire as (transfigured) hunger, a reasonably straight manifestation of Freud's theory of human instinct. So, I suppose, is it manifested in *Genesis*, in the apple, which is still fresh in discussion, blatantly so in the remarriage comedies, and not just because the names of Adam and of Eve appear among the seven titles of the comedies I have taken into account.

3

Given, as in *Pursuits of Happiness,* the idea of remarriage, hence of marriage, as requiring the creation of the woman (hence recreation, hence recreation of the human), the general pertinence of the events of the story of marriage in *Genesis* is understandably blatant; and in writing each chapter I kept the pertinence largely confined to its blatant moments, as the comedies of remarriage seem to do. In other words, I left my sense of the pervasive bearing of the *Genesis* story largely implicit. I want to explore the connection an explicit degree or two further on this introductory occasion, if only to renew the experience of the comedies and so to recapture the sense of the importance there can be in showing a set of major melodramas to be derivable from those comedies.

"And when the woman saw that the tree was good for food, and that it was pleasant to the eyes, and a tree to be desired to make one wise, she took of the fruit thereof, and did eat, and gave also unto her husband with her; and he did eat." Evidently the woman eats first and, as the serpent had predicted, does not die; though perhaps something in her has died, her innocence, her blindness to her existence. But what is the promised connection with knowledge? Is it her knowledge that she and the man are separate, since she can disobey? And is this knowledge expressed in her "giving also unto her husband," as opposed to taking for herself alone? Or is there no knowledge on earth until the man eats "with her"?—for the serpent's beguiling her with the idea of having her eyes opened is not said to be accomplished until it can be said that "the eyes of them both were opened, and they knew" (that they were naked); only together is knowledge possessed. But is this *why* she gave to her husband? The tale is careful to account for her taking the fruit from the tree—she had been told of its powers, reassured about them, and saw for herself that the tree was pleasant and good for food. What does she know of the man and see in him? One can readily enough impose a speech for her here, insert a temptation, say a test, leading to a question: I know a taste you do not know. Will you continue with God's prohibition of this taste, or will you accept his promise to make a helpmeet for you and therefore know what I know?

We have in any case to recognize that eating and knowing for herself did not satisfy the mother of us all—quite as if we are being shown that what it means to bite into knowledge is not that you thereupon close some gap or fill some want of knowledge but that you are thereupon opened to the incessant want of knowledge. Then the first bite explains nothing, since that is what has to be explained. What is the origin of the want, the sense of lack? We know how Freud answered, what he found we missed. But for the moment (perhaps bearing Freud in mind) go back to the thought that, if the woman's eating had an effect of knowledge, which means of wanting to know, then it pertains to a knowledge of her existence as separate from the man's (from the man's knowledge, hence from his existence). Here I adduce a passage from Emerson's "Experience": "It is very unhappy, but too late to be helped, the discovery we have made that we exist. That discovery is called the Fall of Man. Ever afterwards we suspect our instruments. We have learned that we do not see directly, but mediately, and that we have no means of correcting these colored and distorting lenses which we are." I quote a little more than is quite necessary here, always recognizing that the original connection of human existence with skepticism is so readily misplaced, and Emerson's powers of formulation so willingly dismissed.

Then what is wanting—if marriage is to be reconceived, or let's say human attraction—is for the other to see our separate existence, to acknowledge its separateness, a reasonable condition for a ceremony of union. Then the opening knowledge of the human is conceived as the experience of being unknown. To reach that absence is not the work of a moment.

Again from Emerson's "Experience": "If at any time being alone I have good thoughts, I do not at once arrive at satisfactions, as when being thirsty, I drink water; or go to the fire, being cold; no! but I am at first apprised of my vicinity to a new and excellent region of life." It is to be apprised of human existence, of satisfactions not alone in drinking but of, let us say, pouring and tasting. This is about as far as I can claim to have gone in *Pursuits of Happiness* in studying remarriage comedy's open and repeated allusions to the Eden story. When, in the first chapter of that book, I describe the future Lady Eve's opening gesture as "clunking [the man] on the head with an apple," I am emphasizing the clunking obviousness of the allusion (following the opening animated titles of a serpent sporting a top hat and weaving himself through as many letters—as much of language—as time allows) which I note as her "attracting the young man's attention." And while the film makes a comedy of the fact that the woman continually attracts the man's consciousness—not to say baffles it or nets it and pins it, mounts and labels and lectures it—he continues to the end to fail to get his eyes opened to her identity. The comedy is that this does not prevent him from acknowledging her existence, her reality for him, under whatever guise. Indeed it may, as matters stand, be a condition of the acknowledgment—men do not, as philosophy is always saying, know how to value knowledge.

Something I do not do is to trace the asymmetry between the feminine and masculine quests for knowledge back to the myth itself, to the moment of the giving of the fruit of the tree, the thing I have hinted at as the institution of ceremony, which expresses the woman's knowledge that a choice is in question. Taking the fruit from the tree, unlike accepting it from a human hand, is not the same as receiving it. (This does not presume that no taking is grateful nor that no receiving is violent.) The woman surmises, or invents, the difference between nature and civilization, hence marriage. The man's streak of stupidity, or innocence, or brutishness, is sometimes registered in these comedies by his not knowing a crucial difference: in *The Lady Eve* by not knowing the difference between beer and ale; in *Adam's Rib* by not knowing the difference between a slap and a slug; in *It Happened One Night* by a vanity in knowing so many distinctions—for example between the position of piggy-backing and that of a fireman's carry—that the man is blind to the fact that what he is presently doing is abducting the woman into his image of marriage.

In the melodramas, the man's ignorance, or fixation of images, is no laughing matter, and the fact becomes unignorable in these so-called women's films. Both they and the genre of comedy from which they derive take their energy from the woman's story, from her power and process of creation and undoing. In thus raising the question, What does the woman want to know and to be known? the suggestion is lodged that the answer may be more than men can imagine on their own. (Should I rather say?: what the feminine wants known is more than the masculine can imagine. This seems at once trivial and evasive.)

The last time I taught a seminar on these genres of film, in 1989—justified by a new sense of them as participating in the ideas of Emersonian perfectionism—a piece of my preparation was to read Elaine Pagels's recently published *Adam, Eve, and the Serpent.* There I found a reverberatory set of observations:

> Accompanying the spread of Christianity . . . was a revolution in sexual attitudes and practices. Yet when we explore Jewish and Christian writers from the first centuries of the common era, we find that they seldom talk directly about sexual behavior, and they seldom write treatises on such topics as marriage, divorce, and gender. Instead they often talk about Adam, Eve, and the serpent. . . . Many people who have . . . discarded the creation story as a folk tale nevertheless find themselves engaged with its moral implications concerning procreation, animals, work, marriage, and the human striving to "subdue" the earth and have dominion over all its creatures. . . . What I intend to show . . . is how certain ideas took their definitive form during the first four centuries as interpretations of the Genseis creation stories, and how they have continued to affect our culture and everyone in it, Christians or not, ever since. (Pp. xviii, xix, xxiii)

Such observations struck me, in retrospect, as confirming my experience of those Hollywood comedies and as bearing on their popularity, confirming in particular my sense that they are to be trusted in unpredictable detail to be participating in (in the continuing seriousness and unresolution of) an ancient set of quarrels. Since major early exponents of those quarrels were, at random, Saints Paul, Jerome, Ambrose, and Augustine, am I saying that those films are as good as the thoughts of saints, or anyway as the stained glass that depicts their concerns? Not understanding what "as good" would mean here, I simply claim that to deny the bearing of those thinkers and of such films on one another is to deprive oneself of a way to know what thinkers of that magnitude are and what films as good as these (as films) can be.

Prompted by Pagels's discussions of a succession of concepts that the founding, mostly Christian, theologians derived from the Adam and Eve tale, I begin to recall moments from the comedies I had passed by in writing *Pursuits of Happiness.* I mention two obvious cases and one doubtful one.

In the first full sequence of *The Awful Truth,* after a prologue in some Athletic Club—virtually defined as simultaneously a haven from women and a preparation for them, call it a male beauty salon—an early gesture of the woman toward the returned man, when they are left alone in their house, is to pluck an orange from a basket of oranges, look at it, and toss it across the room to him. Very much not an apple, but hardly less mysterious. Surely it is reasonable to ask whether somebody or other having to do with the film intended the orange as an allusion to the famous apple. (Reasonable, at any rate, somewhat early in one's experience of such films. Eventually, so it seems to me, it becomes more urgent to understand how a film so knowing as this one is able to disguise its knowingness, as it were to feign indifference to itself, in the manner of certain other great beauties.) A reasonable answer is to discover why the film might want such an allusion to the apple (intention is an expression of wanting); that is, to find what its use is for the allusion; how, in other words, it can contribute to an understanding of, participate in, the event to which it alludes.

A difference from the apple is that this orange has writing on it, a word that gives the man the lie: it is stamped "California" whereas the man had wished it thought (hadn't he?) that he had brought the basket from Florida, the other American Eden. On this reading, the woman's gift of this piece of fruit is giving something *back*, a response to something that has already happened. She does not seem particularly surprised or dismayed by her discovery of the trace of writing, as though she already knew all that mattered, that the man was hiding something, putting distance between them. In which case she may toss the orange not to accuse but to assure him: having already absorbed the knowledge he thought to withhold, she may wish to declare that the risk to the marriage is not from her. He had elaborately tried to get her to believe otherwise by cultivating a suspicion about the self-evidently harmless singing teacher she had been out with all night. But the risk is from his need for an unannounced privacy, that is, from a fear of some unnamed exposure, hence of some shame (as opposed to some guilt, as from some involvement outside the marriage, which we do not know of). In recognizing that his desire is for some adventure beyond the present dispensation of their marriage, the woman's tossing the orange can express her consent to enter the further adventure with him, sparing him the task of asking first. This makes the orange-tossing a kind of dumb show anticipating her later implied offer in becoming his sister. It is not inconceivable that something he wants is simply to be given freely the two weeks of unquestioned freedom he has just stolen, thus to be trusted implicitly.

I call the singing teacher "self-evidently harmless," but to arrive at this self-evidence was the work of something like a century. His name is Armand Duvall, the name of the lover in Dumas's *La Dame aux Camelias,* retained (slightly mispelled) by Robert Taylor in the Cukor/Garbo *Camille,* a figure who in the meantime had become Alfredo in Verdi's *Traviata.* So the jokes in *The Awful Truth* about Armand's "continental mind" and Jerry's American maleness (as cloaked in Cary Grant) take a slap at Armand's/Alfredo's final ineffectiveness in rescuing Marguerite/Violetta, and at the same time raise a question about Jerry's self-evidently greater interest for a new (American) woman, thus furthering the ground on which to discern the taint of villainy in maleness as such, as explored in remarriage comedy. Even Grant's piano-playing here—in a quite professional vaudeville duet with the dog in contention—is rendered suspicious, in retrospect, in Cukor's repeated association of male piano virtuosity with madness or villainy—the Baron in *Camille* and Charles Boyer in *Gaslight,* but also John Barrymore in *Bill of Divorcement* and Conrad Veidt in *A Woman's Face.* Further concerning the harmonic reaches of *La Dame aux Camelias* into our genres, I ask how, in the depicted struggles to decide on a name for Bette Davis's character in *Now, Voyager,* we understand her being named Camille by the continental mind in that world (Paul Henreid). He had there, as Armand/Alfredo elsewhere, talked and drawn the woman out of her half-world circle of women into a south of momentary freedom. Again the woman gives over this figure because of some trouble in his invisible domestic life, but she remains justly grateful to him. In entering another life she wears, out of what she names her "idiosyncrasy," significant white camelias she alone buys for herself. This whiteness signals, but evidently to no one any longer, at once an availability and an illic-itness, a condition that in her is marked with Violetta's/Garbo's transcendence of male rescue.

Arguments about the orange-tossing readily read back into the Eden story. The woman in Eden may also be understood as responding to her knowledge that the man already desires the forbidden fruit, and she goes first in order to turn that very desire into marriage, as if she is his mind reader. Or, consonantly, she may be giving back the gift as if to undo the idea of herself as a gift from one male to another. I think of Barbara Stanwyck as Jean, the future Lady Eve, contesting her father's magic by saying, "I'm not your daughter for free, you know." The man might well like to disparage her both as a reader of his mind and as acting on her own: "And the man said, The woman whom thou gavest to be with me, she gave me of the tree, and I did eat." (In the recent essay on *Macbeth* mentioned earlier I associate melodrama with the contest of interpretations and with marriage as made of, and unmade by, mind reading.)

Another silent translation of *Genesis* into the remarriage arena occurs in the opening sequence of *Adam's Rib*—again after a prologue—in which our first glimpse of Adam is of him asleep and of Amanda (like "woman," "Amanda" is a word containing a letter or two or three alongside "man") having arisen from (I mean by) his side, going to bring them back food. *Genesis* says: "And the Lord God caused a deep sleep to fall upon Adam, and he slept; and he took one of his ribs . . . and the rib . . . made he a woman, and brought her unto the man." As with every other assignable event of the story, Adam's sleep has interested theologians, but I do not know of a consensus or a central contention concerning it. The fact of the man's sleeping is emphasized in the film *Adam's Rib* by the woman's curiosity about his dreaming, telling him that he made noises in the night. In my chapter on the film, noting this, I go on to say that she in effect understands his dream to be manifested in his opposition to her taking the case in opposition to him in court; or more accurately, understands it as demanding her opposition to him in court. More pertinent here than the argument I produce in *Pursuits of Happiness* for this interpretation is the bearing of Amanda's curiosity about the dream on Eve's story, in which the story of a transgressive gift is associated with a sleep during which a bargain between males is effected about women; about, as said, women as gifts, satisfactions, a bargain the woman in each case acts to break. This idea seems capped by Amanda's giving back, or rather giving away, a suspicious, not wholly unwelcome, hat that Adam had presented to her.

The overlooked third case from remarriage comedy I cite in relation to the *Genesis* story—the case I referred to as doubtful—puts a moment from *The Philadelphia Story* that I had passed over as obvious filler, even boring, together with a moment from *Genesis* that I knew I did not understand, or did not know how I was understanding. Near the end of that film, after we have seen the pairs mixed up in the forest—Mike (James Stewart) having taken Tracy (Katharine Hepburn) off for a swim and a quasi-declaration, quasi-denial, of mutual love; Dexter (Cary Grant) and Liz (Ruth Hussey) having gone off to compose their counterblackmail blackmail—Dexter invites Liz for a morning swim to complete the all-night party and conspiracy. Liz declines, saying she'll wait to take that pleasure with Mike, and Dexter asks her whether she isn't running a risk in waiting for him so long. She replies in effect that Mike still has things to learn and that she wants for the time being to stay out of his way. We know that Mike is thirty and a writer of short stories, almost a poet, a maker of word-objects. What has he to learn? In *Genesis,* when the Lord God said to himself—upon warning the man that if he eats of the tree of knowledge he will surely die—"It is not good that the man should be alone; I will make him an helpmeet for him"—he thereupon formed every beast and every fowl "and brought them unto Adam to see what he would call them." Why the detour? Why not proceed directly to create the woman, as seems to have been done in the case of recognizing the need for the man ("there was not a man to till the ground")? This may be understood as God's way of letting Adam learn that nothing but woman will be, and will be called by him, his helpmeet: the existence of no other being will contradict his being alone.

But what happens more immediately in the "detour" is Adam's invention of names; said otherwise, his discovery of language. Then an understanding of the necessity for delaying the appearance of the woman is that in order that something be a helpmeet, namely stand in that relation of other to a human being, that being must have equally the capacity to name, and the man must name her, know her, as his, his to know, and to be known by ("bone of my bones, flesh of my flesh"). Say accordingly that Liz is waiting for Mike to acquire his own names for things, sufficient experience to his name to allow him to experience, to recognize, who she is, to name her. (If this seems a bit much to ask of a connection with a narrative detour in *Genesis,* might it help—and in which direction—to ponder Dexter's promise, or threat, to Tracy, at the denouement of *The Philadelphia Story,* "to get those eyes [that is, hers] open," which puts these words of the serpent this time in the voice of the man?)

Then Amanda contesting Adam's dream or image of her is a contesting of something about his naming of her, either the way of it or the what of it. That the equality and privacy of naming is an issue for them is made explicit when the court reporter stops the trial for a point of clarification after they have each called the other or described the other as, let me spell it, "Pinky." "Pinky? That's a name?," the reporter asks, to which Hepburn replies, "Yes, Pinky; y for him, i-e for me." But in the noises he has made in the night another name may have surfaced, something still private but like the other names for her that emerge as he is packing up to leave with his anger, names like "competitor," and "the new woman," to which he says he's not sure he likes being married, a speech ending with his ugliest crack at her, implying a range of names: "I like there to be two sexes." This however is itself in response to an ugly twist she had the previous night given to a name for him, for both of them in case there really is only one human gender—I suppose this means, in cases where the fact of human sexuality as such appears psychically more original than the division into human sexes—as she kicks him, in a rage at having, she insists, not been slapped by him but slugged, crying out, "Let's all be manly!" They have for the moment lost their memory and their imagination of one another.

Naming the woman is characterized throughout the remarriage comedies as the man's generic requirement to claim her, which is to be understood as his recognizing his commitment to her, his willingness for the tie. That the claim be entered by the man and then, while appreciated, contested by the woman, is a pair of equally essential laws of the genre. This pretty clearly places the genre's extraordinary exchanges within what Hollywood at that time would have called the battle of the sexes. Catherine Clément incorporates it differently, for instance, in speaking of Puccini's *Turandot:* "What the worried, murmuring crowd says in the Peking night implies the ferocious and loving battle between women and men."[1] Julia Kristeva elsewhere elaborates: "It is a commonplace, and the changes, radical as they may be, that feminism has forced upon our morals have not upset this one aspect of erotic life: women want marriage. . . . The feminist struggle has given a boost to libidinal vitality by means of phallic competition, through the amatory war underlying identification with the other sex. Nevertheless, couples, held in contempt, have come together again, homosexual or heterosexual, mothering or sadomasochistic."[2]

I am reminded of one of the philosophical gags in *Pursuits of Happiness* that I remain, probably unduly, proud of, where I reformulate the dialectic of the legitimacy of marriage—marrying as declaring that you are already married—by saying, in a kind of comic purloining of Kant's aesthetics, that it is the capacity of a pair to take pleasure in one another without a concept, a pleasure of exclusiveness and devotedness not determined by predicates taken from church, state, or the fact of children. I have gone on to ask whether, sometimes to assert that, it is equally not determined by the division of genders, that in this genre the structure may invite couples of the same sex. But the only instance I know in which this is proved in a convincing work is in George Cukor's last finished film, *Rich and Famous* (a remake of the marvelously interesting film *Old Acquaintance,* from four or more decades earlier, with Bette Davis and Miriam Hopkins), where the principal pair, who after years of comings and goings wind up at midnight in Connecticut with a kiss, is made up of two women (Candice Bergen and Jacqueline Bisset).

Descriptions such as "amatory war" and "ferocious and loving battle between women and men" do not fit the events of the melodramas of the unknown woman. In these melodramas the man is either impotent to claim and hold the woman (*Now, Voyager; Stella Dallas; Blonde Venus; Letter from an Unknown Woman;* in a sense *The Marquise of O—*), or else he is reactively potent and brutal in his demands (*Gaslight,* in a sense *The Marquise of O—*). I speculate that there is an antagonism in the melodramas (typically civilized in manner) that preempts or displaces the battle of the sexes. I discuss the amatory wars of the comedies as struggles for acknowledgment; in the melodramas this is avoided or renounced: the man's struggle there is, on the contrary, a struggle against recognition. The woman's struggle is to understand why recognition by the man has not happened or has been denied or has become irrelevant, hence may be thought of as a struggle or argument (with herself) over her gender.

4

The appearance of the concept of gender prompts me, on a final revision of this Introduction, to insert a section here, before concluding this account of developments in my thinking through certain film melodramas in relation to a certain form of film comedy, sketching what explanation I have for my repeated reluctance to attempt to catch the tide of debate on this issue of gender at any time since I began writing about these films. This insertion is not to excuse intellectual unfashionableness nor to deplore intellectual fashion, but to note—something I imagine the fashions I feel closest to, however also distant from, might themselves endorse—that there is no single narrative that will essentially capture some imagined totality of events to be taken as constituting our present intellectual context.

While I take it for granted that, over the years since I began publishing installments of my thoughts about Hollywood remarriage comedy, feminist film theory has, as a growing body of work in many voices, come to constitute the most influential and fruitful in the field of professional film studies, I found my chance, or took the chance, to position my findings explicitly in relation to some passages of that work only during the writing of the last of the essays to appear here, that on *Stella Dallas*. My belatedness here is actually consistent with my conviction, especially in recent years, that I should not speak in explicit relation to the developing complexities of feminist issues in film unless specifically invited to. (This is understandably bound up with my growing preoccupation with the question of philosophy's right or claim to its arrogations of voice in matters it takes as of universal or necessary interest.) *Stella Dallas* turned out to provide the invitation, indeed the command, since an explicit and (to my mind) essential subject or question of that film, as I read it, is the extent to which a male voice can be listened to in arriving at that subject. Nevertheless, my belatedness deserves some account here on its own, so here briefly:

I have been at the work I do for a long time, as these things go. My *World Viewed: Reflections on the Ontology of Film* appeared in 1971, following a few years of thinking about how to teach film in an aesthetics course and publishing anticipations of it; and the earliest installment of what became *Pursuits of Happiness* appeared in 1976, having been presented at a film conference a year earlier, the year, I would learn much later, in which Laura Mulvey's landmark statement for feminist film studies appeared, "Visual Pleasure and Narrative Cinema." I do not know who I thought would read *The World Viewed* (in my *Gaslight* chapter here I express a similar ignorance about my wishes for the first philosophical essays I had been publishing), but surely and vaguely I imagined that, among others, some philosophers as well as some film theorists might find promptings in its treatment of representation, skepticism, the senses, and what English-speaking philosophy calls the problem of "other minds." So that the failure of the book to elicit critical response struck me as no more surprising in the case of the one field than in the case of the other. I was drawn to philosophize, as I would eventually come to say, within a sense of the persistent rift in the (Western) philosophical mind between shunning institutions of philosophy, roughly those nameable as French-German and American-English. I knew of almost no one else who felt similarly drawn or, perhaps I should say, felt similarly pained by a philosophical silence in that space. So while I continued on my way, along with scattered others, I confess to periodic hesitations about whether one should, in all propriety, go on saying hello so often when there is so often no hello back.

A sign of change, or a response to this awkwardness, came my way a few years ago when an influential contributor to the field of film studies, Dudley Andrews, sent me a paper he was to deliver at a regional literary association meeting explaining why *The World Viewed* was never received in the dominant centers of academic film study. The general reason given in the paper was that in 1971 American academic film studies was still in its formative stages, and its founders were preoccupied with the monthly, even weekly, onrush of material originating mostly in France and then in England. This made a certain sense to me, and I took Andrews's paper not as a sign that things might soon change so much as a civil noting of plausible value whose neglect should not be taken personally; and I think I took that kindly: while it goes without saying that the field of film studies owes me no explanation, I was grateful for the sense that an explanation might rationally be wondered about. But the implication that the silence was not to be taken as hostile was put to a test when later the same year I received from the editors of *Critical Inquiry* a letter submitted to them by Tania Modleski rebuking, or I think I may say denouncing, them and me for the appearance in its pages of my double essay on *Now, Voyager* (reprinted as Chapters 3 and 4 of this book). Apart from hypotheses about my motives, Modleski asserts that I "[fail] to cite any of the women working in [my] area." Since I went back to that pair of essays and counted some twelve women I had cited (including Modleski), I gathered the charge was that I had cited no writing by a woman specifically on *Now, Voyager*. That is true; and it is also true that I cite no man on the subject. Of the few texts by women that I had found on the film, none could be taken as having anticipated what I was led to speak about concerning that film (understandably, since my work on melodrama proceeds straight out of my work on remarriage comedy), and all contained, to my ear, as I said, a note of condescension toward the film (or contempt toward Hollywood) that I found misplaced but that I did not want to argue about. I suppose, really, that I felt it would have been pointless to discuss these issues in isolation from a consideration of the massive and decisive achievements over the past two decades of feminist thinking in literary and in cultural studies, something I was not, am not, prepared to attempt. I accepted the editors' invitation to respond to Modleski's letter, which I did at some length, and both are printed in the Autumn 1990 issue of *Critical Inquiry*. (I add that the following year Teresa de Lauretis, in response to reading that pair of my essays, after a conversation when we met at the Dartmouth School of Criticism and Theory, told me of a text ["Fantasia," by Elizabeth Cowie, published in 1984 in *m/f*, a journal I had not known] that really had anticipated a climactic topic of my essays—the film's quite clear notation, within the bounds of deniability, of Charlotte Vale's [latent?] homosexuality. De Lauretis valuably examines the relation between Cowie's and my readings in her recent notable set of texts in *The Practice of Love: Lesbian Sexuality and Perverse Desire* [1994].)

Modleski subsequently expanded her charge against me—not me alone—in the opening chapter of her *Feminism without Women* (1991) where she names, dismissively, an important piece of the philosophical circumstances of the material to be presented here, its Emersonian background. She quotes there, from the text of the *Stella Dallas* lecture that I had presented at a conference we were both participants in (my lecture was a slightly earlier version of Chapter 5 of this book), where I raise the question: "Does this idea of the feminine philosophical demand serve to prefigure, or does it serve once more to eradicate, the feminine difference?—to articulate or to blur the difference between the denial to the woman of political expression and a man's melancholy sense of his own inexpressiveness." Modleski evidently refuses this as a genuine question from me since she describes me as "canny enough" to ask it. What I was doing was reporting something I felt I had discovered about male thinking, namely the tinge of self-imposed melancholy or pathos arising from a self-imposed suppression specifically of the male philosopher's feminine voice (not by me identified with a general female feminine voice). The sense of this self-suppression is a late entry in my various interpretations over the years of philosophical skepticism, and it is a principal burden of the postscript to "Ugly Duckling, Funny Butterfly," that is, Chapter 3 of this book.

Modleski draws the Emerson connection with my work from the interpretation of Emerson in David Leverenz's "The Politics of Emerson's Man-Making Words." The pertinent passage she quotes from Leverenz ends this way: "Emerson's ideal of manly self-empowering reduces womanhood to spiritual nurturance while erasing female subjectivity. 'Self-Reliance' takes for granted the presence of faceless mothering in the mind, an ideal state of mental health that he sums up in a memorable image: 'The nonchalance of boys who are sure of a dinner.'" It happens that I had alluded to just that passage from "Self-Reliance" near the beginning of the section that now follows this inserted, belated one, and I would like to avert unnecessary misunderstanding about it if I can. Emerson's passage runs as follows:

> The nonchalance of boys who are sure of a dinner, and would disdain as much as a lord to do or say aught to conciliate one is the healthy attitude of human nature. A boy is in the parlor what the pit is in the playhouse; independent, irresponsible, looking out from his corner on such people and facts as pass by, he tries and sentences them on their merits, in the swift, summary way of boys, as good, bad, interesting, silly, eloquent, troublesome. He cumbers himself never about consequences, about interests; he gives an independent, genuine verdict. You must court him; he does not court you. But the man is as it were clapped into jail by his consciousness. As soon as he has once acted or spoken with *éclat* he is a committed person, watched by the sympathy or the hatred of hundreds, whose affections must now enter into his account. There is no Lethe for this. Ah, that he could pass again into his neutrality! Who can thus avoid all pledges and, having observed, observe again from the same unaffected, unbiased, unbribable, unaffrighted innocence,—must always be formidable. He would utter opinions on all passing affairs, which being seen to be not private but necessary, would sink like darts into the ear of men and put them in fear.

The words quoted from Leverenz do not seem to me to meet this passage. Leverenz is surely right to sense—if this is what is implied—a certain intimacy on Emerson's part with the "boy," whatever that figure turns out to betoken; but "Self-Reliance" throughout can be taken as about the condition of its writer, so its audience, as definitively one in which the condition of the boy is unattainable, inimitable. If so, it is not easy to see what it means to say that the image of the boy "sums up" Emerson's ideal state. Emerson's intimate but reserved appreciation of the boy's spectacle, his concerned pride in it, strikes me as his declaring himself to be, as much as a supposed mother, the provider of the sure dinner. In the preceding paragraph he had articulated the phantasm: "Do not think the youth has no force, because he cannot speak to you and me. Hark! in the next room his voice is sufficiently clear and emphatic. It seems he knows how to speak to his contemporaries. Bashful or bold then, he will know how to make us seniors very unnecessary." This seems the report of a scene Emerson commonly witnesses, and given his time and place it probably would have been a boy and not a girl thus speaking. But that force is directed not against girls—if it had been a girl speaking, Emerson's point would have remained unchanged (we are free to imagine that he would indeed welcome the change) —but against "us seniors." The image is of what Emerson calls "innocence," rebuking the terrible thing that has happened to us seniors with our "experience," from which we learn nothing new. If one thinks this empty, or worse, from where does one call upon the power of change? The alternative is to accede to the idea that what is called one's subject position exhausts one's subjectivity. (Empirically, I suppose, that is so often what happens—to "seniors," who so often put aside their best things. Then of course the work that art or philosophy may do becomes pointless. But this gets contentious.)

"The healthy attitude of human nature" is not the surety of a dinner, which is a description that gently mocks the unexamined ease with which promising youth assumes its disdain; the healthy attitude is disdain itself, specifically disdain of good opinion. Whatever Leverenz's phrase "ideal state of mental health" adds to or subtracts from Emerson's phrase "healthy attitude," it should not imply that Emerson finds an ideal state now to exist, or to expect that one exactly could. It does not exist in the boy's nonchalance, which will pass with experience, for better or worse. The verdicts he delivers today are recalled by Emerson not because their justice is final but because their inspiration is clear, their responsibility discharged in responsiveness, their morality and politics ("good and bad") still alive ("innocent"), still part of what is "interesting, silly, eloquent, troublesome." Nor does the healthy attitude exist in "the man," whose experience, or "consciousness," commits itself to remembrances ("There is no Lethe for this") and to the surveillance of affections (not the reciprocation of them).

I can, I hope, appreciate the refusal to listen to the experience of what Emerson calls the man, to refuse that economy of the successes and failures of pleasure. (Wasn't that refusal, and showing it to be practical, the power or promise of Mulvey's "Visual Pleasure and Narrative Cinema"?) But how does it help the cause of women, or any emancipation, to listen, for example to Emerson, just long enough to find a profitless interpretation of what he says?

An answer to that question would be a function, I imagine, of answers to questions of the politics of essentialism and anti-essentialism in debating feminism that are at issue in Modleski's *Feminism without Women.* Whether the kind of transfigured (anti-) essentialism I discuss (for example in *The Claim of Reason*) in interpreting Wittgenstein's idea of a criterion bears on that debate is—given what I have just now been saying—not for me to say. So the point of taking up again a charge against me from Tania Modleski perhaps comes to the wish to keep open my way of considering film against a hasty, inaccurate condemnation of that way by Modleski, as for instance in the following terms: "The 'faceless mothering' in the mind referred to by Leverenz is an especially apt term given Cavell's use of the text *Stella Dallas,* the archetypal story of a mother's self-*effacing* sacrifice of her child for the child's own social advancement." I trust that the reader will verify, in my text on the film, printed here as Chapter 5, that my "use" of the archetypal story in *Stella Dallas* is to demonstrate the *overturn* of the received archetypal story of self-effacing sacrifice, to reveal it instead in the Stanwyck *Stella Dallas* as a story—or as the cover for a story—of self-liberation and self-empowering, epitomized precisely as the claiming of a face. (I was helped to this account by an essay of William Rothman's, cited in my Stella chapter.) I presented essentially the same text to six or seven university audiences in the years 1989 through 1991, and most of the discussions took this point with considerable surprise, indeed with initial disbelief, and wished to go over what is quite straightforward evidence for my counteraccount of Stella's behavior and her power of consciousness in the film. "Going over" the evidence, with due suspicion, is precisely what my reading asks for: I find that the pain in imagining Stella's stage of isolation on that reading is intenser than the pain of the received reading of sacrifice, intenser enough to account for the all but universal wish not to recognize the possibility of that counterreading.

5

To say—taking up again Liz's exchange with Dexter near the end of *The Philadelphia Story*—that there is no helpmeet prior to language amounts to saying that there is no human desire without the capacity to make oneself intelligible; so it amounts to saying that there is no human desire without the imagination of one to whom one may be intelligible, hence the capacity to remain unintelligible, to live without, the frightening capacity to wait. Perhaps this can be seen, in the woman's recognition of her isolation at the close of the melodramas, as being in a position of madness—to pose the question but without the answer of madness, without its methods. I relate this isolation to Emerson's wish for us, inspired by the power of youth's judgment upon us, to pass again into our neutrality, an image of claiming again the power of judgment over our lives. And I relate this, this rediscovery or reclaiming of the fact of our existence, to Thoreau's definition of the discovery that we exist (which Emerson had called, on its melancholy side, the Fall) as our being beside ourselves in a sane sense, and hence with *Walden's* pun on morning (sounding at once like grieving and like dawning) to mark the line between melancholy and ecstacy. The stage is marked by Descartes early in his second Meditation: "I am something real and really existing, but what thing am I?"

The woman's isolation is associated in the films of unknownness with some register of her relation to the transcendent—grounded in a cosmic symbology of light and darkness, of enclosure and the imagination of freedom. I think of Ingrid Bergman, standing against the sky, almost at the end of *Gaslight*: "It's been a long night"; of Greer Garson, apparently having worn out hope, near the end of *Random Harvest*: "The mist is rising"; of Bette Davis at the close of *Now, Voyager*: "We have the stars"; of Joan Fontaine, throughout

Letter from an Unknown Woman, speaking beyond the grave from a
letter countersigned by a nun; of Barbara Stanwyck, silent at the
end of *Stella Dallas,* walking to and from an ecstatic vision of
another world. How are such things to be understood in relation
to remarriage comedy's apparently opposite tropism, its ending
firmly, studiously, turning the couple back into their unsponsored,
risky reality, picking up the secular thread?

The most brutal assertions of this-worldliness occur, appropri-
ately, in what in *Pursuits of Happiness* I characterize as the blackest
of the remarriage comedies, *His Girl Friday.* I quote again from its
epitomizing exchange of antitranscendence: Bruce (Ralph Bellamy), planning to marry Hildy (Rosalind Russell) and take her
away to Albany, free of the squalor of Walter (Cary Grant) and his
world of headlines and corruption and human interest stories, is
praising life insurance to Walter: "Of course it doesn't help you
much while you're alive. It's afterwards that's important." Walter
laughs heartily; Bruce's evident confusion about who and how life
insurance is to help *might* have been a good joke. But seeing that it
is Bruce who tells it, Walter stops laughing abruptly, saying, "I
don't get it!" And yet *His Girl Friday* climaxes with Walter's claim
that an "unseen power" watches over his newspaper. No doubt this
invokes nothing beyond, say, gambler's luck—but then what is
gambler's luck? Walter's conviction that nothing in the world is to
be taken at face value is a conviction in things unseen that is not
less than an unshakable, unslakable, faith.

Then is the derivation of the melodramas from the comedies
to be seen, in this matter of transcendence, as a refusing of the
irreverence of the comedies, a transforming or displacing of their
laughter by denying their sense of distance from another realm,
perhaps by sentimentalizing it? These are difficult and important
questions, ones I could not venture upon, as things now stand for
me, without taking into account melodrama's relation to tragedy
and, yet more urgent, to opera. Take the figure of the singer to be
occupying a visible world in which to be discovered and in the same
breath to be invoking an invisible world from which to be heard.
Then transcendence is so fundamental to the experience of opera
that immanence (*this* spirit in *this* body) becomes its issue. (This
is a theme of the last of the three chapters of my *Pitch of Philosophy.*)

Since such an account is not in question here, I close these
remarks by citing Peter Brooks's fine and influential book *The*

Melodramatic Imagination, published in 1976, in which I have found much profit, and also problems, still awaiting the attention they deserve. It is an encouraging book for one who senses that the concept of the melodramatic has been (philosophically) under-valued and understudied, in comparison with the value attached to and the study devoted to the tragic, the comic, and the ironic; and particularly interesting for one who, sharing Brooks's sense that the emotionality and, let's say, superreferentiality of the melodramatic mode contrast significantly with the sensibility of poststructur-alism; contrast most sharply in its deconstructive turn, with its preference for the intra- and the contratextual effects of a text. This connection suggests to my mind an ironic connection between deconstruction and logical positivism, a consequence, of course, of their different (immeasurably so, so far) hostilities toward the metaphysical; but equally a consequence—less noticeable because more widely shared—of their hostilities toward the ordinary, construed as the banal, the staple of melodrama.

Brooks extends the line of those who find in the melodramatic the essential gesture of theater as such—a line notably indebted to Eric Bentley—and in that gesture of excess, of the histrionic, of the hysterical, find an explanation for the essential popularity of the genre of melodrama. Whether this is an explanation or a repetition of the question, the association of popularity with the theatrical is a reminder that the hostility shown the ordinary in positivist and deconstructive practices are extremes of philosophy's chronic flight from, perhaps in reaction to an absorption in, the ordinary or everyday. It is a flight, or retreat, figured, for example, whether positively or negatively, in Plato's cave, in Dante's dark wood, in Rousseau's chains, in Emerson's jail, in Thoreau's caged woods, in Nietzsche's and Poe's crowds, in Wittgenstein's rough ground (in opposition to pure ice).

A way of articulating the originality of Wittgenstein's *Philosoph-ical Investigations* is to note the virtual explicitness with which he interprets metaphysics as a kind of melodramatic answer to a melo-dramatic discovery: the discovery is the one that Descartes charac-terizes as causing him "astonishment," namely that he does not know the basis of his conviction that the world, and he in it, exists, the presentation of skepticism; the answer is what Wittgenstein calls (a fantasy of) a superorder of superconcepts (*Philosophical Investigations,* §97) arrived at by a process of the subliming of our signs (for example, §94), a latter-day version of what Hume had described as being wrought upon, in philosophizing, by "the *intense* view" (*Treatise of Human Nature,* 1.4.7). (If we put together Descartes's presentation of skepticism's moment of astonishment at the discovery that we do not know we exist, with Emerson's interpretation of the Fall of Man as the melancholy discovery that we exist [as fallen], then skepticism appears as the denial of the Fall, not of the supposed mythical event (for which it may be said to supply a secular interpretation), but of the myth's impression of our finitude, an impression of unsurveyable entanglement, for which skepticism would substitute an impression of fixed, intransigent limitation.)

There are even recognizably melodramatic scenes reported in *Philosophical Investigations,* as for example: "I have seen a person in a discussion on this subject strike himself on the breast and say: 'But surely another person can't have THIS pain!'" Such a scene is worth pondering in light of the idea of the melodramatic as the locus of "excessive" expression. Here the locus is precisely (also) one of the emptiness of expression, in which, that is, nothing is meant, a locus of another shade of madness. (The complexity in Wittgenstein's genealogy of the meaningless, perhaps in comparison with positivism's fixing of the subject, would best further our discussion at this stage of it.) The coincidence of madness, emptiness, and excess or exaggeration, dots my various considerations of skepticism. This coincidence should, I think, put into question such a formulation as this from Brooks's *Melodramatic Imagination:* "The nineteenth-century novel needs such a theatricality . . . to get its meaning across, to invest in its renderings of life a sense of memorability and significance" (p. 13). If, on the contrary, we sense that a certain theatricality is the sign of an inability to mean, to get our meaning across, then such writing comes across to us by understanding this desperation, figuring our hidden screams, and then understanding us despite ourselves, despite our inexpressiveness, the poverty and pathos of all expression. Here is a possible site of explanation for melodrama's popularity.

My philosophical placement of the melodramatic as the hyperbolic effort to recuperate or to call back a hyperbolic reliance on the familiarity or banality of the world bears relations—clear and perhaps not so clear—with Brooks's idea of the mode of the melodramatic as a response to what I gather is understood as a historical event, the loss of conviction in a transcendent basis for the distinction between good and evil. This loss has, on Brooks's account, led to an intuition of the "moral occult," a region or source of lost order the melodramatic attests to and is meant to reach.

> The desire to express all seems a fundamental characteristic of the melodramatic mode. . . . The world is subsumed by an underlying manichaeism, and the narrative creates the excitement of its drama by putting us in touch with the conflict of good and evil played out under the surface of things. . . . The center of interest and the scene of the underlying drama reside within what we could call the "moral occult," the domain of operative spiritual values whch is both indicated within and masked by the surface of reality. The moral occult is not a metaphysical system; it is rather the repository of the fragmentary and desacralized remnants of sacred myth. (pp. 4, 5) The heightening and the hyperbolic, the polarized conflict, the menace and suspense of the representation may be made necessary by the effort to perceive and image the spiritual in a world voided of its traditional Sacred, where the body of the ethical has become a sort of *deus absconditus* which must be sought for, postulated, brought into man's existence through the play of the spiritualist imagination [p. 11]. By the end of the Enlightenment, there was clearly a renewed thirst for the Sacred, a reaction to desacralization expressed in the vast movement we think of as Romanticism [p. 16]. The melodramatists refuse to allow that the world has been completely drained of transcendence; and they locate that transcendence in the struggle of the children of light with the children of darkness, in the play of the ethical mind [p. 22]. What we have called "the moral occult," the locus of intense ethical forces from which man feels himself cut off, yet one he feels to have a real existence somewhere behind or beyond the facade of reality, and which exerts influence on his secular existence, stands as an abyss or gulf whose depths must, cautiously and with risk, be founded [p. 202].

Valuable as these thoughts assuredly are, it is hard to take them up clearly since they seem to invoke so many of the modern fates or echoes of the, let's say, beyond.

How is the distance between "the facade of reality" and "a real existence of [ethical forces] behind or beyond" imagined to be spanned? Does it continue Kant's distinction between the transcendental, the conditions of the possibility of knowledge, and the transcendent, that which defies knowledge? But then we will hardly think of what is beyond as "the moral occult." It is just the moral realm. Does the distance in question then deny the Kantian distinction? This could explain the thought that the loss of the sacred creates the occult—since it is the negation of Kant's claim that the moral provides the ground of the religious (the realm of the sacred), not the other way around. Kant could be wrong about this, but the coherence of his position proves that its denial (namely the claim that the sacred provides the ground of the moral realm, of its open, public acceptance, hence that the closing of the sacred is what occludes the moral) is not necessary but rather argumentative. The cost for a theory of melodrama in assuming the denial of Kant is the loss of Kant's understanding of the denial: for Kant, to place the moral as the dependent of the sacred is to plunge into one of the various forms of madness he calls transcendental illusions, among which are skepticism, fanaticism, and magic (say, occultism).—But why put this reversal of Kant as the assumption of a *theory* of melodrama, since isn't it the assumption of melodrama itself? But this is my point: Brooks seems to me to picture melodrama as a response to an event, as if we understood the event and what it means that the response is one of excess; whereas my suggestion is that the event is of melodrama itself—the regicide itself, for instance, not alone its consequence.

Kant's idea of spiritual derangement is, roughly, that we are each put into the position of attempting to provide a transcendence in our, as it were, private experience, a link with the beyond that only membership in a realm of law can sanely provide. It is like searching for the power of a word when the conditions of language have been lost. We might say that the word would have to become absolutely expressive, as with a metaphysical voice. (We move here into territory explored at some length in my consideration of Derrida's treatment of Austin's theory of performative utterances, in the second lecture of *A Pitch of Philosophy*.) Brooks, as cited, notes: "The desire to express all seems a fundamental characteristic of the melodramatic mode." (One thinks here of silent movie acting, before the inherent exaggerations of film were under control, or of the classical postures of elocution, or of hysteria.) Yet I ask for the provenance of this "all."

My writing about film began under the pressures, among others, of recognizing a continuous response to skepticism in Wittgenstein's scenes of excess (for example, "Couldn't I imagine having frightful pains and turning to stone while they lasted?" (§283); "Yes, but there is *something* there all the same accompanying my cry of pain. . . . And this something is what is important—and frightful" (§296)). In Chapter 4, "Postscript," I further situate a formulation I propose in *The Claim of Reason* for Wittgenstein's idea of a private language: "The fantasy of a private language, underlying the wish to deny the publicness of language, turns out . . . to be a fantasy, or fear, either of inexpressiveness, one in which I am not merely unknown, but in which I am powerless to make myself known; or one in which what I express is beyond my control"—so a fantasy of suffocation or of exposure (p. 351; quoted below p. 157). Accordingly, I am led to stress the condition that I find to precede, to ground the possibility and the necessity of, "the desire to express all," namely the terror of absolute inexpressiveness, suffocation, which at the same time reveals itself as a terror of absolute expressiveness, unconditioned exposure; they are the extreme states of voicelessness. (I claim that these are the polar states expressed in the woman's voice in opera.) As a characterization of solipsism, this crisis of expression is for me a characterization of what has become of human exchange as such (or as widespread as, say, the consequences of the French Revolution, the event reasonably emphasized by Peter Brooks).

Does Brooks's speaking of "a sort of" *deus absconditus* imply that we know a Pascalian idea of a hidden God surely to be a thing of the past? But the possibility is directly under investigation in Nietzsche's *The Gay Science* (§125), in the parable about the Madman searching for God. The concluding position of the woman of the unknown woman melodramas, which I earlier named structural madness (I might say symbolic, as opposed to imaginary and to real), now associated with an incommunicability of the transcendent, might perhaps usefully be studied in conjunction with that parable, which runs as follows:

> Have you not heard of that Madman who lit a lantern in the bright morning hours, ran to the market place, and cried incessantly, "I seek God! I seek God!" As many of those who do not believe in God were standing around just then, he provoked much laughter. Why, did he get lost? said one. . . . Or is he hiding? Is he afraid of us? The madman jumped into their midst and pierced them with his glances.
>
> "Whither is God?" he cried. "I shall tell you. *We have killed him—*

you and I. All of us are his murderers. But how have we done this? How were we able to drink up the sea? Who gave us the sponge to wipe away the entire horizon?" What did we do when we unchained this earth from its sun? Whither is it moving now? Wither are we moving now? Away from all suns? Are we not plunging continually? . . . Are we not straying as through an infinite nothing? . . . Has it not become colder? Is not night and more night coming on all the while? Must not lanterns be lit in the morning? Do we not hear anything yet of the noise of the gravediggers who are burying God? Do we not smell anything yet of God's decomposition? Gods too decompose. God is dead. . . . What water is there for us to clean ourselves? . . . Is not the greatness of this deed too great for us?

"I come too early; my time is not come yet. This tremendous event is still on its way, still wandering—it has not yet reached the ears of man. Lightning and thunder require time, the light of the stars requires time, deeds require time even after they are done, before they can be seen and heard."

By the lantern of the enlightenment, remnant of reason, someone effects to seek the God who has absconded because of the beams of that very light. And while the conjunction of mad screaming with banal intellectual teasing is a staple of the comic view, when we have become the clown the irony becomes the color of melodramatic pathos. (An unbeliever asks whether the absconded one is hidden, evidently thinking he is asking whether one who never arrived has left, conceivably even imagining that the joke, if there is one, has been played just on the madman. Is it a wonder he is driven mad?)

We may feel in the parable that we are in at the obstetrical scene of melodrama, born crying into the world with an inexpressible tale. But where is the excess? If we have killed God—if, let us say, we are implicated in the creation of the occult—then the question, for example, about where we shall find water to clean ourselves seems a reasonable one. Then perhaps it is the idea of this killing, to pick up a recent thread, which is (was already) excessive. But what if someone heard about this event from someone causally connected with someone who saw it happen? "Night and more night coming on. . . . It has not reached the ears of man." In another mood I would put this with something we know Nietzsche's ears had heard, Emerson's words in "Politics": "We think our civilization near its meridian, but we are yet only at the cock-crowing and the morning star." Utter understanding; utter disagreement. What do Europe and America hear of one another?

Suppose the secularity of remarriage comedy shows that its moral perfectionism really can survive, can retain itself within, the unknown woman melodrama and its manichean, demonic lights. Then, in all fragility, we have it attested that our intelligibility to one another is so far a match for the heydays of chaos reaching our ears.

Following the cue of the light, of the rising
and falling of the light as a cause of madness, and
considering that this rising and falling is the light by which
we see the figures on the screen, we have to ask whether
there is something in the light of film that is
inherently (not, of course, inveterately) maddening.

1

Naughty Orators: Negation of Voice in <u>Gaslight</u>

OMETHING IN THE LANGUAGE OF THE unknown woman melodrama must bear, as I was saying, the weight borne by the weight of conversation in the case of remarriage comedy. In turning our attention now to *Gaslight* I identify this opposing feature of language as that of irony, a negation of conversation, a recognition of one's isolation—a piece of knowledge to which the women of our melodramas, in transcending marriage, have to show themselves equal. Sadistic irony riddles the exchanges of *Gaslight,* from the coil of words with which this husband (Gregory, played by Charles Boyer) incessantly lashes this wife (played by Ingrid Bergman) ("Paula, don't get hysterical"—when he's driving her to dissociation; "You're not beginning to imagine things too, are you Paula?"—when all of his time with her is spent suggesting things for her to imagine); to the irony of such directions as those of the opening words of the film, "Stand back. Stand back." said by an anonymous policeman to a depicted audience outside the house of murder, but in some viewing bound to be taken by us as directed to us as audience, in that case, however, ambiguously, ironically, since it could be meant either as a warning to protect ourselves from what is coming or as a tip to seek a perspective from which to command a better view; to the full-throated melodramatic climax of ironies in which the woman confronts her husband alone—brandishing a knife with which she might free him or kill him, and doing neither quite, or perhaps both—and delivers to him her *cogito ergo sum,* her proof of her existence, which I might translate for this film roughly as, "Now I exist because now I speak for myself; and in particular because I speak in hatred and to you, who have always pretended to understand me, and pretended not to understand me, and who I now know will alone understand my every word and gesture" (as if, in our mysterious world, to exist is to take revenge). I call this late moment Paula's aria, and its declaration causes, or is caused by (that is, it is the same as), her metamorphosis, or creation, which is what one should expect of the assertion of the *cogito* that, as in Descartes, puts a close to skeptical doubt.

The melodrama of *Gaslight,* in turn, reveals the *cogito* as occurring in an explicit context of irony and madness. The overt content of the wife's declaration to her husband is that she is mad, that she is just what he has suggested she is and driven her to be— or is this itself irony? (I do not know that philosophers have ever spoken explicitly of irony in relation to the *cogito,* but hardly any have failed to find some demonic bewilderment over it, sometimes speaking of a peculiar circle in Descartes's argument, sometimes wondering whether the *cogito* is really an argument exactly at all. One is after all apt to wonder: if I am supposed to exist only if I acknowledge that I do, claim my existence, who was I before I acknowledged it, and before whom is it that I claim it, since every other's existence must be under the same necessity of acknowledgment that mine is under? Some such bewilderment must have helped keep the *cogito*'s fascination alive for three-and-a-half centuries, for it is improbable that its life is due to some as yet unfathomed intricacy of argumentation.) Now the association of the *cogito* with a scene, or play, of madness formed the crossroads of a notable early moment within the developments of French thought over the past two or three decades that have transformed the study of literary criticism and theory: I mean the crossroads of Derrida's taking up of the treatment of Descartes in Foucault's *Madness and Civilization: A History of Insanity in the Age of Reason.* I will want to come back to this moment as a way of defining my own early stake in writing of such matters—a stake I am sure was internal to my being drawn to think about film. But first let us get deeper into what this film has to say for itself, how it accounts for the woman's turn to her freedom for the source of energy that allows her to claim her existence at last. What becomes of her; what is she metamorphosed into?

That the woman frees herself from her husband in forms of madness and irony suggests that the portrait of marriage we are given in this film is precisely the way of life that the women of both the comedy of remarriage and of the derived melodrama of the unknown woman all shrink from, live so as to find freedom from. In *Gaslight* we are given the perfect contradiction of the education and creation sought in remarriage comedy: in this melodrama the woman is meant to be decreated, tortured out of a mind altogether.

The imaging of her terror of madness by the lowering and raising of the light in the gas lamps in her room and by the obscure sounds originating over the room are, I have found in discussions of the film, quite unforgettable—people who saw the film only on its first release, some fifty years ago, at once identify the film when reminded of these features. But these features are generally falsely remembered as being planned by the husband to drive his wife mad: the devices to this end that the husband actually plans consist rather of insinuating to his wife, then accusing her, then "proving" to her that she forgets things and hides things and steals things.

The general order of these events is roughly as follows. After the opening sequence of the young Paula escorted at dusk out of her dead aunt's house, Paula's story is picked up ten years later, in a set of sequences in Italy, opening with her singing lesson with her aunt's old teacher and closing with the morning after her wedding night with a man she had met some two weeks earlier (he is the pianist, it happens, who had been her accompanist at the singing lesson) to whom she promises the house she owns—uncannily like the house in a little square in London that the man has just intimately confessed to her that he has always dreamed he might live in one day with a woman he loves. Back in London, after reopening the house, and following Gregory's suggestion to board up in the attic all the furnishings of the house, which are associated with Paula's memories of her aunt, Paula's deterioration—beyond her mounting bouts of panic in response to Gregory's various demonstrations—shows in her inability to go out of the house alone for an afternoon walk, in her incapacity to oppose Gregory's violent disapproval of inviting guests into her house, in her failure to make her wishes credible to her servants, punctuated by her being isolated under the fluctuating gaslight. When at a formal party at the house of Lady Dalroy, a friend of her aunt's, Paula publicly breaks down under a fresh private accusation of Gregory's, a young detective from Scotland Yard (played by Joseph Cotten)—a friend of this household and an admirer as a youth of Paula's celebrated aunt—divines the urgency of the situation and seizes an opportunity that night to be admitted into Paula's house after her husband has taken her home and gone out again. The detective contrives to regain Paula's confidence in her memory and then in her own senses and intellect sufficiently to ground her belief in his tale that the man she has accepted in marriage is the murderer of her aunt. Of the countless significantly recountable details in the film, I mention two that occur after the detective then leaves to intercept Gregory's usual return to the house: (1) that of the almost deaf cook who, meaning to protect Paula, precipitates what seems a final recurrence of Paula's self-doubt by "confirming" Gregory's wild denials that a stranger had visited the house while he was absent—so the world of women is drawn into conspiring with the maddening world of men; and (2) that of Cukor's homage to Hitchcock, who might have made a film using this material, as the camera stays for what feels like too long a time fixed at Paula's door after she has shut it behind her to await developments as the detective leaves, and then moves as if in Paula's sleep-walking pace, distractedly, to discover Gregory entering the house from above—forcing open the barred door to the attic—an unnerving moment of exposure and vulnerability, as if after all we have been shown, we recognize for the first time that this obsessed maniac has actually been pursuing his obsession just a few feet from the woman victimized by it, by her having to deny it, as if we also have been denying some part of it, some part of our own victimization by it, a late recognition that we are blind to the direction from which danger comes.

Only marriage given a historical development that empowers it to save could have the power of this marriage to destroy. The decreation of the woman works first to destroy Paula's confidence in her memory, hence to destroy her memory. Some of the first words of the film are those of a man (some kind of official guardian, a solicitor one supposes) saying to the young Paula, whose guardian aunt has been murdered, "No, no, Paula. Don't look back. You've got to forget everything that's happened here" (when she has exactly nothing to look forward to); and later her husband Gregory will say to her, "You're becoming forgetful, Paula" (when she has returned to the scene of her past and wants exactly only to look forward). So not only individual men are destroying her mind, but the world of men, in its contradictions with itself, is destroying for her the idea and possibility of reality as such. This seems roughly to be what was happening in Freud's treatment, or in Freud's case history of his treatment, of the patient he called Dora. (Freud's behavior toward Dora was so described by Steven Marcus when, in an essay on this case history in 1974, he redirected the attention of American literary-psychoanalytic culture to this material so prominently featured by Freud and now so prominently under discussion, particularly in feminism.)[1]

The process of controlled amentia is one that is to render the woman of *Gaslight* stupid, say self-stupefying: she does not know what the fairly obvious sounds of tramping are on the floor above, and she does not know why, hence soon not even whether, the gas lamp is obviously lowering in her room—self-stupefying, but in such a way that what she imagines cannot be dismissed, either by her or by us, as ordinary stupidity, any more than Descartes's suggestion that he might only be dreaming that he is sitting before his fire can be dismissed by him or (if we follow him) by us as ordinary stupidity. Let us say that it is in both cases hyperbolic stupidity. (Of course I am offering a little gag here about what philosophers have learned from Descartes to call hyperbolic doubt, but I would not have my gag too simply interpreted. It is meant to question whether this philosophical description is satisfying; but it is at the same time meant to affirm that some such philosophical description is at this place necessary.) How is the woman's over-coming of her stupefaction, her access to knowledge, represented?

The access is initiated upon the appearance of the young man, the man from outside, called the detective, whose access to the house the woman at first shrinks from. The detective gains her confidence by producing the match to the aunt's mysterious single glove that she kept in her case of mementos; this matching is an adventurous mode of identifying an authentic contact. (This matching may well prompt us to ask how it was that Gregory first gained his girl's confidence—it is quite clear that Paula has known no other man romantically.) The young man confirms the reality of her sensations (that there is tramping, that the light dims)—call them expressions of the reality of her inner life—and then explores this reality with therapeutically detective-like questions concerning when the light goes down and when it comes up again. Her knowledge dawns, and the night of self-stupefaction begins to end, on his pressing the question, "You know, don't you Mrs.

Anton? You know who's up there," as she confirms his assertion of her knowledge by at first denying it: "No. No. He can't be." Here again there is a remarkable structural resemblance to perhaps the central crux of Freud's treatment of Dora, his insistent claim to her that she possesses a piece of knowledge that is important to his theory and that she persists in disclaiming (a piece of sexual knowledge, you may be sure).

I cannot say that I am surprised by this early, repeated intrusion of the case of Dora into these deliberations, and since I welcome it, and will cultivate it for a few moments, I should perhaps explain why I am not surprised. I have suggested that some internal connection between the discoveries of psychoanalysis and the means of film narrative is argued in their each originating, in the closing years of the nineteenth century, in the study of the sufferings of women. The originating role of women in psychoanalysis is becoming a familiar topic as interest increases in Freud's early cases: besides the Dora case there is principally the sequence of cases, all concerning women, reported in Freud and Breuer's *Studies on Hysteria* (1893–1895). That our interest in film, as expressed in the astonishingly rapid discoveries of narrative technique in the new medium, especially in its adaptations of melodrama and romance, is equally a function of the study of women is not something to attempt to argue for now. I mostly offer the idea as my intuition of the fascination of film, without denying the reasonably obvious fact that human males have also significantly occurred in major films, but suggesting that while men primarily appear in contexts of mutual competition and of uniform or communal efforts (in work, in adventure, in prison, in war) it is individual women who have given film its depth, as if lending it their own fascination. (It is an open question for me whether Charlie Chaplin and Buster Keaton would exactly be exceptions to this idea.)

I begin to speculate about why it is that women play this originating role in both of these developments by way of continuing to think about the history of skepticism in Western culture, particularly about its inception or representation in Shakespeare and Descartes, especially with respect to philosophical doubts about the existence of what philosophy calls others minds—as though both psychoanalysis and film testify that by the turn of the twentieth century psychic reality, the fact of the existence of mind, had become believable primarily in its feminine (some may say passive) aspect. (This should help us to see why in Wittgenstein's *Philosoph-ical Investigations*, in his study of the question of the other, the pervasive example is that of pain.) But doesn't this line of specula-tion assume that both psychoanalysis and cinema are themselves interested in testimony as to the existence of mind, that it is part of the value of both that they provide modern testimony, testimony acceptable to a modern sensibility, as to psychic reality? Yes.

Freud's brutal insistence to Dora of her knowledge precipitates her termination of the analysis, and part of the crux of her case is whether her leaving is a realistic rebuke to Freud's bullying or whether it is a denial that confirms the truth of his claim. Another part of the crux (taking up Freud's reporting of the case as one in which he learned of the power of countertransference, having failed to take into account his identification, call it, with the woman) is the extent to which psychoanalysis is, and presented itself to Freud as, the theft of women's knowledge, that knowledge which, suppressed, caused the conditions psychoanalysts were first asked to see, conditions of hysteria. Gregory's "Don't get hysterical, Paula" is said to her suggestively, so this figure further encodes a resemblance to psychoanalysis in the man's power of hypnosis or suggestion, and it thus invokes the—again current—criticism of the scientific pretensions of psychoanalysis, that it coerces the confessions it claims as its evidence. And, to be sure, if all psycho-analysts were, and were by the psychoanalytic process compelled to be, essentially like Gregory Anton, the criticism would be valid. (Why, one should accordingly ask, is this such a critic's picture of the psychoanalyst?—recognizing that a Gregory Anton might also ask *that* question.)

A last line of comparison I invoke between *Gaslight* and the Dora case concerns the sense in Freud's account that the woman had been handed over to him by her father, as if to help continue her obedience to, or subservience within, the world of men. This might at first seem to be Paula's case as well, as she moves from the hands of the lawyer into that of the singing teacher, and from there into the hands of the piano player. But both Gregory and the detec-tive arrive as from Paula's aunt, thus from a connection with the world of women (called for by the genre of the unknown woman): it is surely because of Gregory's association with the aunt's singing teacher that we imagine his general route into Paula's confidence; and the missing glove is a direct sign of the bearer's having been *sent* by the aunt, as if to overcome false emissaries. That the glove is also presented as if by a child, the boy to whom the aunt has entrusted the memento (a sign of an undoubted memory), is also to the point: it invokes in the child another figure called for by the genre, and at the same time it presents the young detective as not quite or just another grown man; he is in effect a part of Paula's childhood.

Her childhood is invoked poignantly the night of Lady Dalroy's musicale and dinner party. The anticipation of the evening gives Paula courage for the single time in the process of her decreation to oppose Gregory and to command the obedience of the scornful maid Nancy, declaring her intention to go to the party alone if necessary. Then, the opening exchange with Lady Dalroy gives a vivid picture of Paula in command of her faculties: "You're Paula Anton; I'm sure you don't remember me." "Indeed I do, Lady Dalroy. I was at the children's party here, and there was a magician." The combination of her powers of decision and command and of her intact memory, in particular her memory of her childhood, within the orbit of a powerful woman, poses a threat to Gregory's plan, and he uses this outburst of Paula's confidence, the show of the woman she might have been, might be, as the occasion to crush her hopes at their strongest. His defeat of her on this critical ground prepares her for the crisis, in which she accepts her fate of being declared and confined as mad. This sequence thus repeats the rhythm of the maddening established by Gregory in the preceding sequence, where he had countermanded Paula's invitation to the inquisitive neighbor (the spinster figure, Miss Thwaites, played by Dame May Whitty) to come into the house, and then bullied Paula, with sweet reasonableness, into agreeing that she *could* have had the woman in if she had really wished it (thus suggesting that Paula's problem is her own metaphysical, intellectual occultism, and not social and psychological violence; it is what metaphysics chronically suggests). Then out of the blue Gregory announces, having somehow begun playing a tune from *Die Fledermaus* on the piano (to change the mood, or cover it), that they are going out to the theater this evening, so clearly there is no time now for a visitor. Paula is stunned with elation, and Gregory charmingly, teasingly gets her to deny, as if it were the reverse of the truth, the childish thought that he is a bad man who keeps her a prisoner. As she lets her spirits extend into a whirling dance to his music, and fills the

room with painful laughter and uncertain singing—it is the only
recurrence of her singing voice after the early lesson with Signor
Guardi—Gregory breaks off the music and begins a methodical
strangling of Paula's rising spirits by accusing her of the meaningless action of having taken a picture from the wall and hidden it.
(The passage into and out of dancing is one of immense cinematic
and theatrical bravura, on the part both of actress and of director.
I find in it an allusion to the passage in *A Doll's House* near the end
of Act 2 in which Nora is being instructed in dancing by male
piano playing. Nora's husband is replaced at the piano by Dr. Rank,
friend of the household, who encourages a wilder dancing which
her husband then puts a stop to, saying, "This is sheer madness. . . .
You've forgotten everything I taught you"; and having just said,
"Nora darling, you're dancing as if your life depended on it," which
she confirms. The power of demonic piano playing possessed by a
foreign or invasive male with some shadow over him is a figure, as
noted earlier, that appears in several of Cukor's films.)

It is worth noticing here, for those who still have difficulty
believing just how well made well-made movies can be, that Paula's
memory of the magician plays ironically into her blindness to Gregory's strategy at the party, which is precisely to make a watch magically appear. He had earlier held her bag open, and waited (as if
keeping the camera running) until she turned to see him, unmistakably, drop the brooch he had given her into her bag—a perfectly
ordinary bag. The new trick of making the watch appear matches
and caps the trick of making the brooch disappear. His feeling
around the outside of the soft bag until he discovers the outline of
the hard watch (in close-up) is in a sense his most intimate gesture
toward her since their embraces in the opening sequences of the
film.

Here we might consider that we witness the gaslight dimming
only in her bedroom. (We witness its return to normal only at the
last, in her husband's room, near the end of her interview with the
detective. Artfully, the return to normal is shown to be as much
the cause of fear, as much an event to be aghast at, as the dimming.)
It is specifically her bedroom that her husband twice abandons her
in, or to, in extreme terror—the first time in terror, as she puts it,
"of this house, of myself," the second time in terror of her sentence
to a madhouse, I mean to a different madhouse. (She had described
her house to her new husband, the place to which that husband

has already confined her, as "a house of horror.") What goes on in her bedroom with him are scenes of psychic torture, prepared by the woman's sense that she is fated to horror, that her desires are twisted and incomprehensible to the one figure in her life who now defines reality for her, that these normal, human desires are by no means to be satisfied but to be deplored and humiliatingly confessed. This is figured in the opening sequence of Paula's and Gregory's guided tour of the Tower of London (preceding the sequence of their viewing the Crown Jewels), as Paula discovers that the brooch Gregory had given her is missing, and the institutionally confident voice of the tour guide (continuing in voice-over) accompanies her imagination as he picturesquely describes the method of torture on the rack. Gregory's impotence seems to me implied in various ways; for example, by his nameless fear of the young man; by his flirtatiousness in response to the overtures of the housemaid (played by Angela Lansbury); by his implying, when he asks the maid to explain her makeup secrets to his wife, that his wife is unattractive to him; and by the gross, general displacement rendered in his obsession with jewels. But I am not here concerning myelf with Gregory's story. It is in a sense inessential. (The essential or first question in considering his relation to Paula is whether he does or does not fully recognize the thing that everyone else knows who knows Paula well—that she strikingly resembles her aunt. That we are not given the means to know whether Gregory fully recognizes this, or cares about it, suggests to me the irrelevance of this man's story—as if there is nothing remarkable in this telling of its twistings, as if all women face equivalent turns in the men to whom they give themselves in marriage.) And I urge that before coming further to terms with what the sequences in her bedroom may betoken—in particular before proffering some obvious Freudian symbolism of jewels and Gregory's fetishizing of them as all this film knows of the relationship between this man and woman—we have more evidence to ponder concerning how that relationship is to be described.

The detective describes it as one in which Paula is "being systematically driven out of her mind," and grateful as we are for his practicality and enlightenment, here and hereafter, he does not satisfy our more speculative, or let us say dramaturgical interests. For example, when Paula asks how her husband could be up in the attic, the detective answers by describing the path he takes "over

Here the path is opened for considering Paula to be responding to lowering lamps and noises in the attic as to a ghost story, or ghost play. (Then where does that place us?)

the roof," rather than responding to her evident wish to know how her husband could be doing such a thing at all. A way of describing the mode of torture that is systematically driving Paula out of her mind is to note that she is being deprived of words, of her right to words, of her own voice. Sometimes this happens by her being made ashamed to describe what she sees and hears (the dimming light, the noise—one might disgracefully call them fragments of a primal scene); sometimes by her being made to know that her protestations of innocence will not be believed, and her desire for companionship will not be heard; and sometimes by her being offered a simple description, such as "My watch is gone," and being invited to supply the speech-act of blaming, as if every fact accuses her.

The idea of deprivation of the right to words alerts us again to the ways the therapeutic process is pictured in this film. Upon the detective's confirming the dimming of the light, the woman says, "You saw that too? Then it really happens. . . . Now I can tell you.

Every night when my husband goes out. . . ." She stops, startled by
hearing her own words. The man continues for her, carrying on
her words: "The light goes down. Then what?" And she is able to
go on: "I hear things. . . . I watch. . . . Then the light goes up." A
hesitation again, and again the man continues: "And he comes
back." And again she can take the words on: "Yes. Always quite
soon after." A dog would have had no trouble making such a
connection. Only a human being could be *prohibited* from making
it, from subjecting herself to her own words, having her own
thoughts. In *The Claim of Reason*[2] I call something like this "having
a voice in your own history," and compare the ways by which one
may be so denied (deny oneself) in philosophy and in politics. This
denial of voice is not the loss of speech, a form of aphasia, but a
loss of reason, of mind, as such—say of the capacity to count, to
make a difference. The image of this denial that haunts Paula—
and that men keep telling her to forget—she reveals to Gregory
moments after they reopen the house in London, as she recites her
discovery of her murdered aunt: "She had been strangled. . . . Her
lovely face was all—No! I can't stay here!" The young detective, in
giving her an explanation, in a sense, of what she saw, bringing
her back from strangulation, reintroducing her to language (demonstrating that her words are not shameful, but ordinary and
perfectly credible, that the act of speech is hers to define), returns
her to her voice—becoming, one can say, her voice teacher.

Here something of the uncanny power of the medium of film—
its natural surrealism and violence—shows through. Suppose we
take the film as an exploration of the question Paula asks her
singing teacher in the film's first sequence proper (after the brief
prologue): "I have no voice, have I?" The maestro answers: "The
trouble is not with your voice alone. Your heart is not in your
singing any more." He does not answer the question of her having
a voice so far as it concerns a special talent or gift that Paula is questioning in herself, and he goes on to suggest that she is in love, and
tells her to forget tragedy (alluding to her aunt's murder, but also
somehow to the meaning of singing), and urges her to take the
chance of happiness—which, he adds, is better than art, thus
explicitly raising the question both of what happiness is and what
art means. The question of the possession of a voice and of the
meaning of singing is set up by the prologue, in which, more fully,

the vaguely official man says to the child Paula, as they drive in a hansom away from the house:

> "No, no, Paula. Don't look back. You've got to forget everything that's happened here. That's why you're going to Italy, to see Signor Guardi. He was the best friend your Aunt ever had and he'll be yours too. Perhaps Signor Guardi will make you into a great singer as she was. Wouldn't you like that?"

The young Paula (who when we next see her in Italy ten years later seems barely twenty years old) continues to look bewildered and speechless, as well she might. Where in the history of (let us say legitimate) theater could one imagine a play opening with words such as: "Perhaps Signor Guardi will make you into a great singer. Wouldn't you like that?" One could imagine Groucho Marx saying it to Margaret Dumont, or W. C. Fields to a ten-year-old brat whom he fears and despises and offers to strike. But film has the power also to slip past comic censorship and to design for us a fantasy we are to find our own way out of.

From the interrupted singing lesson with Signor Guardi Paula goes to meet Gregory in the corner of a courtyard flanked by barred windows, where he says, "I've waited for you so long," and she replies, "We've only known one another two weeks"—to which he counters, "I've waited all my life," his words steeping language in ironies from which it may never recover. After her later voice lesson from the young detective she goes again to meet Gregory, this time ascending forbidden stairs alone, as if into her mind— literally into the space above her bedroom from which the mad- dening noises originated, and finds the man roped to a chair. She asks the detective to let her speak to her husband alone, eagerly locks herself together with her husband in the attic room as the detective reluctantly leaves, and launches into her aria of revenge. Signor Guardi had stopped the early, literal singing lesson with the words, "This opera is tragedy, Signorina, a thing you seem inca- pable of understanding. Did you never hear your Aunt sing Lucia? You *look* like her." "But," responded Paula, "I don't sing like her." Now, at the end of the film, we are given her version of the mad song, prompted, as in *Lucia,* by the violent end of her marriage, and bearing certain earmarks of her aunt's performance.

We know that her aunt performed so that only one person in

her audience knew the secret of what she was hiding in plain view: the royal jewels sewn into her gown among worthless stones. Now, Paula uses her voice so that her husband (or someone who is, as it were, identified with his position—fixed to a chair, in reversed roles with her, subject to her vengeance, us) alone is in a position to know the open significance of her spectacle of madness, of what is sewn into her mind. She intones:

> "Are you suggesting that this is a knife? I don't see any knife. You must have dreamed you put it there. . . . Are you mad, my husband? Or is it I who am mad? Yes. I am mad. . . . If I were not mad I could have helped you. . . . But because I am mad I hate you, and because I am mad I have betrayed you [thus she defines the speech-act of her voice lesson with the detective], and because I am mad I am rejoicing in my heart without a shred of pity, with glory in my heart."

Her *cogito* thus comes to the singing of her existence, and she chants this existence, accepts herself, as mad. (The mood is helped by the apparent allusion to Macbeth's hallucinated dagger.) Nor is she, so far as I understand, recovered from this state as the film ends. After calling the detective back into the attic room to "Take this man away," she has only two or three small sentences left to say. Walking out onto the roof balcony of the house with the detective (the route she refused to cut her husband free, in cutting herself free, to take) she says, "This will be a long night"—something madness can know about itself. This time the detective speaks allegorically (one hopes), as melodrama will, about the weather: "It's already starting to clear." But this is a mere courtesy. His going on to ask, "Will you let me come and talk to you sometime?" is a subtler and more practical courtesy; he does not expect that Paula will talk to him. She is back where she started, or stopped, at best—the place from which she was to be rescued from her fears and her ignorance of the world by marriage to a mysterious stranger. Her identification, through the aria, with her dead aunt has rescued her from that rescue, but the world of women here seems to hold no further hope; it cannot conceive of it. Women's options in this universe—apart from the exceptional aristocratic title (such as that possessed by Lady Dalroy) and outside the state of matrimony (if these women are indeed to be understood as being outside, rather than serving as further figures for present states of matrimony)— are the flirtatiousness of the maid, the deafness of the cook, or the shocked spectatordom of the spinster; a set of options perfect for maintaining the perfect liberty and privilege of the male.

The figure of a magician and piano player who exercises a hypnotic control over a singer is bound at some stage to invoke Svengali, a figure from the late nineteenth century that has also been associated with the early practice of Freud and Breuer. But Svengali loved Trilby, and the voice upon which he lavished his unearthly skill was hers. In his cultivation of it he took control of it, but the world-historical singing that resulted is no more accurately described as his voice ventriloquized through her than as her voice possessed by him. The joint inhabitation here is no doubt at best a parody of love, but it is not a parade of hatred: distinctions are to be made. It is a parody, moreover, this sharing of the same voice, that comedies of remarriage look for a sane version of—that is, show it to be worth looking for a sane version of.

Another association to mysteriously absorbed singing keeps impinging on my consciousness, doubtless because Svengali is a Jew, and surely because this particular material began coming together during my time in Jerusalem (on and off through the spring of 1986). The events of Kafka's story "Josephine the Singer, or the Mouse Folk" are generally accepted, I believe, as modeling something about the Jews, I suppose about the dispersion of the Jews, particularly in the story's relation to prophecy. My association turns on two thoughts in the story: on Kafka's question whether the singer creates the people for whom she sings, or the other way around; and on his question whether a singer can, as it were, express a people who did not themselves already sing, and hence whether one should really call what she does singing, since it is not different from what goes on every day—whether we call it chanting, or beseeching, or saying. The allegory drawn this way seems no more apt for the relation of a prophet or perhaps a philosopher to a people than for an artist (of a certain stripe) to a public, and perhaps especially, as I will suggest, to a movie public (where the public is apparently openly *all* of the people, the populace, whose lives are not different—are they?—from screened lives).

It was the conjunction of film with madness, skepticism, and the *cogito,* together with the issues of discipleship and of the finding of one's voice, that prompted my earlier citing of Derrida's review of Foucault. Articulating this conjunction of themes forms one sort of response to a question repeatedly directed to me, in various guises, which I might formulate in this way: What is film that it invites you to discuss philosophical issues of this kind, and why specifically do you wish to accept the invitation from film (when there are so many other places)? So I will spell out this response a little in terms of a fragment or two in answer to another demand equally often pressed upon me in recent years—to say how I understand my relation to philosophical developments in France over the same years as those in which I have been doing my work, say the past three decades, especially to that of Derrida. I hope that these fragments will provide an efficient measure of the level of discussion that my concluding descriptions of this woman and her film will lay claim to—that is, the level my descriptions will claim that this woman and her film lay claim to.

I note two autobiographical moments in Derrida's reflections on Foucault's *Madness and Civilization,* moments in his lecture of March 4, 1963.[3] I may be the last person I know to read this lecture of Derrida's, and I dare say he is past interest in the reactions it elicits. But I have claimed that American intellectual time is in any case different from European, beginning with the birth of American thinking in Emerson, who in the 1840s and 1850s was writing as if before the post-Kantian split between the German and the English traditions of philosophy—as if it need not have taken place. One could say either that I am still a generation late, or else that I am, as in a good tragedy, working my way backward to a recognition.

The first of Derrida's autobiographical moments I note is his opening ironic declaration that "having formerly had the good fortune to study under Michel Foucault, I retain the consciousness of an admiring and grateful disciple" (p. 31); the second moment is his closing declaration that "I philosophize only in *terror,* but in the *confessed* terror of going mad" (p. 62). These moments cast in their elaboration, an uncanny light on certain of my own preoccupations in those years around 1960—preoccupations, or a facet of my preoccupations, that there would still perhaps be no particular point in stressing, no ready circle of interest in, apart from the delayed resonance of contemporary intellectual developments in France (which is doubtless part of the reason why I am now questioned particularly about my relation to them). Derrida speaks of discipleship (unironically, I take it) in terms of "start[ing] to speak," or, shall we say, finding a voice:

> The disciple's consciousness, when he starts, I would not say to dispute, but to engage in dialogue with the master or, better, to articulate the interminable and silent dialogue which made him into a disciple—this disciple's consciousness is an unhappy consciousness. . . . As a disciple, he is challenged by the master who speaks within him and before him, to reproach him for making this challenge and to reject it in advance, having elaborated it before him. (P. 31)

And Derrida, in confessing the terror of going mad, is responding to his characterization of philosophy as "perhaps the reassurance given against the anguish of being mad at the point of greatest proximity to madness" (in the preceding sentence he had spoken of the philosopher's reflecting of the *cogito* for the other, that is, for oneself, as a relationship in which "meaning reassures itself against madness and nonmeaning" [p. 59]).

The title essay of my first book, *Must We Mean What We Say?*[4] (from a talk delivered in 1957), characterizes the ordinary language philosophers—whose work I therein claim to inherit, specifically by placing myself in the relation of discipleship to Austin—as "continuing—while at the same time their results are undermining—the tradition of British Empiricism: being gifted pupils, they seem to accept and to assassinate with the same gesture" (p. 21n.19). The gesture, in particular, is one of "reminding ourselves of *what we should say when*," which turns out to be a matter of reinserting or replacing the human voice in philosophical thinking, that voice that philosophy finds itself to need to deny, or displace. (It is this denial of voice that, for me, determines philosophy's drive to the hyperbolic. How this relates to Derrida's findings concerning the denial of writing is no small matter, at least for me.) Four essays later, in the context of thinking about Beckett's *Endgame*, I characterize philosophical profundity as taking the shape of madness, and summarize Wittgenstein's philosophical procedures as declaring, or confessing, that there is "no other philosophical path to sanity save through madness" (p. 127). These statements about replacing the voice and about the mad itinerary of sanity could be the epigraphs to *The Claim of Reason*. That book of mine is about skepticism as sketched, for example, in

Descartes's *Meditations*—skepticism interpreted as the repudiation of language (or reason) by itself—and about the recovery from this repudiation as the return, if it is possible, from tragedy, say from the community's expulsion. But this early congruence of Derrida's and my interests in discipleship, voice, Cartesian skepticism, and madness takes place within as yet immeasurable differences.

A banal but decisive difference between us lies—or did, all those unknown years ago—in our accounts of Descartes's hyperbolic doubt (something we both contrast with what we both call "natural" doubt). For Derrida this is a turn to excess or exaggeration (and hence oddly resembles Austin's view of the matter, as when Austin says: "Some philosophers are prone to argue that because I *sometimes* cannot know that therefore I *never* can");[5] whereas for me the hyperbolical is a turn to emptiness (sometimes I say a craving for nothingness), a wish to exist outside language games—not so much as it were beyond language, perhaps, as before it. Both excess and emptiness express the human wish to escape the human—the desire for the inhuman, or the demonic.

A sublime difference between us lies—or did—in our conceptions of philosophy, a path of difference drawn, to my mind, by an affinity, one hard for me to characterize, one that takes philosophy to exist only in its questioning of itself, its threats to itself. The difference is suggested, in those of Derrida's reflections that I confine myself to, in his division of nonphilosophy from philosophy: "Foucault would be correct . . . if we were to remain at the naive, natural, and premetaphysical stage of Descartes's itinerary, the stage marked by natural doubt" and not come to "the properly philosophical, metaphysical, or critical phase of doubt" (p. 52). I would like to say: for me there is no itinerary, say no approach, to philosophy; rather philosophy comes upon me, approaches me, like a conversion. This may seem a trivial difference, but it is to my mind as important as the division as such between philosophy and nonphilosophy. The difference may be read in that strain or moment of philosophizing when philosophy does not recognize itself as having a history. Being a master of (whatever else) what may be thought of as the history of Western philosophy, Derrida recognizes (or did) himself and philosophy as having something like a history, preceded by a line or lines of thinking beginning with the Greeks. I believe that no American (North American? Middle American?) conceives this of himself and his or her philosophy. (Derrida might perhaps reply that he does not assume history, especially not one continuity of history, but rather plays with, or plays off, history. Then I might reply: No American philosopher plays off history. If Emerson does something of the sort, it is not out of a sense that the history may be taken to be his, but in the knowledge that it is not.) Analytical philosophy is of course made, as science is, always to escape its history. On this ground, where the myth of pure thought dwells, Thoreau is for once and in full irony at one with the later Americans, as when he says: "The oldest Egyptian or Hindoo philosopher raised a corner of the veil from the statue of the divinity . . . and I gaze upon as fresh a glory as he did, since it was I in him that was then so bold, and it is he in me that now reviews the vision. . . . No time has elapsed since that divinity was revealed,"[6] which is to say that there is no history for philosophy, always only an origin, which the present preserves or fails.

For Derrida the land of thought is fully occupied, as it were, by the finished edifice of philosophy, one that has genuinely been built by the impulse to philosophy, so that room for thought must be made, say by a process of reading or writing or following on by the pedagogy called deconstructon; whereas for an American the question persists whether the land of thought has as yet been discovered, whether it will be today, and whether it is at best occupied by fragments, heaped in emergency, an anthology of rumor. (My picture here is, perhaps, of the transcendentalists pouring over Coleridge's collection of excerpts and comments called *Aids to Reflection*.) Might one find some ground to deconstruct before there are any philosophical foundations in place? As if language is from the beginning a standing source of distortion. It seems a vision motivating what leads both to Beckett and to logical positivism.

And one can perhaps say that working to avert foundation, in advance, is precisely what Emerson and Thoreau were doing in founding, or deconfounding, American thinking. Certainly they found the way to thought, could not avoid the way, that drew their writing to the long coastlines of madness. I understand Emerson to be writing in general in the procedure of what in "Self-Reliance" he calls self-reliance, which he there defines as "the aversion of conformity." Conformity is the state in which society sees to it that its members live, the state, accordingly, in which we mostly do live. This state is characterized by Emerson as voicelessness—or, say, hyperbolic inexpressiveness—and thus as a form of madness. Writing in the aversion of conformity is a continual turning away from society, hence a continual turning toward it, as for reference—as if the philosopher is a dervish between madness and sanity. One might call this process of writing deconformity. Since walking, feet on the ground, is more Thoreau's speed, he puts the matter a little differently: "With thinking we may be beside ourselves in a sane sense," which closely translated means that thinking aspires to ecstasy; hence Thoreau is broadly implying that the thinking we on the whole go in for leaves us beside ourselves in an insane sense, which he specifies as despair; we would say depression, or melancholia.

Now, since in Emerson's and Thoreau's world philosophers have not yet as a group separated themselves from the community, they cannot assume that they are writing for identifiable philosophers, and so they are reticent about declaring their own fears of madness—put this as the threat that they will not be able to guide, or ride out, their accession to ecstasy. Reticent not for themselves but because of the directness of the implication (they call it the conviction) of their fellow countrymen: one would not want too openly to invite another to the risk and party of madness who has not already shown his or her readiness for it. They leave themselves dismissible, protecting society from wrong access to them, if they can, as when the writer of *Walden* successively identifies himself with the bird of awakening (the rooster), the bird of prophecy (the owl), and the bird of madness (the loon): you may take him or leave him alone, which is where and what he is. In a land without an edifice of thought, in which the first cabins of thought are still under construction, there is no question of wishing to go back, as if historically or pedagogically or archaeologically, to the day of thought's founding—its metaphysical point of departure from chaos, or emptiness, or madness. The question is rather one of detecting these departures and arrivals each day. (Emerson's founding question he can express, in the opening sentence of "Experience," by asking "Where do we find ourselves?"[7] So, for example, when in *The Claim of Reason* I interpret certain famous parables in Wittgenstein's *Investigations* (that of the idea of a private language, and the related one of the person who insists on saying that there must be something boiling in a picture of a boiling pot), I say that they are meant to draw out the bits of madness or emptiness that philosophers, being human beings, are subject to under the pressure of taking thought (p. 336). And if Wittgenstein's interlocutors in those places (which is to say, any of the voices Wittgenstein contends with in himself, as a philosopher) suffer moments of madness and emptiness, then where not in the moments of the *Investigations,* where not in the event of philosophy? I go on to say that a philosopher's failing to recognize these outbreaks, to confess their madness, as it were, is itself a sign that the outbreak is shared. Moreover, since I am there placing myself in opposition to certain standing interpretations of those parables of Wittgenstein's, I am naming certain fellow professors of philosophy as sharing these outbreaks or bits of madness. That I mean this naming impersonally, and include myself within this term of criticism, will not altogether set aside the suspicion that I am stepping beyond the bounds of academic manners, even if my remarks are seen as a compliment to philosophical genuineness. Were my immediate audience Foucault—and, say, Artaud, or Bataille, or Blanchot, or Lacan, or Deleuze, or Derrida—the issue of the bounds of manners would itself be shared. But as matters stand the cultural (or say stylistic) distance between American and French intellectual life sometimes strikes me as maddeningly untraversable; too near to ignore, too far to go. So, naturally, I am reticent in my self-revelations, as I am reticent in giving away the positions of my masters, Emerson and Thoreau. (Then what am I doing now? Why now?)

Derrida's weaving of irony and openness in his claims for discipleship bears further thought. Since I find our voices passing and repassing in the experiments I have made with certain of the passages of an early essay of his, and of certain others, I am led to take his reflections on discipleship as, more generally, or more specifically, reflections on reading at its most faithful—as if at its most faithful reading consists of this competition or mutual inhabitation or mutual subjection of voices. Then one had better be careful of what it is one is drawn to read faithfully. This takes me back to my interest in film—I mean to my practice of working out such concepts as I am invoking here sometimes in relation to film and to films, and specifically back to the mad song in *Gaslight*.

I APPROACH IT by inquiring into the film's title, into gaslight. In a definitive remarriage comedy made three years earlier, Preston Sturges's *The Lady Eve,* a supporting character tells the lady (Barbara Stanwyck) that he has just conned the film's sucker/hero (Henry Fonda) with the story of "Cecelia, the Coachman's Daughter," which he calls a "gaslight melodrama"; this character goes on to describe it as one of those impossibly old-fashioned popular productions about innocence and villainy set in a dualistic, heavily symbolic universe, dealing in events of dispossession and of the loss and the finding of identities, and so on—the sort of thing that sophisticated con artists like themselves laugh about and are beyond believing. The bigger and better laugh for us, more or less implicit, is that *The Lady Eve* is thus declaring a certain relation, to be defined, between the con game(s) of its own depiction and the equally venerable con game(s) of melodramatic narrative. Our *Gaslight* is such a production as Sturges comically alludes to, with this decisive difference; it is a film, yet one, let us say, that is lit by the same light as gaslight melodramas (by the same mood, transfigured)—as is declared in the opening shot of a lamplighter lighting a street lamp, which illuminates the screen. (Cukor's own *Adam's Rib* analogously declares its affiliation with classical melodrama in depicting a mock film melodrama—an imitation two-reeler called a "Too Real Epic"—of villainy and innocence and the rescue from dispossession. Since this affiliation is not just alluded to but shown within film itself, and still within a certain mode of comedy, the melodrama is itself presented comically, in this case as a home movie, thus attesting to the underlying unity of the world of film as well as to the domestic provenance of a certain genre of melodrama.) But what is this "decisive difference" of film? What is the work of film? (I will not here take in evidence the fact that an arc lamp projector is directly a form of gaslight.) If this film belongs among the defining members of a genre, it ought to tell a piece of this difference.

Following the cue of the light, of the rising and falling of the light as a cause of madness, and considering that this rising and falling is the light by which *we* see the figures on the screen, we have to ask whether there is something in the light of film that is inherently (not, of course, inveterately) maddening. Here I think of my emphasis, in speaking of photography, of photography's metaphysically hallucinatory character, its causing us to see things that are absent: it makes things present to us to which we are not present. Hence I call film a moving image of skepticism. In viewing film we know ourselves to be in Paula's condition of victimization, in need of ratification, if so far without her bad luck—as if to be human is to be subject to the madness of skepticism. An acknowledgment of film's maddening light is expressed narratively in *Gaslight* as the connection between the wife's incomprehensibly (to her) fluctuating light and the apparently (to us) all too comprehensible actions of her husband. The film links Paula's fear of hallucination with the idea of hypnotism. ("Don't look at me like that," she cries, shielding her eyes. Have we stood back from that, from looking at her like that?)

But another feature of this narrative of rising and falling light is quite readable. That gas lighting works throughout a given household in such a way that one jet lowers or rises according to whether another jet, elsewhere in the house, is raised or lowered, is a phenomenon drummed in by the dialogue. We are never shown Paula lighting her own, or any other, lamp; hers waxes and wanes (inversely) with her husband's. Read this as: the woman's supply is drawn off by the man's unacknowledged need of it, and specifically by his unacknowledged, assumed power to demand it (his literal draining of her is not even part of his conscious deviousness). Then, in addition to the theme of hallucination as an interpretation of hypnotism, we are given the theme of vampirism; one life the sapping of another's, an interpretation of a certain state of human intimacy.

Emerson portrays what I understand this state to be in a passage from "Fate":

> Jesus said, "When he looketh on her, he hath committed adultery."
> But he is an adulterer before he has yet looked on the woman, by the superfluity of animal, and the defect of thought, in his constitution. Who meets him, or who meets her, in the street, sees that they are ripe to be each other's victim.[8]

Emerson's gesture here, following Jesus' internalization of the law, is to interiorize the matter further—unless characterizing the

condition as "fate" externalizes it. Either way, this mutual victimization, sapping of one another, vampirism, is what Emerson spots
as adultery; and since this state is to be seen between a pair in the
common street—I take the scene as one of encountering them
together, or putting them together, any ordinary day—we see the
state of public intimacy (call this marriage) as itself a state of adultery. Put into Emerson's structure of Fate, what this means is that
the given or conforming condition of marriage as adultery is what
we are fated to. Hence this condition is exactly something that self-
reliance calls upon us to challenge, to turn upon through our
equally primitive capacity to think in aversion to the given: Fate is
not itself our metaphysical fate, but an opening choice; we can
(this is the Kantian fact of reason) turn the account into freedom,
which is thus always an eventual condition. Strictly, I suppose,
adultery would be the name of any given, fixed relation to others
(the word *adultery* stems from a word meaning other); in Emerson's
understanding of conformity, it is the sapping of self-reliance, of
acting from one's own light. Then marriage, as it is given, would
be the perfected state of this adulterating, conforming fixation.

What are the conditions under which the woman of *Gaslight*
starts to act in her own light, takes on her voice, the power of voice
sufficient to turn upon her husband, terminate her marriage (call
it her marriage to fate), a voice found in the power of freedom,
initially, of madness? A practical fictional condition, as befits the
help of the good young detective, is that her husband is, let us say,
disarmed and restrained—that is, roped to a chair. A psychological
fictional condition is her assumption of identity with her aunt. But
what does this identification consist in? I have said that Paula's mad
song, her aria of revenge, succeeds or inherits her aunt's mad song
from *Lucia*. This implies that the camera and its transfigurations,
under projection, can turn, for one thing, human speech into
singing. So the question becomes: How has this star, this human
figure of flesh and blood, call her Ingrid Bergman, called upon the
camera to lend her this transfiguration? Part of the answer would
be to say what a star is, what it is about such human beings that
invites this favorable photogenesis. It is not knowable a priori, but
this film should be consulted on the matter.

We are told that the aunt's performances were double: a public
one, and simultaneously a private one, in which the precious tokens
of intimacy she was concealing from her public were displayed in

plain view. A public is, logically, required for something to be hidden in plain sight; the concept of intimacy in question is accordingly that of secrecy; it is the concept of intimacy that Gregory would steal. Paula performs for her husband fictionally in isolation, but with the knowledge that what is in plain view can never be displayed for him; he was always turned from it; what is in plain view is herself, her appeal for intimacy. Is she hiding her existence? Even if we see how to say yes to this, she is not keeping it a secret from Gregory; so for that very reason he is not in a position to penetrate it. And we might also say that what is concealed from him is revealed to and by the camera and its director, from whose hiddenness is determined what of the woman will be rendered to her public as in plain view—in view of which it is up to each of us to turn toward her and her film, in intimacy, knowing the gifts we render one another, or to turn from her and her film, in more or less common, appreciative ignorance. So both Svengali and Gregory are types—radically opposed types—both of the director and his or her camera, and of what you might call a film's dispersed public.

One moral to be drawn from this allegory—whether you think these relations healthy or unhealthy, escapable or inescapable, worth or not worth the fame and ecstasy they provide—is that what attracts the favorable powers of the camera and the projection of its work is a certain willingness and capacity of the star for exposure—say, for making herself visible with, as Paula puts it, "glory in her heart." A certain willingness for visibility is the way Emerson puts his version of the *cogito*'s demand in his taking on of Descartes for America, and his claim that we are ashamed to say "I am," afraid of the exposure of ourselves to the consciousness of others (say, of otherness, so of exposure to ourselves); from which Emerson draws the conclusion that we mostly do not exist, but haunt the world, ghosts of ourselves. When the detective first sees Paula, he says he thought he saw a ghost. He is registering her resemblance to her dead aunt, of course, a resemblance we have already learned from Signor Guardi, and from the portentous portrait of the aunt in costume, to be striking; but the detective is surely also responding to a quality of Paula's own bearing—of, let us say, her being bound but unclaimed. The price of Descartes' proof of human existence, of the mind's inability, as it were, to doubt itself, to doubt that it doubts, is that our relation to our bodies is attenuated; the price of Emerson's proof of human existence, our exposure to the consciousness of otherness (say our subjection to surveillance), is that our relation to ourselves is theatricalized, publicized. It is no wonder that it is in melodrama, and in movies, that such matters are worked out.

Not only there, of course, so I have still not answered why it is there among other places that I seek to trace their working out. What then is my more general interest in film as such beyond, as it were, my interest in particular films? I will answer here and now, in concluding, by stating five assumptions in three plus two sentences.

I assume that movies have played a role in American culture different from their role in other cultures, and more particularly that this difference is a function of the absence in America of the European edifice of philosophy. And since I assume further that American culture has been no less ambitious, craved no less to think about itself, than the most ambitious European culture, I assume further still that the difference everyone recognizes as existing between American and European literature is a function of the brunt of thought that American literature, in its foundings in, for instance, Emerson and Whitman and Poe, had to bear in that absence of given philosophical founding and edifice, lifting the fragments that the literature found, so to speak, handy and portable. Finally, I assume that American film at its best participates in this Western cultural ambition of self-thought or self-invention that presents itself in the absence of the Western edifice of philosophy, so that on these shores film has the following peculiar economy: it has the space, and the cultural pressure, to satisfy the craving for thought, the ambition of a talented culture to examine itself publicly; but its public lacks the means to grasp this thought as such for the very reason that it naturally or historically lacks that edfice of philosophy within which to grasp it.

Its film prepared to satisfy the craving for thought, and its public therefore deprived of recognizing the economy of its satisfaction, American culture casts its film and its film's public in the relation that is described in "Josephine the Singer" as existing between Josephine and her public. Each will think that it is the creator of the other: and film's public, for all its periodic adoration of its art, will fall to doubting the specialness and beauty of its art, and its own need for it; it will even come to doubt that its art is an art—that it sings—at all.

Postscript (1988)

The allegory of spirit through images and consequences of gaslighting may, if it does not put one off, put one on to wanting some (further) explanation of the connection. (The founding connection, for the work represented in my text, is always the fate of spirit as the fate of voice; so that strangulation and vampirism— the victimizations, respectively, of the aunt and of Paula—are psychically linked thefts, say of freedom, or separateness, differ- ence.) Beyond specifying the connection of rising and dimming gaslight with the ideas of vampirism, and of the husband's oblivi- ousness of his need, and of the woman's fear of the normal, I have suggested a connection with the man's incessant accusations or insinuations of the woman's metaphysical obscurity (described by him variously as her behaving "meaninglessly," as her "sleep- walking," finally as her being "mad"). Here I note his final announcement of his own metaphysical obscurity: "Don't try to understand me. . . . The jewels were a fire in my brain." (The *Amer- ican Heritage Dictionary* provides the meaning with which "gas" was coined by the chemist van Helmont (d. 1644) as "an occult principle supposed to be present in all bodies"—like, say, certain ideas of the mind. How this extends the etymological connection of "gas" with "chaos"—either as empty space or as disorder (or pre-order?) is a nice question.) Derrida, in response to my presen- tation, observed that "gas" and the fateful German Geist ("spirit," "mind," etc.) are related words. So, of course, are further varia- tions, which I have signaled within my text—Paula's being marked as a ghost, and her fear (or amazement) at events of rising and falling gaslight describable as her being aghast at them. Derrida's observation was not meant as an explanation of the connection, but it increases the pressure for one.

The extent to which, or sense in which, such domestic melo- dramas are ghost stories—a matter coming to another head, in Ibsen, in *Ghosts*—is laid out in the question the detective asks the constable after they have followed Gregory only to have him disap- pear into the fog, like a ghost: "You don't suppose he could have gone into his own house do you? . . . Why should a man walk out

A way of describing the mode of torture that is systematically driving Paula out of her mind is to note that she is being deprived of words, of her own voice. Sometimes this happens by . . . her being offered a simple description, such as "My watch is gone," and being invited to supply the speech-act of blaming, as if every fact accuses her.

of his own house, all the way around the corner, just to get back where he started from?" If we translate this as: "Why would he wish to enter his house unseen?" the answer is irresistible: in order to haunt the house, which is a way of inhabiting it. Here the path is opened for considering Paula to be responding to lowering lamps and noises in the attic as to a ghost story, or ghost play. (Then where does that place us?) This suggestion is confirmed by Gregory's last accusation of Paula, that her madness is inherited from her mother, who, he claims to have discovered, died in an insane asylum—himself now the fabricator of a ghost story, fictionalizing Paula's history as well as her perceptions. (In not considering Gregory's own story, I am not considering the extent to which he seems to come to believe his fabrications.) Paula had said to Gregory the morning after their wedding night that her mother died in giving birth to her, and that she never knew her father. It is a very questionable tale, not to say a haunting one, since Paula's "aunt" might have had her reasons for telling Paula the story: it could cover such a fact as that Paula's mother was indeed mad; or the fact that Paula is the "aunt's" child, whom it would have been most inconvenient for a famous actress, in a secret liaison with a royal figure, to acknowledge as hers (as theirs?). But the question for us is what Paula thinks of the story, why she speaks of it as knowing no more than these few words about so massive a matter of her life. She attaches great feeling and significance to the memory of her aunt's going over for her, on special occasions, the stories associated with her collection of theatrical mementos; but the child seems not to have asked about, nor to have had, mementos associated with the figure she calls her mother. As if she does not feel she has the right to know something, or as if she already knows something. Now consider again: Who does Paula know to be in the attic? And before all: Who did she know was there before she knew? And who am I to want to know what Paula knows—to speculate, for example, about Freud's observation, in discussing second marriages in his 1931 essay "Female Sexuality," that a woman's problems with her (first) husband will repeat her problems—Freud says, "disappointments"—with her mother. (A poltergeist is a ghost that manifests itself by noises and rappings. Evidently also by thumps and scraping. It stems from a word meaning to cry out.)

Explanation of the connection between gaslight and spirit may be taken as the tenor of the explanation given by the cook Elizabeth when Paula, drained, manages to scream down the stairwell for Elizabeth to come up. Entering Paula's room and, in response to Paula's question, assuring her that there's no one in the house to cause any dimming, Elizabeth adds: "But the gas comes in pipes; and I expect there gets more gas in the pipes at some times than there does at others." Paula sees the possibility: "Yes. Yes. I suppose that could explain it." It does not explain the ensuing noises, however, and it does not really in itself match what calls for an explanation: it does not connect the specific conduits between the seen and the unseen. (And can film do what Kant could not do?) But the dimension Elizabeth's explanation invokes of gas coming in pipes, and of having more or less gas put into the pipes, and not ones joining merely the rooms within this house, but one's linking this house with numberless other houses, is the dimension of a social organism in which this house functions, bound in the

Paula's mad song, her aria of revenge, succeeds her aunt's mad song from _Lucia_. . . .
How has this star, this human figure of flesh and blood, call her Ingrid Bergman, called
upon the camera to lend her this transfiguration?

networks of dependence of a vast city. Hence the dimension is an
allegory of those features of (modern) life that Gregory can depend
upon, without planning, that support the deference and secrecy
his plans require—the obedience of servants; the nightly visits to a
"studio" where he does mysterious, unshareable work; power to
exclude all other people and all other places from his marital privacy.
I do not have to say that his occupations are, allegorically, characteristic of the society that supports them to observe that his evil is, for
all its exotic trappings, utterly, unutterably, unoriginal—like the
preoccupations of melodrama.

My putting Gregory's unoriginal power to inflect the possibilities of ordinary social exchange toward mystery and evil, together
with his devotion to metaphysical obscurities, betrays perhaps my
memory of a conjunction Austin records in his "Other Minds":

The new trick of making the watch appear matches and caps the trick of making the brooch disappear. . . . A conjunction Austin records in his "Other Minds": "The wile of the metaphysician consists in asking 'Is it a real table?' . . . and not specifying what may be wrong with it. . . . *What are you suggesting?* . . . Conjurers, too, trade on this. 'Will some gentleman kindly satisfy himself that this is a perfectly ordinary hat?' . . . We haven't the least idea what to guard against."

"The wile of the metaphysician consists in asking 'Is it a real table?' (a kind of object which has no obvious way of being phoney) and not specifying or limiting what may be wrong with it, so that I feel at a loss 'how to prove' it is a real one. . . . *What are you suggesting?*" (Austin's emphasis). To which Austin appends the following footnote: "Conjurers, too, trade on this. 'Will some gentleman kindly satisfy himself that this is a perfectly ordinary hat?' This leaves us baffled and uneasy: sheepishly we agree that it seems all right, while conscious that we haven't the least idea what to guard against." Let us grant that Austin is too quick to invoke "the wile of the metaphysician" as the cause of our "feeling at a loss how to prove" reality. Evidently Austin would exempt himself, and his more candid philosophical procedures, at a stroke from the tendency of human unguardedness to mount systematic defenses, at devastating intellectual cost, against philosophical "suggestion" ("I cannot see all of any object so I cannot know with certainty that there is a table here").

Still, the condition of unguardedness and suggestibility that Austin isolates is traded on by psychological torturers (as often as not, no doubt, self-torturers)—a more extensive species than professional metaphysicians and magicians. Austin's philosophical animus in his appeals to ordinary language is explicitly to counter the skeptic, portrayed in the guise of trickster. But if skepticism reappears as (self-)torture, then Austin's portrayal does not reveal steps by which skepticism is to be defeated, but, on the contrary, gives the ground of its continued success, its open threat, say our openness to suggestion. (This should be related to a common criticism of deconstruction, that it partakes of the metaphysics it seeks to overcome. I have said that Austin underestimates the craving of metaphysics [ours for it, its for totality]. Does one believe [really] that Derrida underestimates the craving? My indebtedness to Austin is spelled out a little in the ensuing chapter.)

On the subject of obviousness and oblivion, or light and darkness, I pose again a question for those with the fixed idea that Hollywood film of the golden age (whose trade is, let us say, obviousness and oblivion) cannot know and explore the subjects I have been working out here, cannot, as it were (whether or not it recognizes itself in the terms in which I have described it), in certain of its signature works, assume responsibility for itself. What is the evidence for this idea? Should I regard what I have written here as evidence against it? But if indeed the conviction in Hollywood's metaphysical or magical ignorance is a fixed idea, then nothing would count as evidence for or against it. One would have instead to locate some spiritual trauma that has caused the fixation. It must be a late version of the trauma sustaining the idea that Emerson cannot know what he does, that to know his work just cannot be his work. It is a point on which America's admirers and its detractors eagerly agree.

His response to the assault of the ensuing
repeated images is to cover his eyes with the outspread fingers
of both hands in a melodramatic gesture
of horror and exhaustion.

2

Psychoanalysis and Cinema: Moments of <u>Letter from an Unknown Woman</u>

WHEN THE MAN IN Max Ophuls' film *Letter from an Unknown Woman* reaches the final words of the letter addressed to him by the, or by some, unknown woman, he is shown—according to well-established routines of montage—to be assaulted by a sequence of images from earlier moments in the film. This assault of images proves to be death-dealing. His response to finishing the reading of the letter is to stare out past it, as if calling up the film's images; and his response to the assault of the ensuing repeated images is to cover his eyes with the outspread fingers of both hands in a melodramatic gesture of horror and exhaustion. Yet he sees nothing we have not seen, and the images themselves (as it were) are quite banal—his pulling the veil of the woman's hat up over her face, the two of them at the Prater amusement park in winter, her taking a candied apple, their dancing, his playing a waltz for her on the piano in an empty ballroom. *An apparently excessive response to apparently banal images*—it seems a characterization of a response to film generally, at least to certain kinds of film, perhaps above all to classical Hollywood films. But since Max Ophuls is a director, and this is a film, of major ambition, the implication may be that the man's response here to the returning images of the film and of his past—his horror and exhaustion— somehow underlies our response to any film of this kind, perhaps to major film as such, or ought to. It seems a particular mode of horror that these hands would ward off, since we may equally think of the images looming at this man not as what he has seen but as what he has *not* seen, has refused to see. Then are we sure that we have seen what it is up to us to see? What motivates these images? Why does their knowledge constitute an assault? If *Letter from an Unknown Woman* were merely the high-class so-called woman's film it is commonly taken to be—as the bulk of the melodramas I refer to here are generally taken to be—it and they could not justify and satisfy the imposition of such questions of criticism.

Remarriage comedy, in effect enacting what Freud calls the diphasic character of human sexuality, displays the nostalgic structure of human experience. Since these films, being major achievements of the art of film, thus reveal some internal affinity of the phenomenon of nostalgia with the phenomenon of film, the popular nostalgia now associated with movies stands to be understood as a parody, or avoidance, of an inherent, treacherous property of the medium of film as such. The drama of the remarriage genre, the argument that brings into play the intellectual and emotional bravery of the distinctive, lucid pairs whose interactions or conversations form the interest of the genre—Irene Dunne and Cary Grant, Barbara Stanwyck and Henry Fonda, Katharine Hepburn and Spencer Tracy—turns on their efforts to transform an intimacy as between brother and sister into an erotic friendship capable of withstanding, and returning, the gaze of legitimate civilization. They conduct, in short, the argument of marriage. In *The Philadelphia Story* (directed by George Cukor in 1940) this ancient intimacy—here between Katharine Hepburn and Cary Grant—is called, twice, growing up together. In *The Awful Truth* (directed by Leo McCarey in 1937) the woman (Irene Dunne) actually, climactically, enacts a role as her husband's sister (the husband is again Cary Grant), in which this high-minded society lady blatantly displays her capacity for low-down sexiness.

The transformation of incestuous knowledge into erotic exchange is a function of something I call the achievement of the daily, of the diurnal, the putting together of night and day (as classical comedy puts together the seasons of the year), a process of willing repetition whose concept is the domestic, or marriage, however surprising the images of marriage become in these films. "Repetition" is the title Kierkegaard gives to his thoughts about the faith required in achieving marriage; and the willing acceptance of repetition, or rather eternal recurrence, is the recipe Nietzsche discovered as the antidote for our otherwise fated future of nihilism, the thing Nietzsche calls "the revenge against time and its 'It was'"—a revenge itself constituting a last effort not to die of nostalgia.

Nietzsche explicitly invokes the concept of marriage in his prophetic cry (in *Thus Spoke Zarathustra*) for this redemption or reconception of time. (In German *Hochzeit* [literally, high time] means marriage or wedding. In the section called "Of Great Events," Zarathustra says it is now *die höchste Zeit* [the highest time]; moreover, in the section called "The Seven Seals," Zarathustra explicitly enough presents his symbol of eternal recurrence as "the wedding ring of rings [*dem höchzeitlichen Ring der Ringe*]—the Ring of Recurrence.") These ideas of repetition may be said to require of our lives the perpetual invention of the present from the past, out of the past. This seems to be the vision of Freud's *Beyond the Pleasure Principle,* in which death—I take it to comprehend psychological death—comes either through the success of this invention, that is, the discovery of one's own death (hence, surely, of one's own life, say, of one's willingness to live), or else through the relapse of the psychological into the biological and beyond into the inorganic, which may be viewed as countermodes of repetition.

In writing *Pursuits of Happiness* I incurred a number of intellectual debts that I propose here not to settle but somewhat to identify and organize—in effect, to rewrite certain of my outstanding promissory notes. My initial business is to continue to confirm a prediction of *Pursuits of Happiness* to the effect that there must exist a genre of film, in particular some form of melodrama, adjacent to, or derived from, that of remarriage comedy, in which the themes and structure of the comedy are modified or negated in such a way as to reveal systematically the threats (of misunderstanding, of violence) that in each of the remarriage comedies dog its happiness. My next main business will be to say how I cloak my debt to the writing of Freud, which means to say what I conceive certain relations of psychoanalysis and philosophy to consist in. My concluding piece of business, as a kind of extended epilogue, will be to produce a reading of the moment I invoked in opening these remarks, a man's melodramatic covering of his eyes, from the Ophuls film from which I have adapted the title of the new genre.

THE PREDICTION THAT some form of melodrama awaited definition was based on various moments from each of the comedies of remarriage. In the earliest of the definitive remarriage structures, *It Happened One Night,* the pair work through episodes of poverty, theft, blackmail, and sordid images of marriage; in *The Awful Truth* the pair face distrust, jealousy, scandal, and the mindless rumoring of a prospective mother-in-law; in *His Girl Friday* the pair deal with political corruption, brutal moralism, and wasting cynicism; in *The Lady Eve* with duplicity and the intractableness of the past; in *The Philadelphia Story* with pretentiousness, perverseness, alcoholism, and frigidity.

But it is in the last of the remarriage comedies, *Adam's Rib,* that melodrama threatens on several occasions almost to take the comedy over. The movie opens with a sequence, in effect a long prologue, in which a wife and mother tracks her husband to the apartment of another woman and shoots him. Played by the virtuoso Judy Holliday, the part is continuously hilarious, touching, and frightening, so that one never rests content with one's response to her. An early sequence of the film proper (so to speak) consists of the screening of a film-within-a-film, a home movie that depicts the principal pair coming into possession of their country house in Connecticut, in which Spencer Tracy twice takes on comically the postures and grimaces of an expansive, classical villain, threatening, with a twirl of his imaginary mustache, to dispossess Katharine Hepburn of something more precious than country houses. These passing comic glimpses of the man's villainous powers recur more disturbingly toward the end of the film, when he in turn tracks his spouse and confronts her in what he might conceivably take to be a compromising situation, and for all the world threatens to shoot her and her companion (David Wayne). What he is threatening them with soon proves to be a pistol made of licorice, but not too soon for us to have confronted unmistakably a quality of violence in this character that is as genuine—such is the power of Spencer Tracy as an actor on film— as his tenderness and playfulness. I say in the chapter on *Adam's Rib* in *Pursuits of Happiness* that Tracy's character as qualified in this film declares one subject of the genre as a whole to be the idea of maleness itself as villainous, say sadistic. (Having made his legal point, Tracy turns the candy gun on himself, into his mouth, and proceeds to eat it—a gesture that creates its comic effect but that also smacks of madness and of a further capacity for violence and horror hardly less frightening on reflection than the simple capacity for shooting people in anger.) The suggestion I drew is that if the masculine (I should say, male heterosexual) gender as such, so far in the development of our culture, and in so beautifully developed a specimen of it as Spencer Tracy, is tainted with villainy, then the happiness in even these immensely privileged marriages exists only so far as the pair together locate and contain this taint—you may say domesticate it, make a home for it—as if the task of marriage is to overcome the villainy in marriage itself. Remarriage comedies show the task to be unending and the interest in the task to be unending.

The taint of villainy leaves a moral cloud, some will say a polit- ical one, over these films, a cloud that my book does not try, or wish, to disperse. It can be pictured by taking the intelligent, vivid women in these films to be descendants of Nora in Ibsen's *A Doll's House,* who leaves her husband and children in search of what she calls, something her husband has said she required, an education. She leaves saying that he is not the man to provide her with one, implying both that the education she requires is in the hands of men and that only a man capable of providing it, from whom it would be acceptable, could count for her as a husband. Thinking of the woman of remarriage comedy as lucky to have found such a man, remarriage comedy studies, among other matters, what has made him, inescapably bearing the masculine taint, acceptable. That she can, with him, have what the woman in *The Awful Truth* calls "some grand laughs" is indispensable, but not an answer; the ques- tion becomes how this happens with him.

This prompts two further questions, with which we are entered into the melodrama of unknownness. What of the women who have not found, and could not manage or relish a relationship with such a man, Nora's other, surely more numerous, descendants? And what, more particularly, of the women of the same era on film who are at least the spiritual equals of the women of remarriage comedy but whom no man can be thought to educate—I mean the women we might take as achieving the highest reaches of stardom, of female independence so far as film can manifest it—Greta Garbo and Marlene Dietrich and, at their best, Bette Davis and Barbara Stanwyck and Ingrid Bergman, perhaps a few others.

The price of the woman's happiness in the genre of remarriage comedy is the absence of her mother (underscored by the attrac- tive and signal presence, whenever he is present, of the woman's

father) together with the strict absence of children for her, the
denial of her as a mother—as if the woman has been abandoned,
so far, to the world of men. Could remarriage comedies achieve their
happiness in good faith if they denied the possibility of another
path to education and feminine integrity? It would amount to
denying that the happiness of these women indeed exacts a price,
if of their own choice, affordable out of their own talents and tastes,
suggesting instead that women without these talents and tastes are
simply out of luck. Such an idea is false to the feeling shown by
these women toward women unlike themselves—as, for example,
Rosalind Russell toward the outcast woman in *His Girl Friday,* or
Irene Dunne toward the nightclub singer whose identity she takes
on in *The Awful Truth,* or Claudette Colbert toward the mother
who faints on the bus in *It Happened One Night.* It is as if these
moments signal that such films do not stand in generic insulation
from films in which another way of education and integrity is
taken.

With one further feature of the way of education sought by
Nora's comedic progeny, I can formulate the character I seek in a
melodrama derived from the comedy of remarriage that concerns
those spiritually equal women (equal in their imagination of happiness and their demand for it) among those I am calling Nora's
other progeny.

The demand for education in the comedies presents itself as a
matter of becoming created (not, eventually, *by* anyone other than
herself, and not *for* anyone), as if the women's lives heretofore have
been nonexistent, as if they have haunted the world, as if their
materialization will constitute a creation of the new woman and
hence a creation, or a further step in the creation, of the human.
This idea has various sources and plays various roles as the theory
of remarriage develops in *Pursuits of Happiness.* Theologically, it
alludes to the creation of the woman from Adam in *Genesis,*
specifically its use by Protestant thinkers, impressive among them
John Milton, to ratify marriage and to justify divorce. Cinematically, it emphasizes the role of the camera in transforming human
figures of flesh and blood into psychic shadows of themselves, in
particular in transforming the woman, of whose body more than
is conventional is on some occasion found to be revealed (today
such exposure would perhaps be pointless), so that Katharine
Hepburn will be shown pointedly doing her own diving in *The*

Philadelphia Story, or awkwardly crawling through the woods in a wet, clinging dress, or having her skirt torn off accidentally on purpose by the man in *Bringing Up Baby,* or being given a massage in *Adam's Rib.* The most famous of all such exposures, I guess, is that of Claudette Colbert showing some leg to hitch a ride in *It Happened One Night.* Dramatically, the idea of creation refers to a structure Northrop Frye calls Old Comedy—he is, however, thinking primarily of Shakespearean drama—in which the woman holds the key to the happy outcome of the plot and suffers something like death and resurrection: *All's Well That Ends Well* and *The Winter's Tale* would be signal examples. I take Hermione in *The Winter's Tale* to be the other primary source (along with Ibsen's Nora) of the woman in remarriage comedy, understanding that play as a whole, in the light of the film genre, as the greatest of the structures of remarriage. *The Winter's Tale* also proves (along with *A Doll's House*) to underlie the women of the derived melodrama of unknownness, since while Hermione's resurrection at the close of the play (which I interpret as a kind of marriage ceremony) is a function of Leontes's faith and love, it is before that a function of Paulina's constancy and effectiveness, and the ceremony provides Hermione not just with her husband again (to whom she does not at the end speak) but as well with her daughter again (to whom she does speak).

In remarriage comedy the transformation of the woman is accomplished in a mode of exchange or conversation that is surely among the glories of dialogue in the history of the art of talking pictures. The way these pairs talk together I propose as one perfect manifestation of what Milton calls that "meet and cheerful conversation" (by which he means talk as well as more than talk), which he, most emphatically among the Protestant thinkers so far as I have seen, took to constitute God's purpose in instituting sexual difference, hence what is generally called marriage. But now if deriving a genre of melodrama from remarriage comedy requires, as I assume, the retaining of the woman's search for metamorphosis and existence, it nevertheless cannot take place through such ecstatic exchanges as earmark the comedies; which is to say that the woman of melodrama, as shown to us, will not find herself in what the comedies teach us marriage is, but accordingly in something less or conceivably more than that.

Then the sense of the character (or underlying story or myth) of film I was to look for in establishing a genre of melodrama may be formulated in the following way: a woman achieves existence (or fails to), or establishes her right to existence in the form of a metamorphosis (or fails to), apart from or beyond satisfaction by marriage (of a certain kind) and with the presence of her mother and of her children, where something in her language must be as traumatic in her case as the conversation of marriage is for her comedic sisters—perhaps it will be an aria of divorce, from husband, lover, mother, or child. (A vast, related matter, which I simply mention here, is that what is normally called adultery is not to be expected in these structures, since normally it plays no role in remarriage comedies—something that distinguishes them from Restoration comedy and from French farce. Thus, structures such as *Anna Karenina* and *Madame Bovary* are not members of what I am calling the melodrama of the unknown woman. In this genre it will not be the threat of social scandal that comes between a woman and a man.)

But what is the emphasis on unknownness for? What does it mean to say that it motivates an argument? And what has the argument to do with nihilism and diurnal recurrence? And why is it particularly about a woman that the argument takes place? What is the mystery about her lack of creation? And why should melodrama be expected to "derive" from comedy? And what is it that makes the absence of a woman's mother a scene of comedy and the presence of her mother a scene of melodrama? And—perhaps above all—what kinds of questions are these? Philosophical? Psychoanalytic? Historical? Aesthetic? If, as I hope, one would like to, answer "All of these, at least," then one will want to say how it is that the same questions can belong to various fields that typically, in our culture, refuse to listen to one another.

The questions express further regions of what I called the intellectual debts incurred in writing *Pursuits of Happiness,* ones I had the luxury then of mostly leaving implicit. The debt I have worked on most explicitly in the past several years concerns the ideas of the diurnal, and of eternal repetition, and of the uneventful, as interpretations of the ordinary or everyday.

The concept of the ordinary reaches back to the earliest of my debts in philosophy. The first essay I published that I still use— "Must We Mean What We Say?" (1958)—is a defense of so-called ordinary language philosophy as represented by the work a generation or so ago at Oxford of J. L. Austin and at Cambridge of the later Wittgenstein. Their work is commonly thought to represent an effort to refute philosophical skepticism, as expressed most famously in Descartes and in Hume, and an essential drive of my book *The Claim of Reason* (1979) is to show that, at least in the case of Wittgenstein, this is a fateful distortion, that Wittgenstein's teaching is on the contrary that skepticism is (not exactly true, but not exactly false either; it is the name of) a standing threat to, or temptation of, the human mind—that our ordinary language and its representation of the world *can* be philosophically repudiated and that it is essential to our inheritance and mutual possession of language, as well as to what inspires philosophy, that this should be so. But *The Claim of Reason,* for all its length, does not say, any more than Austin and Wittgenstein do very much to say, what the ordinary is, why natural language is ordinary, beyond saying that ordinary or everyday language is exactly not a special philosophical language and that any special philosophical language is answerable to the ordinary, and beyond suggesting that the ordinary is precisely what it is that skepticism attacks—as if the ordinary is best to be discovered, or say that in philosophy it is only discovered, in its loss. Toward the end of *The Claim of Reason,* the effort to overcome skepticism begins to present itself as the motivation of romanticism, especially its versions in Coleridge and Wordsworth and in their American inheritors Emerson and Thoreau. In recent years I have been following up the idea that what philosophy in Wittgenstein and Austin means by the ordinary or everyday is figured in what Wordsworth means by the rustic and common and what Emerson and Thoreau mean by the today, the common, the low, the near.[1]

But then *Pursuits of Happiness* can be seen as beginning to pay its philosophical debts even as it incurs them. I have linked its films' portrait of marriage, formed through the concepts of repetition and devotion, with what, in an essay that compares the projects of Emerson and of Thoreau with—on an opposite side of the American mind—those of Poe and of Hawthorne, I called their opposite efforts at the interpretation of domestication, call it marriage. From this further interpretation of the ordinary (the ordinary as the domestic) the thought arises (as articulated in the Introduction) that, as in the case of literature, the threat to the ordinary that philosophy names skepticism should show up in film's

favorite threat to forms of marriage, namely, in forms of melodrama. This thought suggests further that, since melodramas
together with tragedy classically tell stories of revenge, philosophical
skepticism will in return be readable as such a story, a kind of
violence the human mind performs in response to its discovery of
its limitation or exclusion, its sense of rebuff by truth.

The problem of the existence of other minds is the formulation
given in the Anglo-American tradition of philosophy to the skeptical question whether I can know of the existence (not, as primarily
in Descartes and in Hume, of myself and of God and of the
external world, but) of human creatures other than myself, know
them to be, as it were, like myself, and not, as we are accustomed
to asking recently with more or less seriousness, some species of
automaton or alien. In *Pursuits of Happiness,* I say explicitly of only
two of the comedies that they are studies of the problem of the
existence of the other, but the overcoming of skeptical doubt can
be found in all remarriage comedy: in *It Happened One Night* the
famous blanket that empirically conceals the woman and thereby
magnifies her metaphysical presence dramatizes the problem of
unknownness as one of splitting the other, as between outside and
inside, say between perception and imagination (and since the
blanket is a figure for a film screen, film as such is opened up in
the split); in *The Lady Eve* the man's not knowing the recurrence of
the same woman is shown as the cause of his more or less comic,
hence more or less forgivable, idiocy; in *The Awful Truth* the
woman shows the all-knowing man what he does not know about
her and helps him find words for it that take back the divorce; in
Adam's Rib the famously sophisticated and devoted couple demonstrate in simple words and shows and in surrealistic ordinariness
(they climb into bed with their hats on) that precisely what neither
of their sexes knows, and what their marriage is the happy struggle
to formulate, is the difference between them; in *The Philadelphia
Story* the man's idea of marriage, of the teaching that the woman
has chosen to learn, is his willingness to know her as unknown (as
he expresses it, "I'll risk it, will you?").

OTHER OF MY intellectual debts remain fully outstanding, that to
Freud's work before all. A beholdenness to Sigmund Freud's intervention in Western culture is hardly something for concealment,
but I have until now left my commitment to it fairly implicit. This

has been not merely out of intellectual terror at Freud's achievement but in service of an idea and in compensation for a dissatisfaction I might formulate as follows: psychoanalytic interpretations of the arts in American culture have, until quite recently, on the whole been content to permit the texts under analysis not to challenge the concepts of analysis being applied to them, and this seemed to me to do injustice both to psychoanalysis and to literature (the art that has attracted most psychoanalytic criticism). My response was to make a virtue of this defect by trying, in my readings of film as well as of literature and of philosophy, to recapitulate what I understood by Freud's saying that he had been preceded in his insights by the creative writers of his tradition; that is, I tried to arrive at a sense for each text I encountered (it was my private touchstone for when an interpretation had gone far enough to leave for the moment) that psychoanalysis had become called for, as if called for in the history of knowledge, as if each psychoanalytic reading were charged with rediscovering the reality of psychoanalysis. This still does not seem to me an irrelevant ambition, but it is also no longer a sufficient response in our altered environment. Some of the most interesting and useful criticism and literary theory currently being produced is decisively psychoanalytic in inspiration, an alteration initiated for us most prominently by the past three or so decades of work in Paris and represented in this country by—to pick examples from which I have particularly profited—Neil Hertz on the Dora case, Shoshana Felman on Henry James's "The Turn of the Screw," and Eve Kosofsky Sedgwick on homophobia in *Our Mutual Friend*.[2] And now my problem has become that I am unsure whether I understand the constitution of the discourses in which this material is presented in relation to what I take philosophy to be, a constitution to which, such as it is, I am also committed. So some siting of this relation is no longer mine to postpone.

I content myself here with saying that Freud's lifelong series of dissociations of his work from the work of philosophy seems to me to protest too much and to have done harm whose extent is only now beginning to reveal itself. I call attention to one of those dissociations in which Freud's ambivalence on the matter bleeds through. It comes in chapter 4 of *The Interpretation of Dreams*, just as he has distinguished "the operations of two psychical forces (or we may describe them as currents or systems)." Freud goes on to

say: "These considerations may lead us to feel that the interpretation of dreams may enable us to draw conclusions as to the structure of our mental apparatus which we have hoped for in vain from
philosophy." [3] Given that this feeling is followed up by Freud in the
extraordinary chapter 7, which ends the book, a piece of theoretical
speculation continuous with the early, posthumously published
"Project for a Scientific Psychology," the ambiguity of the remark
seems plain: it can be taken, and always is, so far as I know, to
mean that our vain waiting for *philosophy* is now to be replaced by
the positive work of something else, call it psychoanalysis (which
may or may not be a "scientific" psychology); but the remark can
equally be taken to mean that our *waiting* for philosophy is at last
no longer vain, that philosophy has been fulfilled in the form of
psychoanalysis. That this form may destroy earlier forms of philosophizing is no bar to conceiving of psychoanalysis as a philosophy.
On the contrary, the two thinkers more indisputably recognized as
philosophers who have opened for me what philosophy in our age
may look like, such as it interests me most—Wittgenstein in his
Philosophical Investigations and Martin Heidegger in such a work as
What Is Called Thinking?—have both written in declared opposition to philosophy as they received it. Heidegger has called philosophy the deepest enemy of thinking, and Wittgenstein has said that
what he does replaces philosophy.

The idea of "replacing" here has its own ambiguity. It could
mean what the logical positivists roughly meant, that philosophy,
so far as it remains intelligible, is to become logic or science. Or
it could mean what I take Wittgenstein to mean, that the impulse
to philosophy and the consequences of it are to be achieved by
replacing, or reconceiving, the ground or the place of the thus
preserved activity of philosophizing. And something like this could
be said to be what every original philosopher since at least Descartes
and Bacon and Locke has illustrated. It is as if in Wittgenstein and
in Heidegger the fate to philosophize and the fate to undo philosophizing are located as radical, twin features of the human as such.

I am not choosing one sense of replacement over the other for
Freud's relation to philosophy. On the contrary, my sense remains
that the relation so far is ambiguous or ambivalent. Such matters
are apt to be discussed nowadays in terms of Freud's preoccupation
with what is called priority or originality—issues differently associated with the names of Harold Bloom and Jacques Derrida. So it

may be worth my saying that Bloom strikes me as unduly leveling matters when he speaks of Freud's crisis in *Beyond the Pleasure Principle* as obeying the structure of a poet's demand, against his precursors, for equal immortality.[4] Freud's problem there was less to *establish* his originality or uniqueness than to determine whether the cost or curse of that *obvious* uniqueness might not itself be the loss of immortality. I find that I agree here with what I understand to be Derrida's view (of chapter 2 anyway) of *Beyond the Pleasure Principle*—that in it, and in anticipation of his own death, Freud is asking himself whether his achievement, uniquely among the sciences (or, for that matter, the arts) in being bound to the uniqueness of one man's name, is inheritable.[5] This is the question enacted by the scenes of Freud the father and grandfather circling the Fort/Da game of repetition and domination, looking so much like the inheritance of language itself, of selfhood itself. What is at stake is whether psychoanalysis is inheritable—you may say repeatable—as science is inheritable, our modern paradigm for the teachable. If psychoanalysis is not thus inheritable, it follows that it is not exactly a science. But the matter goes beyond this question. If psychoanalysis is not exactly (what we mean by) a science, then its intellectual achievement may be lost to humankind. But now if this expresses Freud's preoccupation in *Beyond the Pleasure Principle* and elsewhere, then this preoccupation links his work with philosophy, for it is in philosophy that the question of the loss of itself is internal to its faithfulness to itself.

This claim reveals me as one of those for whom the question whether philosophy exists sometimes seems the only question philosophy is bound to, that to cease caring what philosophy is and whether it exists—amid whatever tasks and in whatever forms philosophy may appear in a given historical moment—is to abandon philosophy, to cede it to logic or to science or to poetry or to politics or to religion. That the question of philosophy is the only business of philosophy is the teaching I take from the works of Wittgenstein and of Heidegger whose inheritance I have claimed. The question of inheritance, of continued existence, appears in their work as the question whether philosophy can be taught or, say, the question how thinking is learned, the form the question takes in *Beyond the Pleasure Principle*. It is perhaps primarily for this reason that my philosophical colleagues in the Anglo-American profession of philosophy still generally (of course there

are exceptions) hold Wittgenstein or Heidegger at a distance, at
varying distances from their conceptions of themselves.

What would be lost if philosophy, or psychoanalysis, were lost
to us? One can take the question of philosophy as the question
whether the life of reason is (any longer) attractive and recognizable, or as the question whether by my life I can and do affirm my
existence in a world among others, or whether I deny this, of
myself, of others, and of the world. It is some such question that
Nietzsche took as the issue of what he called nihilism, a matter
in which he had taken decisive instruction from Ralph Waldo
Emerson. I persist, as indicated, in calling the issue by its, or its
ancestor's, older name of skepticism; as I persist in thinking that to
lose knowledge of the human possibility of skepticism means to
lose knowledge of the human, something whose possibility I envision in *The Claim of Reason,* extending a problematic of Wittgenstein's under the title of soul-blindness.

It is from a perspective of our culture as having entered on a
path of radical skepticism (hence on a path to deny this path) from
the time of, say, Shakespeare and Descartes—or say from the time
of the fall of kings and the rise of the new science and the death of
God—that I see, late in this history, the advent of psychoanalysis
as the place, perhaps the last, in which the human psyche as such,
the idea that there is a life of the mind, hence a death, receives its
proof. It receives its proof of its existence in the only form in which
that psyche can (any longer) believe it, namely, as essentially
unknown to itself, say unconscious. As Freud puts it in the closing
pages of *The Interpretation of Dreams:* "The unconscious is the true
psychical reality" (5:613). This can seem a mere piece of rhetoric on
Freud's part, arbitrarily underrating the reality of consciousness
and promoting the unconscious out of something like a prejudice
that promotes the reality of atomic particles over the reality of flesh
and blood and its opposable things—and certainly on less, or no,
compelling intellectual grounds. But when seen in its relation to,
or as a displacement of, philosophy, Freud's assertion declares that
for the mind to lose the psychoanalytic intuition of itself as unconscious would be for it to lose the last proof of its own existence.
(One may feel here the need for a dialectical qualification or limitation; this loss of proof, hence of human existence, is specific to the
historical-political development in which the individual requires
such a proof before, as it were, his or her own eyes, a private proof.

The question may then be open whether, in a further development, the proof might be otherwise possible, say performed before the answering heart of a community. But in that case, would such a proof be necessary? Would philosophy?)

How easy this intuition is to lose (the mind's [psychoanalytic] intuition of its existence as unconscious), how hard the place of this intuition is to find—the place of the proof of existence constituted in the origin of psychoanalysis as a fulfillment of philosophy—is emblematized by how obscure this or any relation of philosophy and psychoanalysis is to us, an obscurity our institutions of learning serve to enforce. (I do not just mean that psychoanalysis is not usually a university subject and only questionably should become one; I mean as well that philosophy is, or should become, only questionably such a subject.) The tale to be told here is as yet perhaps untellable, by us and for us in America—the tale of Freud's inheritance (inescapable for an ambitious student of German culture of Freud's time) of the outburst of thinking initiated by Kant and then developed continuously by Fichte, Schelling, Hegel, Schopenhauer, and Nietzsche. One possible opening passage of this story is from the same closing pages I just cited from *The Interpretation of Dreams*: "What I . . . describe is not the same as the unconscious of philosophers. . . . In its innermost nature it [that is, psychical reality, the unconscious] is as much unknown to us as the reality of the external world, and it is as incompletely presented by the data of consciousness as is the external world by the communication of our sense organs" (5:614, 613). Freud allows himself to dismiss what he calls "the unconscious of philosophers" (no doubt referring to what some philosophers have referred to with the *word* "unconscious") without allowing himself to recognize that his connecting in the same sentence the innermost nature of psychic reality and the innermost nature of external reality as equally, and hence apparently for the same reasons, unknown, is pure Kant, as Freud links the unknown ground of both inner and outer to a realm of an unconditioned thing-in-itself, which Kant virtually calls the It (he spells it "X").[6] Kant's linking of the inner and the outer sounds like this: "The conditions of the *possibility of experience* in general are at the same time the *possibility of the objects of experience*."[7] Heidegger, in *What Is Called Thinking?* quotes this passage from Kant and from it in effect rapidly derives the tradition of German so-called Idealism. He adduces some words of Schelling,

in which the pivot of inner and outer sounds this way: "In the final and highest instance, there is no being other than willing. Willing is primal being and to [willing] alone belong all [primal being's] predicates: being unconditioned, eternity, independence of time, self-affirmation. All philosophy strives only to find this highest expression."[8] The predicates of being unconditioned and of independence of time will remind us of Freud's predicates of the unconscious. Schelling's lectures in Berlin in 1841 were, as noted in Karl Löwith's *From Hegel to Nietzsche,* attended by Engels, Bakunin, Kierkegaard, and Burckhardt. And 1841 is also the year of Emerson's first volume of essays. His volume sounds, for example, this way: "Permanence is a word of degrees. Every thing is medial."
"It is the highest power of divine moments that they abolish our contritions also . . . for these moments confer a sort of omnipresence and omnipotence, which asks nothing of duration, but sees that the energy of the mind is commensurate with the work to be done, without time. . . . I unsettle all things . . . I simply experiment."[9] Compared with the philosophical culture of Schelling's audience, Emerson's mostly had none; yet his philosophizing was more advanced than Schelling's, if Nietzsche's is (since Emerson's transcendental realm is not fixed; the direction or height of the will is in principle open). Heidegger claims for his quotation from Schelling that it is the classic formulation of the appearance of metaphysics in the modern era, an appearance that is essential "to understand[ing] that—and how—Nietzsche from the very start thinks of revenge [the basis of nihilism] and the deliverance from revenge in metaphysical terms, that is, in the light of Being which determines all beings."[10] However remote the fate of such a claim may seem to us here now, it will, if nothing else, at any time stand between us and our desire, however intermittent, yet persistent, for an exchange with contemporary French thought; since Heidegger's interpretation of Nietzsche is one determinant of the Paris of, say, Derrida's Plato and Rousseau and of Lacan's Freud. (It may be pertinent to cite the effort in recent decades to bring Freud within the orbit of German philosophizing, in particular within that of Heidegger's thought, made by the existential-analytic movement [*Daseins-analyse*]. This is no time to try to assess that effort, but I may just note that my emphasis on Freud as, so to speak, an immediate heir of German classical philosophy implies that establishing this relation to philosophy does not require mediation [or absorp-

tion] by Heidegger. The point of my emphasis is that Freud's is to be understood as an alternative inheritance, a competing inheritance, to that of Heidegger. Otherwise Freud's own break with philosophy, his [continued] subjection to it and its subjection to him, will not get clear. Then Wittgenstein's is a third inheritance, or path, from Kant.)[11]

In these paths of inheritance, Freud's distinction is to have broken through to a practice in which the Idealist philosophy, the reigning philosophy of German culture, becomes concrete (which is roughly what Marx said socialism was to accomplish). In Freud's practice, one human being represents to another all that that other has conceived of humanity in his or her life, and moves with that other toward an expression of the conditions which condition that utterly specific life. It is a vision and an achievement quite worthy of the most heroic attributes Freud assigned himself. But psychoanalysis has not surmounted the obscurities of the philosophical problematic of representation and reality it inherits. Until it stops shrinking from philosophy (from its own past), it will continue to shrink before the derivative question, for example, whether the stories of its patients are fantasy merely or (also?) of reality; it will continue to waver between regarding the question as irrelevant to its work and as the essence of it.

It is hardly enough to appeal here to conviction in reality, because the most untutored enemy of the psychological, as eagerly as the most sophisticated enemy, will inform you that conviction is one thing, reality another. The matter is to express the intuition that fantasy shadows anything we can understand reality to be. As Wittgenstein more or less puts an analogous matter: the issue is not to explain how grammar and criteria allow us to relate language to the world but to determine what language relates the world to be. This is not well expressed as the priority of mind over reality or of self over world (as, among others, Bloom expresses it).[12] It is better put as the priority of grammar—the thing Kant calls conditions of possibility (of experience and of objects), the thing Wittgenstein calls possibilities of phenomena—over both what we call mind and what we call the world. If we call grammar the Logos, we will more readily sense the shadow of fantasy in this picture.

FROM THE reassociation of psychoanalysis with philosophy in its appearance on the stage of skepticism, as the last discoverer of

psychic reality (the latest discoverer, its discoverer late in the reces-
sion of that reality), I need just two leaps in order to get to the
interpretation I envision of the moment I began with from *Letter
from an Unknown Woman*. The two leaps I can represent as questions that together have haunted the thoughts I am reporting on
here. Both questions were broached in the preceding essay, on
Gaslight. The first is: Why (granted the fact) does psychic reality
first present itself to psychoanalysis—or, why does psychoanalysis first realize itself—through the agency (that is, through the
suffering) of women, as reported in the *Studies on Hysteria* and
in the case of Dora, the earliest of the longer case histories? The
second question is: How, if at all, is this circumstance related to
the fact (again, granted the fact) that film—another invention of
the last years of the nineteenth century, developing its first master-
pieces within the first decades of the twentieth century—is from
first to last more interested in the study of individual women than
of individual men? My conviction in the significance of these questions is a function, not surprisingly, of my speculations concerning
skepticism, two junctures of it especially. The one is a result of my
study of Shakespeare's tragedies and romances as elaborations of
the skeptical problematic; the other concerns the role of the human
body in the skeptical so-called problem of other minds. I will say
something about each of these junctures.

Since we are about to move into speculations concerning
differences in the knowing of women from that of the knowing of
men, I just note in passing that I am not leaping to but skipping
over the immensely important matter of determining how it is that
the question of sexual difference turns into a question of some
property that men are said to have that women lack, or perhaps
vice versa—a development that helps to keep us locked into a
compulsive uncertainty about whether we wish to affirm or to
deny difference between men and women. As *Adam's Rib* ends,
Tracy and Hepburn are joking about this vulgar error of looking for
a *thing* that differentiates men and women. (It is my claim that they
are joking; it is commoner, I believe, to assume—or imagine, or
think, or opine—that they are perpetuating this common error.
Here is a neat touchstone for assessing the reception of these comedies; perhaps their endings form the neatest set of such touch-
stones.)

In Jacques Lacan's work, the idea of the phallus as signifier is not exactly a laughing matter. The reification, let me put it, of sexual difference is registered, in the case of knowledge, by finding the question of a difference in masculine and feminine knowing and then by turning it into a question of some fixed way women know that men do not know, and vice versa. Since in ordinary, nonmetaphysical exchanges we do not conceive there to be some fact one gender knows that the other does not know, any more than we conceive there to be some fact the skeptic knows that the ordinary human being does not know, the metaphysical exchanges concerning their differences are apt to veer toward irony, a sense of incessant false position, as if one cannot know what difference a world of difference makes. No one exactly denies that human knowledge is imperfect; but then how does that become the skeptic's outrageous removal of the world as such? No one exactly denies that there are differences between men and women; but then how does that become an entire history of outrage? It is from this region that one must expect an explanation for climactic passages of irony that characterize the melodrama of the unknown woman.

When in *Blonde Venus* Marlene Dietrich hands a derelict old woman the cash her husband has handed her, repeating to the woman, in raging mockery, the self-pitying words her husband had used to her in paying her back, to be quits with her, the money she had earlier given him to save his life, the meanness of the man's gesture is branded on his character. When toward the end of *Letter from an Unknown Woman* the man calls out smoothly to the woman, whose visit he interprets as a willingness for another among his endless dalliances, having disappeared to get some champagne, "Are you lonely out there?" and she, whose voice-over tells that she came to offer her life to him, replies, mostly to the camera, that is, to us, "Yes. Very lonely," she has taken his charming words as her cue for general death.

The state of irony is the negation, hence the equivalent in general consequence, of the state of conversation in remarriage comedy. Some feminists imagine that women have always spoken their own language, undetected by men; others argue that women ought to develop a language of their own. The irony in the melodrama of unknownness develops the picture, or figuration, for what it means idiomatically to say that men and women, in denying one another, do not speak the same language. I am not the only male of my acquaintance who knows the victimization in this experience, of having conversation negated, say, by the reactively masculine in others. The finest description known to me of ironic, systematic incomprehension is Emerson's, from "Self-Reliance":

> Well, most men have bound their eyes with one or another handkerchief, and attached themselves to some one of these communities of opinion. This conformity makes them not false in a few particulars, authors of a few lies, but false in all particulars. Their every truth is not quite true. Their two is not the real two [as in the idea of two genders? or of just two Testaments?], their four not the real four [as in the idea of four corners of the earth? or of just four Gospels?]: so that every word they say chagrins us, and we know not where to begin to set them right.[13]

The first of my concluding leaps or questions about the origination of psychoanalysis and of film in the sufferings of women concerns the most theoretically elaborated of the studies I have so far produced of Shakespeare, on *The Winter's Tale*. It has raised unforgettably for me, I might say traumatically, the possibility that philosophical skepticism is inflected, if not altogether determined, by gender, by whether one sets oneself aside as masculine or feminine. And if philosophical skepticism is thus inflected then, according to me, philosophy as such will be. The issue arises as follows: Leontes obeys the structure of the skeptical problematic in the first half of *The Winter's Tale* as perfectly as his forebear Othello had done, but in the later play jealousy, as an interpretation of skeptical, world-removing doubt, is a cover story not for the man's fear of female desire (as Othello's story is) but for his fear of female fecundity, represented in Leontes's doubt that his children are his. Leontes's story has figured in various talks of mine in the past two or three years, and more than once a woman has afterward said to me in effect: If what Cartesian skepticism requires is the doubt that my children are mine, count me out. It is not the only time the surmise has crossed my mind that philosophical skepticism, and a certain denial of its reality, is a male business; but from the dawning of *The Winter's Tale* on me the business seems to me to be playing a role I know I do not fathom in every philosophical move I make. (It is the kind of answer I can contribute to the question who or what Shakespeare is to say that it is characteristically in texts associated with this name that the bearing of the issue of skepticism, and therewith of (modern) philosophy as such, is shown to be establishing itself in, and transforming, our consciousness.)

From the gender asymmetry here it should not be taken to follow that women do not get into the way of skepticism, but only that the passion of doubt may not express a woman's sense of separation from others or that the object of doubt is not representable as a doubt as to whether your children are yours. The passion is perhaps another form of fanaticism, as in part Leontes's is. (*Letter from an Unknown Woman* suggests that the fanaticism is of what you might call love.) And the object of doubt might be representable as one directed not toward the question of one's children but toward the question of the father of one's children. (This is the pertinence of Kleist's *The Marquise of O*—the main reason in its content for what I called its specialness in relation to the melodrama of unknownness.) But how can one know and show that this other passion and this other object create equivalents or alternatives to masculine skepticism?

It is at this juncture of the skeptical development that psychoanalysis and cinema can be taken as asking of the woman: How is it that you escape doubt? What certainty encloses you, whatever your other insecurities, from just this torture? At an early point in my tracking of the skeptic, I found myself asking: Why does my search for certainty in knowing the existence of the other, in countering the skeptic's suspicion concerning other minds, come to turn upon whether I can know what the other *knows*? (*Claim of Reason*, p. 102). So the formulation of what we want from the woman as an access to her knowledge would record the skeptical provenance of the woman's presence at the origin of psychoanalytic and of cinematic discovery. But then we must allow the question: But *who* is it who wants to know? A natural answer will be: The man wants the knowledge. (Would it answer, or motivate, his supposed question: What does a woman want?) This answer cannot be wrong; it is the answer feminists may well give to Freud's handling of the case of the woman he called Dora. But the answer might be incomplete.

At this point two sources of material bearing on psychoanalysis and feminism warrant being brought prominently into play, which I can now barely name. The first is represented in two texts by Lacan entitled "God and the *Jouissance* of The Woman" and "A

Love Letter," which when I came upon them twelve months ago (in
1984) struck me at several points as having uncanny pertinence
to the particular considerations that arise here. When Lacan
announces, "There is no such thing as *The* woman" (sometimes
paraphrased or translated as "The woman does not exist")[14] I was
bound to ask myself whether this crossed the intuition I have
expressed as the task of the creation of the woman. I find that some
of Lacan's followers react to the remark as obvious and as on the
side of what women think about themselves, while others deny this
reaction. I take it to heart that Lacan warns that more than one of
his pupils have "got into a mess" ("G," p. 144) about the doctrines
of his in which his view of the woman is embedded; clearly I do
not feel that I can negotiate these doctrines apart from the painful
positions I am looking to unfold here.

My hesitations over two further moments in Lacan's texts—
moments whose apparent pertinence to what I am working on
strikes me too strongly to ignore—are hesitations directed less to
my intellectual difficulties with what is said than to the attitude
with which it is said. When Lacan says, "I believe in the *jouissance*
of the woman in so far as it is something more" (ibid, p. 147), he
is casting his view of women as a creed or credo ("I believe"), as an
article of faith in the existence and the difference of the woman's
satisfaction. So he may be taken as saying: What there is (any
longer?) of God, or of the concept of the beyond, takes place in
relation to the woman. It matters to me that I cannot assess the
extent or direction (outward or inward) of Lacan's (mock?)
heroism, or (mock) apostlehood here, since something like this
belief is in effect what I say works itself out, with gruesome
eloquence, in the case of Othello, who enacts Descartes's efforts to
prove that he is not alone in the universe by placing a finite, feminine other in the position assigned by Descartes to God (see my
"Othello and the Stake of the Other"). Moreover, letting the brunt
of conviction in existence, the desire of the skeptical state, be represented by the question of the woman's orgasm, is an interpretation
of Leontes's representation of the state of skepticism by the question of the woman's child (following a familiar equation in Freud's
thinking of the production of the child with the form of female
sexual satisfaction, an equation present in Shakespeare's play). So
skeptical grief would be represented for the man not directly by the

question "Were her children caused by me?" but by the double question "Is her satisfaction real and is it caused by me?"

The other source of material (still within my first leap) that I can do little more than name here is the excellent recent collection of essays, subtitled *Freud—Hysteria—Feminism,* on the Dora case.[15] When the case of Dora came up in the discussion of *Gaslight,* it served to focus the resemblance of the relation of Gregory and Paula to a desperate mockery, or interpretation, of a therapeutic relation, one that a particular patient might predictably invite, in therapy, of that relationship. Here I lift up one consideration that speaks specifically to both of the leaps or questions at hand: How does the problem of knowing the existence of the other come to present itself as knowing what the other knows? And: Who is it who wants to know of the woman's existence? The former seems—in the light of the Dora collection—a way of asking what the point is of the "talking cure" (the name of psychoanalytic therapy that Anna O., the woman whose case was reported by Breuer in *Studies on Hysteria,* was the first to use); and the answer to the latter seems routinely assumed to be Freud the man. The contributors to the volume are about equally divided between men and women, and it seems to me that while the men from time to time are amazed or appalled by Freud's assaults upon Dora's recitations, the women, while from time to time admiring, are uniformly impatient with Freud the man. The discussions are particularly laced with dirty talk, prompted generally by Freud's material and drawn particularly by a remark of Lacan's on the case in which, in an ostentatious show of civilization, he coolly questions the position of the partners in Freud's fantasy of Dora's fantasy of oral intercourse. It is in their repetition of Lacan's question, not now coolly but accusingly, that the women's impatience is clearest; it is a kind of structural impatience. To talk to Freud about his talking cure is to be caught up in the logic expressed by Lacan in the formula: "Speaking of love is in itself a *jouissance*."[16] Feeling the unfairness in thus being forced to talk love to Freud, a woman may well accuse him of ignorance in his designs upon Dora, upon her knowledge, not granting him the knowledge that his subject is the nature of ignorance of exactly what cannot be ignored. She may well be right.

The consideration I said I would lift here from the discussions of Dora takes on the detail of Freud's choice of the fictitious name

Dora in presenting his case. Freud traces his choice to the paradigm of a change of name his sister had required of, and chosen for, her maidservant. The women represented in this collection on the whole use this information to accuse Freud of treating the woman he called Dora like a servant, of thus taking revenge on her for having treated him in this way. It is an angry interpretation, which seeks to turn the tables on the particular brilliance Freud had shown in calling Dora's attention to her angry treatment of him in announcing her termination of treatment by giving him two weeks' notice. A less impatient interpretation would have turned Freud's act of naming around again, taking it not as, or not alone as, a wish to dominate a woman, but as a confession that he is thinking of himself in the case through an identification with his sister: as if the knowledge of the existence of a woman is to be made on the basis of already enlisting oneself on that side.

THIS TAKES ME to the other of my concluding leaps or questions, now concerning not generally the genderedness of the skeptical problematic, but specifically concerning the role of the body in the problem of other minds. To counter the skeptical emphasis on knowing what the other doubts and knows, I have formulated my intuition that the philosophical recovery of the other depends on determining the sense that the human body is expressive of mind, for *this* seems to be what the skeptic of other minds directly denies, a denial prepared by the behaviorist sensibility in general. Wittgenstein is formulating what behaviorism shuns—and so doubtless inviting its shunning of him—in his marvelous remark: "The human body is the best picture of the human soul." [17] One can find some such idea expressed in the accents of other thinkers—for example, in Hegel's *Philosophy of Fine Art:* "The human shape [is] the sole sensuous phenomenon that is appropriate to mind"; [18] or again in Emerson's essay "Behavior": "Nature tells every secret once. Yes, but in man she tells it all the time, by form, attitude, gesture, mien, face and parts of the face, and by the whole action of the machine." [19] Freud is expressing the idea in one of his reasonably measured, yet elated, Hamlet-like recognitions of his penetration of the secrets of humanity. In the middle of his writing of the Dora case he turns aside to say: "He that has eyes to see and ears to hear may convince himself that no mortal can keep a secret. If his lips are silent, he chatters with his finger-tips; betrayal oozes out of

him at every pore."[20] Freud's twist on the philosophers here is registered in his idea of our expressions as betraying ourselves, giving
ourselves (and meaning to give ourselves) away—as if, let us say,
the inheritance of language, of the possibility of communication,
inherently involves disappointment with it and (hence) subver-
sion of it.

Expression as betrayal comes out particularly in Freud's phrase
from his preceding paragraph, in which he describes one of what he
calls Dora's "symptomatic acts" as a "pantomimic announcement"
(specifically in this case an announcement of masturbation). Freud
and Breuer had earlier spoken of the more general sense of human
behavior as pantomimic—capable of playing or replaying the
totality of the scenes of hidden life—in terms of the hysteric's
"capacity for conversion," "a psychophysical aptitude for transposing very large sums of excitation into the somatic innervation,"[21]
which is roughly to say, a capacity for modifying the body as such
rather than allowing the excitation to transpose into consciousness
or to discharge into practice. While this capacity is something
possessed by every psychophysical being—that is, primarily
human beings—a particular aptitude for it is required for a given
sufferer to avail herself or himself of hysteria over other modes of
symptom formation, as in obsessions or phobias. The aptitude
demands, for example, what Freud calls "somatic compliance,"
together with high intelligence, a plastic imagination, and hallucinatory "absences," which Anna O. (in *Studies on Hysteria*) taught
Breuer to think of as her "'private theatre.'"[22]

It seems to me that Freud describes the aptitude for hysterical
conversion with special fascination—as if, for example, the alternative choice of obsession were, though no less difficult to fathom,
psychologically rather undistinguished.[23] Breuer and Freud's most
famous statement of the matter, in their "Preliminary Communication" of 1893, is: "Hysterics suffer mainly from reminiscences"
(ibid., 2:7), a statement to be taken in the light of the insistence that
hysterical motor symptoms "can be shown to have an original or
long-standing connection with traumas, and stand as symbols for
them in the activities of the memory" (ibid., 2:95). Hysterical
symptoms are "mnemonic symbols," where this means that they
bear some mimetic allegiance to their origins. Freud will say fifteen
years later, in the "Rat Man" case, that "the leap from a mental
process to a somatic innervation—hysterical conversion . . . can

never be fully comprehensible to us,"[24] a claim I find suspicious coming from him, as though he wishes sometimes to appear to know less than he does, or feels he does, about the powers of women.

In place of an argument for this, I offer as an emblem for future argument the figure of the woman who on film may be understood to have raised "the psycho-physical aptitude for transposing . . . large sums of excitation into the somatic innervation" to its highest art; I mean Greta Garbo, I suppose the greatest, or the most fascinating, cinematic image on film of the unknown woman. (Perhaps I should reassure you of my intentions here by noting that Freud's sentence following the one I just repeated about the psychophysical aptitude in question begins: "This aptitude does not, in itself, exclude psychical health.")[25] It is as if Garbo has generalized this aptitude beyond human doubting—call this aptitude a talent for, and will to, communicate—generalized it to a point of absolute expressiveness, so that the sense of failure to know her, of her being beyond us (say visibly absent), is itself the proof of her existence. (The idea of absolute expressiveness locates the moment in the history of skepticism at which such a figure appears as the moment I characterize in *The Claim of Reason* as the anxiety of inexpressiveness.)

This talent and will for communication accordingly should call upon the argument of hysteria for terms in which to understand it. In Garbo's most famous postures in conjunction with a man, she looks away or beyond or through him, as if in an absence (a distance from him, from the present), hence as if to declare that this man, while the occasion of her passion, is surely not its cause. I find (thinking specifically of a widely reprinted photograph in which she has inflected her face from that of John Gilbert, her eyes slightly raised, seeing elsewhere) that I see her *jouissance* as remembering something, but, let me say, remembering it from the future, within a private theater, not dissociating herself from the present moment, but knowing it forever, in its transience, as finite, from her finitude, or separateness, as from the perspective of her death: as if she were herself transformed into a mnemonic symbol, a monument of memory. (This would make her the opposite of the femme fatale she is sometimes said—surely in defense against her knowledge—to be.) What the monument means to me is that a joyful passion for one's life contains the ability to mourn, the acceptance of transience, of the world as beyond one—say, one's other.

Such in my philosophy is the proof of human existence that, on its feminine side, as conceived in the appearance of psychoanalysis, it is the perfection of the motion picture camera to provide.

HERE I COME upon my epilogue, and a man's hands over his eyes, perhaps to ward off a woman's returning images. *Letter from an Unknown Woman* is the only film in our genre of melodrama that ends with the woman's apparent failure; but as in *Gaslight*, her failure perfectly shadows what the woman's success in this genre of human perplexity has to overcome: the failure here is of a woman's unknownness to prove her existence to a man, to become created by a man. It is a tale the outcome of which is not the transcendence of marriage but the collapse of a fantasy of remarriage (or of perpetual marriage), perhaps in favor of a further fantasy, of revenge, of which the one we see best is a screen; a tale in which the woman remains mute about her story, refusing it both to the man and to the world of women; and a tale in which the characters' perspective of death is not to know forever the happiness of one's own life but finally to disown it, to live the death of another (as they have lived the other's life). (For some this will establish the necessity of psychology; for others, the necessity of politics; for others, the need of art.)

A reading of the film, in the context I have supplied here, might directly begin with the marks of these fantasies, of their negations of the reality, as it were, of remarriage as established in the genre that explores remarriage. For example, the woman in Ophuls's film is shown to be created through metamorphosis, not, however, by or with the man, but for him, privately—as her voice-over tells him (and us) posthumously:

> From that moment on I was in love with you. Quite consciously I began to prepare myself for you. I kept my clothes neater so that you wouldn't be ashamed of me. I took dancing lessons; I wanted to become more graceful, and learn good manners—for you. So that I would know more about you and your world, I went to the library and studied the lives of the great musicians.

What is causing this vortex of ironies, the fact of change or the privacy of it? The idea that woman's work is not to converse with men but to allure them is hardly news, and it is laid out for observation in Ophuls's work, in his participation in the world of fashion and glamour. That the intimacy of allure exactly defeats the intimacy of conversation is a way to put the cause of irony in the film, not alone its incessance in its closing sequences ("Are you lonely out there?") but also at the beginning of their reencounter, as the woman tracks the man back in Vienna until he notices her. He says, "I ought to introduce myself," and she interrupts with, "No. I know who you are"—a remark that could not be truer or more false.

Privacy and irony are in turn bound up in the film with the theme and structure of repetitions. Again this feature here negates its definitive occurrences in remarriage comedy, where repetitiveness is the field of inventiveness, improvisation, of the recurrence of time, open to the second chance; in (this) melodrama time is transient, closed, and repetition signals death—whether the repetition is of its camera movements (for example, the famous ironic repetition of the girl's waiting and watching on the stairs) or its words ("I'll see you in two weeks, two weeks") or its imagery (the woman's denial of chance and her weddedness to fate is given heavy symbolization in the film's endless iteration of iterated iron bars, which become less barriers against this woman's desire than the medium of it). Passing these essential matters, the moment I close with is also one of ironic repetition, and I ask of the woman's returning images: Why are they death-dealing?

Of course, they must make the man feel guilt and loss; but the question is why, for a man whose traffic has been the sentiments of remorse and loss, the feeling this time is fatal. Surely it has to do with the letter itself, beginning as from the region of death ("By the time you read this I may be dead") and ending in the theme of nostalgia ("If only . . . if only . . . "). And, of course, it has to do with the fact that there is a double letter, the depicted one that ends in a broken sentence, and the one that depicts this one, the one bearing the title *Letter from an Unknown Woman,* this film that ends soon but distinctly after, narrated from the beginning, it emerges, by the voice of a dead woman, ghost-written.

The implication is somehow that it is the (ghost) woman who writes and sends the film. What can this mean? That the author of the film is a question for the film is suggested when the man says to his mute servant, who enters as the man has finished reading the letter, "You knew her," and the servant nods and writes a name on a page on the desk on which the letter lies, by the feeling that the servant is signing the letter, and hence the film. No doubt Ophuls is showing his hand here, breaching and so declaring, as it were, his muteness as a director, as if declaring that directing (perhaps composing of any kind) is constantly a work of breaching muteness (how fully, and how well timed, are further questions). But this cannot deny that it is a woman's letter he signs, assigns to himself as a writer, a letter explicitly breaching, hence revealing, muteness.

Moreover, the letter already contained a signature, on the letterhead of the religious order in whose hospital the unknown woman died, of someone styled "Sister-in-charge." Whether or not we are to assume that this is the same locale to which the unknown woman had gone to be delivered anonymously of her and the man's child, her connection with the religious order happens in front of our eyes, as she leaves the train platform after rushing to see the man off for a hastily remembered concert tour. Walking directly away from us, she gradually disappears into blackness at the center of the vacant screen, upon which, at what we might project as her vanishing point, there is a rematerialization, and the figure of the woman is replaced, or transformed into, walking at the same pace toward us, what turns out as it comes into readable view to be a nun. So the woman is part of the world of religion, of a place apart inhabited, for all we see of it, solely by women, a world Ophuls accordingly also assigns himself, I mean his art, in signing the woman's letter. (Whether in claiming the mazed position of the feminine the actual director is manifesting sympathy with actual women or getting even with them; and whether in competing with the feminine other the director is silencing the woman's voice in order to steal it and sport its power as his [his?] own; and whether positive [or negative] personal intentions could overtake the political opportunism [or political insight] of any such gesture; these are questions that I hope are open, for my own good.)

Granted that forces both lethal and vital are gathered here, and granted that the film is the medium of visible absence, I ask again how these forces, in the form of returning images, deal death. Since I mostly am not considering here the narrative conditions of the woman depicted as writing the letter, I leave aside the question whether the vengeance in this act is to be understood as endorsed or reversed in the director's countersigning of it. I concentrate now

on the sheer fact that the images return as exact moments we and
the man have witnessed, or perhaps imagined, together. The
present instants are mechanically identical with the past, and this
form of repetition elicits its own amalgam of the strange and the
familiar. I take it as a repetition that Freud cites as causing the
sense of "the uncanny" in his essay to which he gives that title. Then
this is also a title Ophuls's film suggest for the aesthetic working of
film as such, an idea of some vision of horror as its basis. Freud's
essay includes a reading of E. T. A. Hoffmann's romantic tale "The
Sand-Man," a tale that features a beautiful automaton, something
not untypical of Hoffmann or more generally of the romantic tale
of the fantastic. Freud begins his reading by denying, against a
predecessor's reading, that the uncanniness of the tale is traceable
to the point in the story of "uncertainty whether an object is living or inanimate." [26] Now that point is precisely recognizable as an
issue of philosophical skepticism concerning our knowledge of
the existence of other minds. But Freud insists that instead the
uncanny in Hoffmann's tale is directly attached to the idea of being
robbed of one's eyes, and hence, given his earlier findings, to the
castration complex.

I find this flat denial of Freud's itself uncanny, oddly mechan-
ical, since no denial is called for, no incompatible alternative is
proposed: one would have expected Sigmund Freud in this context
to invoke the castration complex precisely as a new explanation or
interpretation of the particular uncertainty in question, to suggest
it as Hoffmann's prepsychoanalytic insight that one does not see
others as other, acknowledge their (animate) human existence,
until the Oedipal drama is resolved under the threat of castration,
the threat of a third person. (This is a step, I believe, that Lacan has
taken; I do not know on what ground.) Instead Freud's, as it were,
denial that the acknowledgment of the existence of others is at stake
amounts, to my mind, to the denial that philosophy persists within
psychoanalysis, that the psychoanalytic tracing of traumatically
induced exchanges or metamorphoses of objects of love and
subjects of love into and out of one another remains rooted in
philosophy.

And I think we can say that when the man covers his eyes—an
ambiguous gesture, between avoiding the horror of knowing the
existence of others and avoiding the horror of not knowing it,
between avoiding the threat of castration that makes the knowledge

accessible and avoiding the threat of outcastness should that threat fail—he is in that gesture both warding off his seeing something and warding off at the same time his being seen by something, which is to say, his own existence being known, being seen by the woman of the letter, by the mute director and his (her?) camera— say, seen by the power of art—and seen by us, which accordingly identifies us, the audience of film, as assigning ourselves the position, in its passiveness and its activeness, of the source of the letter and of the film; which is to say, the position of the feminine. Then it is the man's horror of us that horrifies us—the revelation, or avoidance, of ourselves in a certain way of being feminine, a way of being human, a mutual and reflexive state, let us say, of victimization. The implications of this structure as a response to film, to art, to others, for better and for worse, is accordingly a good question. I guess it is the question Freud raises in speaking, in "Analysis Terminable and Interminable," of the "repudiation of femininity"— which he named as the bedrock at which psychoanalytic activity is at an end. My thought is that film, in dramatizing Freud's finding, oddly opens the question for further thought—the question, call it, of the differential feminine and masculine economies of the active and the passive.[27]

Emerson devotes the ninth paragraph of "Fate," cited in my previous essay, to a fair intuition, or tuition, of the question:

> Jesus said, "When he looketh on her, he hath committed adultery." But he is an adulterer before he has yet looked on the woman, by the superfluity of animal, and the defect of thought, in his constitution. Who meets him, or who meets her, in the street, sees that they are ripe to be each other's victim. ("Fate," p. 11)

Transcribing so as to isolate a couple of Emersonian master-tones, I read as follows: Our "constitution" is of course both our physiology or individuality, the thing that what agrees with us agrees with, and at the same time it is the thing we are in agreement on; it is the fate at which private and public cross. Who the "we" is who are subject to agreement is given in the slightly later paragraph that begins: "The population of the world is a conditional population; not the best, but the best that could live now." I have argued that the essay "Fate," with a focus on "limitation," takes a focus on "condition" in its register as meaning "talking together," setting out "terms" (of agreement). (It is part of Emerson's interpretation/

obedience to/mastery of/appropriation/substantiation/under-
writing/undermining of Kant.) This merely identifies "the population of the world" as talkers (hence, no doubt, as hearers). Now
grant that Emerson's address to this population—I mean his
writing—is what he has from the beginning defined as his "constitution" (anyway since the seventh paragraph of "Self-Reliance":
"The only right is what is after my constitution";[28] it is what he
means to bring to his nation (but surely not he alone?), as its
bedrock, or say stepping-stone. Then the question of "adultery"
(which is some question of the "other"), the question of victimization, is to be seen, and assessed, in each case of the saying of a
word, the citing of any term, in all our conditions. In writing, hence
in reading, we have to see for ourselves what our relations are—
whether we conform to the demands and the scandals of our
readers, or of our authors, when we do not recognize them as our
own. Emerson's picture of meeting ("him or her") "in the street" is
perhaps one of meeting his reader not at some bedrock but on some
false ground, so that their intimacy victimizes them both, or say
adulterates their originalities.

Perhaps Freud, at the end of "Analysis Terminable and Interminable," pictures the repudiation of femininity or passiveness as a
biological fact because he wishes to conceive that "for the psychical
field, the biological field does in fact play the part of the underlying
bedrock." But suppose the relation of victimization or passiveness
Freud described is, as in Emerson, one he senses between his
writing and his readers, that is to say, his progeny. Then the bedrock
at which psychoanalytic activity ends (whatever the fate of the
biological in psychoanalytic theory) is the fate of psychoanalytic
understanding in its own terms. Psychoanalytic understanding of
the matter of victimization, as of any other matter (for example,
that of psychoanalytic theory and practice), has to take place in
relation to reading Freud, in subjecting oneself to *this* inheritance.
Biology has not lifted this burden from him. If the inheritance is
not to take place "in the street," as victimization, it must take place
in the recognition of, in the reading of, our countertransference to
Freud, as we expect him to, and rebuke him for failing to, read his
countertransference to Dora. Are we then certain what Freud's
"prior" transference to "us" is, who it is we think he thinks we are,
what it is he wants of us? The idea of countertransference here is
meant as a gloss on a moment in an earlier essay of mine in which

I interpret reading as a process of interpreting one's transference to (as opposed to one's projection onto) a text.[29] That idea implies that the fantasy of a text's analyzing its reader is as much the guide of a certain ambition of reading—of philosophy as reading—as that of the reader's analyzing the text. In now specifying the transference in question as of the nature of countertransference (that is, as a response to an other's transference to me) I do not deny the reversal of direction implied in the idea of the text as my reader, but I rather specify that that direction already depends upon a further understanding of a text's relation to me, and that that further relation cannot be said either (or can be said both) to be prior to or/and posterior to any approach (or say attraction) to a text. How could I suppose that this is an issue for women more than for men? Recall that "A Child Is Being Beaten" is a text which Freud ends by using his material to "test" the theories of two competing men, of Fliess and of Adler—which is to say, to beat them.[30] Talk about theory and practice.

I leave you with a present of some words from the closing paragraphs of Henry James's "The Beast in the Jungle":

> The creature beneath the sod [the buried woman companion] *knew* of his rare experience, so that, strangely now, the place had lost for him its mere blankness of expression. . . . [T]his garden of death gave him the few square feet of earth on which he could still most live. . . . by clear right of the register that he could scan like an open page. The open page was the tomb of his friend. . . . He had before him in sharper incision than ever the open page of his story. The name on the table smote him . . . and what it said to him, full in the face, was that *she* was what he had missed. . . . Everything fell together . . . ; leaving him most of all stupefied at the blindness he had cherished. The fate he had been marked for he had met with a vengeance . . .; he had been the man of his time, *the* man, to whom nothing on earth was to have happened. . . . This horror of waking—*this* was knowledge.[31]

James's tale in theme and quality better measures Ophuls's film than the story of Stefan Zweig's from which its screenplay was, excellently, adapted. Such is the peculiar distribution of powers among the arts.

*The joke is
far funnier than
you think.*

3

Ugly Duckling, Funny Butterfly: Bette Davis and Now, Voyager

FOLLOWING this third main installment of a project to define a
companion genre of film melodrama for the genre of remarriage
comedy perspicuously enough to let them both figure as explicitly
and specifically in thinking about philosophical skepticism as I feel
they do implicitly and generally, I append a piece which I call "Postscript" but which has outrun what it follows. There I begin a
response, improvised in tone as in circumstance, to work that has
appeared since my project began, specifically to two essays I have
just read concerning, let's say, gender, or sexual identity, that I want
to respond to at once, that is, in interference with the present
installment. In this business, business is never usual.

Pursuits of Happiness claims that it is the nature of a genre that
when its defining features are negated systematically by other films
then those other films form an adjacent or derived genre. The
process I take as "deriving" the melodrama of the unknown
woman by "negation" from the comedy of remarriage is open and
closed—open in the wish to be taken as speaking provisionally,
closed in the wish *not* to be taken as speaking about *all* film comedy
(precisely not of everything called "screwball comedy," which is
not a genre in the same mode as remarriage comedy) and not of
all film melodrama (and precisely not of everything called "the
woman's film").[1]

One quality of the remarriage comedies is that, for all their
ingratiating manners, and for all the ways in which they are among
the most beloved of Hollywood films, a moral cloud remains at the
end of each of them. And that moral cloud has to do with what is

best about them. What is best are the conversations that go on in them, where conversation means of course talk, but means also an entire life of intimate exchange between the principal pair. We feel that these people know one another, or risk being known, and that they know how to play together (know and accept, you may say, the role of theater in their mutuality) in a way to make one happy and hope for the best. The moral cloud has to do with what that conversation is meant to do, and what I say about those films is that the conversation is in service of the woman's sense of herself as in need of an education. Critically for that reason, I call her a descendent of Nora in Henrik Ibsen's *A Doll's House,* who in one of the most celebrated moments in modern theater, ends a play by closing a door behind her. She leaves the dollhouse saying to her husband that she requires an education and that he is not the man who can provide it for her. The implication is that since he is not this man, he cannot (in logic) be her husband. And implying the contrary as well: if he were, then he would be, and their relationship would accordingly—"miracle of miracles" as Nora puts it—constitute a marriage.

This demand for education has to do with the woman's sense that she stands in need of creation, or re-creation. Now comes the moral cloud. Does creation from, even by, the man somehow entail creation *for* the man, say for his use and pleasure and pride? If not, how does the woman attain independence; how does she complete, as it were, her creation?

Another set of features of the comedies further defines this moral cloud. The woman is virtually never shown with her mother and is never shown to be a mother. Whether the absence of literal mothering is the permanent price or punishment for the woman's happiness, or whether a temporary and mysterious aberration of a disordered world, is not decided. What is decided is that the happiness achieved in remarriage comedy is not uncontaminated, not uncompromised.

I relate this sense of compromise to what I call a taint of villainy in the men of these comedies. It is the feature that most insistently projects their invitation to melodrama. Even in males as charming and, I should like to say, as capable of tenderness as Spencer Tracy and Cary Grant and James Stewart and Henry Fonda, there is reason shown for associating a lingering villainy with the fact of maleness itself—as maleness, or rather masculinity, has been defined, or deformed, in our culture. The implication is that the woman's creation will be completed, furthered, only with the man's. The derived melodrama will then be expected to ask where the woman gets the power to demand the man's transformation, which is to say, where she gets the power to transcend his standing. The melodrama signaled in the tainted male of the comedies suggests that there is a structure of unhappiness that the happiness of the comedies is lucky to escape, even temporarily, even (and always partially by happenstance) partially.

What is this awaiting structure of unhappiness and what may count as transcending it? The structure would have to be one in which what is at stake remains the creation of a woman. (The central women of both the comedies and the melodramas in question are descendants of Nora: sisters so to speak, but with different tastes and talents and chances.) But it cannot be a creation that could happen through conversation with a male, of the fierce and witty kind that defines the comedies, otherwise comic remarriage would be effected. So the woman must achieve her transformation otherwise in the implied melodrama.

In *Now, Voyager,* the woman's transformation happens through a process depicted as, and ponderously symbolized as, metamorphosis. This mode of creation, of as it were molting and rebirth (as Thoreau and Emerson can say) takes place, negating the remarriage structure, very much in the presence of the woman's mother, and in the presence of a child who, while not biologically the heroine's, is hers spiritually, bonded to her, hers to provide a life for. The irony that negates the conversation of the pair in remarriage comedy, the thing that takes the place of their wicked joy in exchanging words, hence in foregoing words, serves to isolate the woman of this melodrama from everyone around her, or almost everyone. It is a question whether it also isolates her from us. Hence I speak of the genre as the study of the unknownness of the woman.

Nothing much to me would be worth trying to understand about such a film as *Now, Voyager*—one of the great films of 1942, one of the four or five most popular films of the period, when Bette Davis was one of the five or six most prominent stars in Hollywood, still widely remembered, from even one viewing five decades ago, as containing the trick with the cigarette in which a man puts two cigarettes between his lips, lights both with one flame, then hands one to the woman—unless one cares for it, cares to find words for it that seem to capture its power of feeling and intelligence, in such a way as to understand why we who have caused it (for whom it is made) have also rejected it, why we wish it both into and out of existence.[2]

I have sketched the body of what I have to say about the film in five segments, around these principal topics: (1) the idea of metamorphosis in the film; (2) Bette Davis and her memorable ways of walking and looking and of delivering lines; (3) the ending sequence and last line of the film ("Oh, Jerry, don't let's ask for the moon. We have the stars.") from which I work to a close with a couple of codas: (4) the longer coda is in effect a reprise of the events of the film that focuses on its study of the changing of names and descriptions of persons, and (5) the shorter is an epilogue on a certain enactment of our philosophical tradition climactically within the film's narrative.

First about metamorphosis. The film is preoccupied with change, a preoccupation laid on with a trowel, as issues in melodrama tend to be laid on with trowels: caring for them depends on whether you can care about matters that demand that openness or extravagance of care. If or when you cannot take such matters this way, then you cannot take such things, for example, as *La Traviata,* or the Tchaikovsky *Sixth,* or the *Revolutionary Etude,* or the tales of E. T. A. Hoffmann, or *Titus Andronicus.* And of course there are moods in which you cannot take them, not with the extravagant seriousness they solicit—perhaps one can think of it as extravagance without excess. Stylistically this calls on a grueling obviousness and repetition of symbology in everything from decor and objects and shadows to names and weather. I will hardly more than point to the film's invocation of metamorphosis through the dramatized image of the butterfly and the consequent or precedent ideas of fledglings and borrowed wings and an ugly duckling and being pigeonholed. Such links are meticulously handled, in tone and characterization, in ways that a film of this period is obliged to handle them, and is exactly capable of handling.

But let us go straight to Davis's, I mean to Aunt Charlotte's (well, but then her as transformed into Renée Beauchamp) two theatrical, or rather cinematic, entrances, the two times she (who?) walks down an incline, the camera beginning at her shoes and

ankles and concluding upon her face. The first time, in the film's
opening sequence, she is descending the staircase of the Vale
mansion for her initial meeting with Dr. Jaquith (Claude Rains).
The second time she is paused before descending a gangway onto
the shore boat for the beginning of the voyage Dr. Jaquith has urged
her to take. This time the camera does not look away as it did the
first time when it cut from her feet to the unfavorable conversation
about her she overhears from the room she is to enter, then cut
back to her naked, unprotected, heavy face, as she tries but fails to
retreat and then enters on a scene in which she is destined for
humiliation; the second time, rather, the camera moves from her
feet up the length of her body to conclude on a gorgeous white
hat, half shading a beautifully modeled face, an image of mystery,
presaging adventure, heralding metamorphosis.

The moment is a useful one in which to resist the temptation to
do a little early symbolic work on the hat. It is easy enough to think
about the hat in some obvious Freudian way; certainly I do not
think it irrelevant that hats are sexual symbols of some kind. In
The Interpretation of Dreams Freud says hats are symbols of the
male sex; the present moment in *Now, Voyager* may contest that.
Let us take to heart Freud's fervent advice not to trust universal
symbols very far, but to look at the specific associations that particular objects inspire in their representativeness in specific contexts.
This particularly fine hat has its own perfectly specific dramatic
associations in this film, which gives, I find, ample cause and
context for speculation or association around it. Immediately, the
hat, as filmed, lends the woman a kind of protection that allows her
to let herself be perceived as an erotic being; eventually it, or rather
its analogue, presides over her letting her mother perceive this,
from whom we know from the beginning the daughter hides her
cigarettes and the novels she reads. The presentation for her mother
is blatantly explicit as she returns home to her mother's room from
her fledgling voyage, dressed (armed?) in another beautifully
becoming wide-brimmed hat, this time not white but black with
experience. From where does this erotic power proceed?

At the level of narrative one is likely to answer flatly that it
comes from the attention paid to her by men on the boat (over-
laying, rewriting, the traumatic break her mother had enforced
between Charlotte and a younger man on a boat trip in an earlier

day that she and her mother had taken together), beginning with
attention from Jerry (Paul Henreid). On the level of cinema
another answer has to be included, given in an early flashback in
which Charlotte remembers remnants from that earlier boat trip
and we see her mother in yet another smart white wide-brimmed
hat, an image that later will be superimposed over Charlotte and
her newfound hattedness just after she has been introduced to
Jerry. The two hats and the two pairs of eyes of the two women in
superimposition almost coincide. This extraordinary cinematic
gesture is disturbing enough on its initial presentation; and it
seems to me to do further work in retrospect (in deferred action,
as Freud names it), as the relationship with her mother later begins
to turn in the daughter's favor. Then we may think back, or really
think further, that while the daughter has called back up that
image of her mother in order, as it were, to inform her, and Dr.
Jaquith, that she is defying her mother's orders, specifically her
injunction to the daughter to isolate herself from the rest of
humanity, she has at the same time found the strength for this defi-
ance through her identification with her mother's power. (If her
fatness suggested one mode of introjection, say cannibalistic, the
figure of superimposition suggests another—let us for the moment

*Cat got your
tongue, Charlotte?*

Camille
Beauchamp.

say metamorphic.) So that it is altogether important that Dr.
Jaquith has painted the mother to the daughter in favorable (if
limited) terms.

But if this daughter's power is defined and contained in her
mother's power (including the power to transcend the mother),
then what does it mean to think of her change, or succession of
changes, as metamorphosis? Does she merely exchange one form
of protection for another (say a woman for a man, or a dismissive
plainness for a dismissive beauty)? (What does "merely" signify
here? Are the only changes that matter metamorphoses?) Dr.
Jaquith raises the question explicitly at the end, seeing her in her
remodeled (metamorphosed?) mansion. He asks her, "Are you the
same woman . . . ?" She answers, "No." But her manner of delivering the monosyllable is one of the oddest in a film of odd deliv-
eries. Jaquith at any rate seems to accept her answer that she is not
the same.

This is to be put together with the quite fantastic moment at
which Jerry, on the night of their dinner together on the ship, for
whom she produces the group photograph of her family (think of
her carrying the photograph with her, even as she had hurriedly
changed into evening clothes, as if it were her identity card), asks

her, "Who is the fat lady with the heavy brows and all the hair?"
When she responds (*she*, it is Bette Davis who takes a pace or two
away and with her back to him replies), "I am the fat lady . . . ,"
Henreid's character is astonishingly able to turn aside what in most
hands would have been an impossible moment and instead, with
a looney courtesy, simply accept the fact that she is changed, which
in that context is to accept the fact that she is the same woman.
(I find that I associate here Nora's interpretation of changing out
of her fancy dress, at the end of *A Doll's House*, with her being
changed.) So that this film proposes the study of human change,
as liberation, as the scene or condition of a doubleness in human
passion (to say the least), an acceptance of the otherness of others
as an acceptance of their difference from, and their sameness
with, themselves.

It has been a developing claim of mine about film since my first
book on the subject, *The World Viewed*, that the most significant
films in the history of the art of film will be found to be those that
most significantly discover and declare the nature of the medium
of film (which is exactly not equivalent to a random running
through of film's various remarkable "effects," nor of its random
ways of self-reflexiveness, of calling attention to its own making).
It is essential to the argument of *Pursuits of Happiness* that a feature
of the medium of film that comes under investigation, and is hence
declared there, in the comedy of remarriage is film's power of metamorphosis or transfiguration. In remarriage comedy, this feature,
as suggested earlier, is expressed as the woman's suffering creation,
which cinematically means the transfiguration of flesh-and-blood
women into projections of themselves on a screen. Hence the obligation in those films to find some narrative occasion for revealing,
within the limits of the law, the woman's body, the body of *that*
actress. This is going on in *Now, Voyager*, but the instance is so
extreme as to suggest further matters. It sometimes happens in
film that a famous face is first shown hidden, or marred, or in some
way unfavorably, perhaps simply as in the plainness of youth or of
some other restricted office, and later revealed in the astonishment
of its familiar power. This does not read to me as some testimony
to accepted beauty: rather on the contrary. It seems to me a realization of the idea Emerson and Nietzsche each phrase (not independently) roughly as the courage to become the one you are. This
possibility, not alone that of beauty, is a source of film's glamour.

I was thinking of
my mother.

(That the idea has debased forms is obvious. What idea lacks debased forms?) One may doubt whether Bette Davis or Barbara Stanwyck or Katharine Hepburn are beautiful. One cannot doubt that each is distinct. Some people are both.

Matters of urgent pertinence are being assumed or bypassed here. I note the incipient question as to why it is the woman's body that is most under pressure. I am not unaware that a certain current in recent feminist film theory may take the answer as obvious: films, perhaps especially of Hollywood, and especially of its so-called Golden Age, just are made to subject women to the appro-priative, unreciprocated gaze of men (Laura Mulvey's "Visual Plea-sure and Narrative Cinema" is the instigating text here.) Such an answer would, to my mind, take there to be no essential difference between, for example, the way Charles Boyer looks at Ingrid Berg-man in *Gaslight,* or the way Spencer Tracy as Mr. Hyde looks at her in *Dr. Jekyll and Mr. Hyde;* and the way Spencer Tracy looks at Katharine Hepburn in *Adam's Rib,* or the way Cary Grant looks at Irene Dunne during her mock nightclub routine in *The Awful Truth*—I mean no difference in the camera's participation in, or delegation of, these gazes (or glances or glares or attentions or appreciations). So then there would be no difference (or merely an

ideology of difference?) between villainous, intractable, vengeful
evil, and what I have named the taint of villainy in the leading
males of remarriage comedy. I can imagine the reply: Of course
such differences do not matter; all the gazes are men's, all the effect
of male eyes. Then how about Charlie Chaplin responding at the
end of *City Lights* to the calamitous gaze of the young woman
whose sight has been restored? Or Bette Davis in *The Little Foxes*
watching her husband die, as if her gaze deprives him of life; or Katharine Hepburn in *Adam's Rib* looking with scorn at her wistful
admirer who has suggested that her husband is traitorous to her; or
Barbara Stanwyck in *The Lady Eve* looking with amazed, excited eyes
at her father as the mug Henry Fonda does a card trick for them:
her gaze hardly needs to *make* anything happen here; or Greta
Garbo in *Ninotchka* laughing as she sees Melvyn Douglas fall off a
chair failing to make her laugh—the man is transfigured by what
he has caused and could not have intended; or Rosalind Russell in
His Girl Friday withering a group of male reporters as she reenters
a room to say, "Gentlemen of the press"; or Mae West delivering
her line running, "Come up and see me"—precisely unimaginable,
I take it, as an offer to be gazed at dominatingly. Still all the same?
and all subject to the camera's fixed gaze, none empowered to

*She [Tina] is
convinced she's an
ugly duckling.*

Who's the fat lady with the heavy brows and all the hair?

instruct the camera in its ways of looking—to, say, the extent men can be instructed? (Again this is not conceived as a final response. I can imagine this objection: the importance of such differences is indeed to be denied. Freedom from the negative instances depends upon freedom from the positive. This objection is like something Emerson likes to say, as in "Self-Reliance": "This one fact the world hates; that the soul *becomes*; for that . . . shoves Jesus and Judas equally aside.")

The taint of villainy functions to acknowledge a background of pain between men and women that the woman of these comedies is willing to include (since the man does not deny it) in a mutually meet and happy conversation committed to turn that pain aside. I do not wish to claim that film in its various manifestations has reached farther than the best thought and feeling of the Western civilization into which it made its entrances. But to assume that the technology and economy of motion pictures emerged in Western civilization, perhaps especially in the Golden Age of Hollywood, exactly and rigidly to reiterate the worst gestures of that civilization, is beyond me. Besides, the pressure on the woman's body is one emphasis in a revised economy of the body; the men in the comedies come in for painful transformations of their own. Then other bypassed questions here of pertinence are: Who or what is the man? What does it mean that the male stars are less apt than the female for change? Who is to ask such questions?

The obligation of transfiguration taken on in the narrative procedures of the melodrama of the unknown woman is less, compared with that of remarriage comedy, one of declaring the (new) existence of the woman than it is one of tracing her (new) identity. And this matter is registered not so much by declaring the fact of this body as by showing its changes of look and circumstance, something that makes changes of costume a defining feature of these films. This is a reason the genre generates historical settings *(Gaslight, Letter from an Unknown Woman),* or narratives that move through significant lapses of time *(Letter* again, and *Stella Dallas,* and *Random Harvest),* or over extreme shifts of environment *(Stella Dallas* again, and *Blonde Venus).*

So here in the case of *Now, Voyager* we must ask, moving to the second of the principal topics of this film I am proposing to sketch: Who is this woman, Bette Davis? What becomes of her on film?

It would be an answer to say: she is the one who can deliver a line—who has the voice, the contained irony, the walk, the gaze, and the glance away, to lay down a line—such as "I am the fat lady with the heavy brows and all the hair." You may laugh a little, or cringe, now just half a century after these events were set to film, as if at the film's very dare to laugh, or merely to cringe, at the violence of the sentiment and the directness of self-presentation that show through the changes in our emotional fashions. But we, most of us, I think, stop laughing or cringing. The feeling in this example is that this actress's perspective shows fatness, so called, to be a further symbolic marker in the film, something that might very well not trouble another mother's daughter (on the contrary), something that stands for any number of specifications, two (further) of which will come out. And she, this actress, is the distinct one who can close a film by saying, "Oh Jerry, don't let's ask for the moon. We have the stars." She is, that is to say, capable of that flair for theater, that theater of flair, exaggeration it may be thought, call it melodrama, that these films of unknownness require. She is a woman capable of the reserves of irony and of fantasy whose particular powers of individuation deprive her of the playfulness her comedic sisters have the talent and the world for. Her experience demands, rather, the capacity to find astonishments and intimacies in a world with little play in it.

There is surely a sense of sacrifice in this group of films; they solicit our tears. But is it that the women in them are sacrificing themselves to the sad necessities of a world they are forced to accept? Or isn't it rather that the women are claiming the right to judge a world as second-rate that enforces this sacrifice; to refuse, transcend, its proposal of second-rate sadness?

My impression is that the weight of current opinion is still inclined to the former of these alternatives. In going on to propose the latter, I am not simply agreeing with those who feel the interpretation of the film to be a function of a political vision. I am claiming that the political stance of the film is feminist, anyway that the nonfeminist interpretation is *no* stronger (hence mine, while it lasts, is to eclipse the nonfeminist or to be eclipsed by it). So that a certain condescension to this film and its generic companions in certain feminist critics, together with the popularity of these films with the wider culture in which they have their origins and with which they are in ideological strife, are matters of importance to me. (What I mean by "a certain condescension" I specify in my "Reply" to Modleski's Letter to the Editors cited in the Introduction.) This political difference concerning these portraits of women exists together with a difference concerning the status of so-called popular culture. What is the basis of the *certainty* that a popular genre of film cannot be as advanced as the advanced (socially, in political sensibility) thought of its time?

How does Bette Davis manage her powers? Here I point simply to a certain hysteria, or hysterical energy, about her character on film. It taps a genius for that expressiveness (as I put the matter in the preceding chapter) in which Breuer and Freud, in their *Studies on Hysteria,* first encountered the reality of the unconscious, the reality of the human mind as what is unconscious to itself, and encountered first in the suffering of women; a reality whose expression they determined as essentially theatrical, a theatricality of the body as such (they spoke of the capacity to form hysterical symptoms as one for "somatic compliance"), seeing the body as a field of incessant significance, but of significance demanding deciphering.[3]

It is Bette Davis's command and deployment of this capacity for

somatic compliance, for the theatricalization of desire and of its
refiguration or retracking that, so it seems to me, made her one of
the most impersonated of Hollywood stars, in a period in which
impersonation was a significant cultural possibility, a living form
of entertainment. If we think of the stars who were most impersonated—among the women, Garbo, Dietrich, Mae West, Katharine Hepburn—Bette Davis would be one of those (I don't know
whether I am remembering something told or shown me or imagining this) impersonated not alone by men and women who did
vaudeville impersonations ("impressions" they were called) but
most taken on by female impersonators. This memory or imagined possibility testifies to a sense that an essential dimension of
Bette Davis's power is its invitation to, and representation of,
camp; an arrogation of the rights of banality and affectation and
display, of the dangerous wish for perfect personal expressiveness.
The wish, in the great stars (to place an earlier point a little differently), is a function not of their beauty, such as that may be, but
of their power of privacy, of a knowing unknownness. It is a democratic claim for personal freedom. It is something Davis shares
with the greatest of the histrionic romantic stars, Garbo and
Dietrich, sometimes Ingrid Bergman, and, among American
women, Barbara Stanwyck.

There is an odd moment in *Now, Voyager* of explicit confirmation that the quality of stardom or magnetism exercised by the
women of these melodramas is not what is called their personal
beauty but lies in their declaration of distinctness and freedom, of
human existence. They are, if goddesses, not ones of love or fate,
but of chance and choice. The moment comes as part of an exchange
between Charlotte and the proper widower to whom she becomes
engaged after her return to her mother's house. The man asks her
why she insists on always wearing a camellia with her evening dress,
a flower moreover she will never let him buy for her. She does *not*
explicitly reply, "Because Charlotte is under other circumstances
the fat lady and under others a woman of adventure known as
Camille; I am protecting you from having to know my times." She
says, rather, in the circumstances now given, "Just a personal idiosyncrasy. We're all entitled to them." Now first, what I have been
saying about Bette Davis's self-definitions, her impersonability, is
that she is endlessly idiosyncratic. Referred to the camellia, her
explanation extravagantly declares, by understatement, her knowl-

edge of this power of her character, this character of her power; as she delivers it she idiosyncratically suppresses her idiosyncratic smile. Do we know her secret? And second, the entitlement to idiosyncrasy is the way John Stuart Mill, in *On Liberty,* describes the form in which, in an imperfect democracy, protection of idiosyncrasy, the heart for it, becomes as important to democracy as liberty itself. Freud's work brings the private knowledge of the cost of protecting and heartening one's idiosyncrasies into public discourse. Or has the idea of bringing it into science been a further way of keeping it from the public?

There is an immediate or gross reason not to accept the work of the film *Now, Voyager* as comprehending Charlotte to be, at the end, sacrificing herself to or for Jerry's world. The immediate and gross reason is that this is essentially the way Jerry wishes to comprehend her. Now we have come to the third of our principal topics, that of the film's closing sequence and final line.

In the library of the house that Charlotte has inherited and made over into her own, Jerry is saying, "No self-respecting man would allow such self-sacrifice as yours to go on indefinitely," and so on. To which Charlotte replies, beginning, "That's the most conventional, pretentious, pious speech I ever heard in my life. I simply don't know you." Now it seems to me that that stays said; that the man never recovers from that indictment or observation; that after this moment he becomes simply superficial, the muddled man to the end. This writing for film is extraordinary. You can take it that the man is still in authority over himself: you *can.* After all he is the charming man with all the cigarettes who has been absolutely indispensable to what has become of this woman. Eternal gratitude is due him; I would not wish to disgrace him for the world. But in this last scene the woman no longer occupies the same level of spiritual existence. He no longer knows where to find her.

Take his saying that she should be free to marry "some man who will make you happy." He had on their voyage said to her, "If I were free, there would be only one thing I want to do, prove that you're not immune to happiness," a little pledge of helpless longing that produced tears from her, which she named there tears of gratitude. We will come back to them. But here at the end she repeats his words, "some man who will make me happy," with the irony and scorn available to one with those eyes, that voice, that body swinging around and lurching away from him in imitation of itself.

(In alluding again to Bette Davis's capacity for somatic compliance, I add Freud's observation that while such a talent is necessary for the development of hysterical symptoms, it is a capacity not necessarily leading to illness. Call it a talent for what a moment ago I called personal expressiveness.)[4] In repeating the man's words she, as it were, studies each of them as she delivers them back, rebuking him for each one. Whereupon he launches into a weirdly inappropriate oration to the effect that what is between them is stronger than both of them, that they cannot destroy it, neglect it as they may, and so on. It is to my mind all ringed, wreathed, with irony, with the sense of things happening at the wrong time, feelings displaced to oblivion.

Are you afraid of getting burned if you get too close to happiness?

The final bit of camp is assigned to him, when at the end he recognizes the fact of some bargain by saying, "Shall we just have a cigarette on it?" It is a high moment of writing for the screen here that we can still take this gesture seriously, allow its mock repetition of a past that is no longer seen in common to maintain an air of sexual and military courtesy, so that it does not repudiate the genuine valorousness in that past. There is a similar cigarette trick in Olive Higgins Prouty's novel; in general the details of closeness and distance throughout the relation of the novel and the film are

I'm immune to happiness.

worth study. Here I merely note that the novel is far more interesting, it incorporates more intelligence, than one might have been led to believe by its fairly total obscurity now. Still, if you take the film in something like the way it presents itself to me, the novel really finds its apotheosis here. But if it can be seen that the novel calls for this film, Jerry reads the film as if it were a novel, and one not at all as good as Prouty's. How that can be done, how an excellent and rich film may be taken poorly (since it is popular, *must* be taken so?), uncinematically, in a sympathetically yet systematically diminished way, remains part of the secret of how these relations work.

After the pair go through the cigarette business this last time, the man asks his last question, "And will you be happy, Charlotte?" (She has become Charlotte for him now, of course. This signals no new identity for her and no further perception of his; on the contrary it signals that there is no longer a question as to what he should call her, that a responsibility for her name is no longer his.) Now here is this woman retracing the reigning concepts of her life—what a mother is, what a child, a home, a husband are, what happiness is—and yet this man stupefyingly asks her whether she will be happy. Evidently she maintains an affection for him, but how is she to answer him now? His late protestation of passion for her has become quite beside the point, no longer welcome. In an earlier day he had elicited her old, tortured capacity for explicit passion, and for that she was fully grateful. I see no reason for her to repudiate that feeling at the end. But while sexual gratitude is truly called for, it has its limits. When in that earlier day she had cried out to him, "These are tears of gratitude, an old maid's gratitude," he would naturally, being Jerry, have felt a demand in them and counted on her resignation, as if her meaning was, in effect, "I know I must not aspire to anything more from you." Beyond Jerry, the meaning can turn differently: "The fat lady with all the hair is eternally grateful. Yet having saved me from the exclusions of that fate, without denying that it was mine, allowing my metamorphosis, you cannot (I assume) be saved yourself. So these tears are from what the world calls an old maid, and they are tears for you, for your limitations, as well as for me and for mine. I assume, that is (correct me if I am wrong), that you cannot aspire to anything more from me."

I seem to have chosen this late moment to register explicitly the dangerous posture of my account of these films about women. I find that to say how I take the films I must from time to time speak for their central women. I feel that I am amplifying their voices, listening to them, becoming them, in films in which, on other accounts, they are unlistened to, being deprived of a voice. (This is fully thematic in *Gaslight*.) But I may be subject to the charge that in taking on a woman's words I am myself joining the list of men I describe in such films who take over or take away the woman's voice. The charge remains to be developed and, so far as I can see how, responded to. In the meantime, I say only that in whatever ways I may be invading Charlotte's privacy or living off her consciousness—risks, temptations, in whatever is called reading—I am not claiming to speak with Charlotte's voice, specifically not with the power represented by her irony, and concealed with it.

And needless to say there are other charges—intellectual, moral, political—that I may be subject to. Some may find the pleasures offered by the film to be horrifying. This was the burden of the intervention of one woman in an early discussion of this material. I interpreted this reaction (but received no confirmation) as taking what happens to the woman in or by the film (above all through the two principal men in it) to be a violation of her that is incomparably worse than any unhappiness in her life with her mother: she is now being told, by the men, by the film world, that her being fat, being plain, wearing glasses, leaving her eyebrows and hair natural, being in general unstylish, makes her unlovable. It follows that my finding transcendence in the film for the woman is desperate, a usual metaphysical consolation that continues the injustice for which consolation is offered. I offer two responses here to this reaction: (1) I am claiming that the heavy symbology of the film—the hair, the hats, legs, shoes, fatness, eye-glasses, flowers, names, transformations of birds and butterflies, the stars and the moon—is not presented unquestioningly, but with room insisted on for the importance of the way these things are appropriated, indeed with different mechanisms of appropriation named or pictured. This will come back. And (2) I am claiming that how these things are appropriated—and marriage, and a child, a home, work in the world—is something that conversation between a woman and a man may rightfully help to determine.

But if instead of a moral *cloud* over these films that the films are made to ponder, as I claim to be the case in remarriage comedies, someone finds that the derived melodramas are from first to last scenes of moral catastrophe that the films pander to distract us from; and if someone accordingly finds that men are not, in general, as a genus, as we stand, *tainted* with villainy (I assume its provenance stretches from the shares men have in the world their kind runs, to what Freud calls the inherent sadistic components of erotic relationships), but are, every one, out-and-out marauders and invaders; and if one finds that the world the woman judges as second-rate is instead a hell on earth that finally extirpates her judgment altogether, so that in seeming to enjoy her having become conventionally, or idiosyncratically, attractive, she has forfeited her mind ever more completely, no longer feels her torture, and the course of her hysteria has only deepened; then of course such a one will not concede the good, I mean rightfulness, of a conversation with men, and then of course my own intervention in these matters is at worst part of the problem, at best baffled by flowers (as the respectable widower, among other perplexities, was). How could I deny the possibility?

We were considering the closing moments of the film and the man's question, after all, "And will you be happy, Charlotte?" And I am taking it that at the end the woman does not forget either her

feeling for or her debt to the man, and that she finds a way to
respond to this question remembering the tact that had been the
condition of their intimacy: "Oh, Jerry, don't let's ask for the
moon. We have the stars." Given that her transcendence of the
world of hated, self-incarcerating ties, of the coin of conventionally
assessed guilt, is underway, she is gallantly providing the man, quite
outclassed, out-lived, with a fiction that they together are sacrificing themselves to stern and clear moral dictates. Whereas for her
what sacrifice there is in view took place on other grounds, in other
seas, before they met, before either of them was born. In her metamorphosis she is and is not what she is; in his incapacity for
change, for motion, he is not what he is not.

We have the stars.

She is and is not what she is. Here is the pivotal irony in this
member of a genre of irony. It is true that she *is* the fat lady, not
merely was true when she was in fact fat. And it is false that she is
the fat lady, and *was* false when she was in fact fat, because she was
always, for example, an ugly duckling, that is, unrecognized. (Her
fatness had not been seen, not by others and, I suppose, not by
her. Jaquith's therapeutic virtue was to be ignorant of it, to know
nothing of its mattering [to her]. This is not everything; but not
nothing.) Every single description of the self that is true is false, is

in a word, or a name, ironic. So one may take the subject of the
genre of the unknown woman as the irony of human identity
as such.

Not just anyone should be expected to recognize this lack of
recognition, the extent to which we are all out of place, ugly duck-
lings. Charlotte's word for the capacity or willingness for this recognition, call it a respect for difference, is as she puts it to Jaquith
that first morning in her room, not being clumsy. (She describes
Jaquith, to himself, as "the least clumsy person" she's ever met,
implying that clumsiness is an essential feature of mortals.) The
opposite of clumsy suggests some kind of gracefulness, but Jerry's
courtesy is not the last word in grace. Clumsy comes from the idea
of being numb, say unresponsive. So the respect for difference
demands responsiveness, specificity of response to the unforeseen,
the perhaps uncategorized, say an improvisation of vision. Jerry's
manners bespeak the indifferent, say the narcissistic. Better polite
than impolite, perhaps, but better yet something else, more. A word
for this something else might indeed be "tact." But the drift in the
way we use and ordinarily bind the idea of the untactful registers
that moralization of morality that deprives us of a good word for
the unclumsy. Our (moralized) idea of tact tends toward the idea
of not mentioning something, not touching on it; not toward an
idea of touching it pertinently, fittingly, painfully if necessary (for
what?). Take this aside on the tact of recognition as an inflection of
Immanuel Kant's taking respect as the basis of moral relationship.
If one says that what one is to respect is the human dignity of the
other, then my gloss on respect (as directed to difference) should
serve to counter the moralization of dignity. What the other values,
or wants to have valued, in himself or herself may be something,
may necessarily be something (so far), quite undignified.

Here I may just make clear where I take Jerry's walking papers
to leave Charlotte in relation to Dr. Jaquith. I say at once that the
story she tells Jerry that they are to have nothing more to do with
one another romantically—which she attributes to Dr. Jaquith as
the condition of her and Jerry's "having Jerry's child"—seems to
me a story and a demand that originates with her. When she said
to Jerry in the final sequence, "Oh I see. . . . It's your pride," she was
registering her perception that what he needs from her now is a
(another) story to save his face. If the demand had originated with
Dr. Jaquith, why would he not have expressed it to Jerry as well as

to Charlotte? My conviction here rests in part on (perhaps it insists on) the difference, or metamorphosis, that has come over Charlotte's relation to Dr. Jaquith. It is my general sense of these melodramas of the unknown woman—manifesting the dark side of remarriage comedies—that like those comedies they explore the question of what it is to constitute a marriage. Specifically it is my sense of Charlotte's reconstitution of the concept of marriage that the ending of her film invites us to conceive that she and Jaquith are married; it would be a way to conceive their arrangement as chaste. How bad a bargain is this for her? This is, visually and as it were spiritually, how I read this pair as, the last time we see them together, they are sitting on the floor of her metamorphosed mansion in the midst of some sort of communal meal, going over their life plans for further metamorphosis together. They are talking in particular about adding a wing to his retreat that is going to house the children whose care is in their hands. She and Jerry may have a child together; she and Jaquith have a life together.

Are you the same woman . . . ?

This is no doubt not a solution open to (or desired by) people very generally. And while obviously a lot of money is not always sufficient to avoid sacrifice, I assume a question raised by such a film is whether a lot of money is always necessary. Both the come-

No.

dies and the derived melodramas typically contain luxurious settings; the role of money is an essential topic for them. Without now saying a word about that, I may say that I hope the films elicit the sort of interest that suggests that they may themselves have useful views of the topic, that "wealth" and "position" are no more to be taken at face value in the films than "marriage" is.

A word about the moon Charlotte proposes she and Jerry not ask for and the stars she says "we" have. The phrase "Don't ask for the moon" has a fixed, idiomatic meaning; "We have the stars" has no such meaning. She is improvising now, on her own. Charlotte's rhetoric makes having the stars seem something less than (a compensation for not) having the moon. But this trades—tactfully —on the conventional, conventionally romantic, reading of the moon. Granted that forgoing the always-vanishing Jerry is painful for this woman, it is at the same time an intellectual relief, to say no more. Let us take "We have the stars"—since it is beyond the security of shared idiom—allegorically, that is, as an interpretation of what stars (literally) are. Then we have them as examples and guides. So to begin with, we have the stars as Bette Davis is a star, hence we have images of independence to aspire to, individuality to the point, if necessary, of undeciphered idiosyncrasy. Further,

we have stars as Emerson and Thoreau had them, as signs of a
romance with the universe, a mutual confidence with it, taking
one's productive habitation on earth; signs of possibility, a world to
think. Is this not enough to go on? I do not claim exceptional
depth for this film's intelligence, only that it and its generic
companions exist in and as opposition to or competition with an
understanding of this woman's choice that reads her and her film
as instancing some hearsay axiom to the effect that the Hollywood
dream factory is capable only of promoting the most vulgar and
most fixated of moony dreams. That axiom treats the woman's film
(as in another age, a woman's novel) with the same dismissiveness
with which it accuses others of treating women. So once again cynicism and sentimentality are shown as made for one another, joined
in dismissing the truth of sentiment.

I come to the first of my codas, on the subject of naming and
the changing of names and of descriptions or, say, signifiers. So
important is this subject to this film about metamorphosis that any
of the matters I took up in my remarks concerning who knows
who you are may be recast in terms of questions about which
names stick and who has the right to use what name for you and
hence whether you are the same person for different people; questions eventually propounding the question whether there is essentially any one person you are.

Parenthetically, this is the question posed in the irony of identifying selves—that they are always before and after themselves. It
might help to consider that this goes into why Martin Heidegger
in *Being and Time* (and after him, in his way, Jean-Paul Sartre in
Being and Nothingness) insists that *Dasein* is not characterized by
predicates but by existentials: it "is" what it is, whatever it is, in a
mode other than, say, a stone is what it is, a different mode of being
(for instance) heavy, stationary, dangerous. The question is not well
theorized in pictures of the self as foundational pellet or some more
ethereal substance, *and* not in *denials* of substance by, I gather,
currently more fashionable pictures of the self as endlessly malle-
able or constructible, say like clay, or continuous, say like a rope.
(Who is supposed to work the clay, or braid the rope?) I think it is
worth following further with Emerson's idea of the self—in its
aspect as mind—as a *consistency*. I am, of course, proposing a
reading of a coin worn almost to illegibility: "A foolish consistency
is the hobgoblin of little minds" ("Self-Reliance"). Perhaps there is

a suggestion here that little minds (whose not?) have in mind a foolish idea of consistency. Then let us take the idea (also) in its sense of viscosity, the degree of texture or firmness or resistance to flow (that of a substance?). Then the alternative to one consistency (call it that of fools) is not an inconsistency but a different consistency. A wiser consistency might be the angel or the star of larger minds. But how about Emerson's less famous sentence that follows the one with the hobgoblin? (a remarkable concept, with both male and female pasts, both hollow spaces and things they may contain): "With consistency a great soul has simply nothing to do."[5] Of course this will (is meant to) seem inconsistent with the idea of consistency as viscosity, so a mind of a certain viscosity will stop there. But how could a self (let us bypass the complication of "soul") have *no* consistency? Well, "simply having nothing to do" may mean that the concept does not apply, that it makes no sense to speak either of consistency or of inconsistency in connection with a great soul, and that then the flow, "beyond" self, is unimpeded, resistance extinguished. This more ancient idea of the absence of self was not alone a metaphysical denial of self as substance but the achievement of a Buddha. Is it ours for the asking or constructing?

In taking up the question of names in relation to such a film, we have to bear in mind that its symbology—in the instance of names as in the instances of hats and shoes and glasses and ivory boxes and smoking and flowers—is, as said, laid on with self-conscious melodramatic strokes.

When Jerry's child Tina tells her father over the phone that her new friend's name (the friend paying for the call) is Vale, she says explicitly (in answer, evidently, to a question asked on the other end), "No. Not the kind you wear on your face"—as though someone is being alerted to a continuing confusion over whether to be a Vale is to veil something, so whether to de-Vale yourself is to unveil something, and to the question what it means that the name Vale (when we first see it and perhaps when Charlotte first saw it) is engraved in stone.[6] It is who Jerry is that Charlotte can accept a change of name from him—a change, of course, of first or given not of last or family name. Dr. Jaquith had said in the opening sequence, "I don't put much faith in scientific terms. I leave that to the fakers and the writers of books." Jerry later, precipitating the pivotal moment of the photograph, turns out to know the scien-

tific, anyway a correct, name of the particular butterfly traced on
Charlotte's borrowed cloak; he calls it a "fritillary," a name whose
further significance is that the woman herself does not know the
name. Does this mean that Jerry is throughout a faker?—and even,
or especially, at the moment when the obscure name, and a change
of names, seems to have some therapeutic power? It is as if we are
being offered a little theory of naming and unnaming. When Charlotte's mother announced "my ugly duckling" she went on to add,
"Of course it's true that all late children are marked," to which Dr.
Jaquith responds angrily, "Often such children aren't wanted. That
can mark them." The exchange suggests that the description "late
children" is itself the mark in question; where moreover "mark" is
itself marked by the significance of being a grade. It is after Jerry
tells Charlotte what kind of butterfly she is cloaked in, or as—the
scientific name marking in its way the butterfly as the classical
image of metamorphosis—that he notices the note pinned to the
back of the cloak, and says, "Somebody must have been playing a
joke on you." She asks him to take the note off; she glances at it
and gives it to him to read. It contains advice about when to wear
the garment, and Jerry responds by saying, "I see. Your wings are
borrowed. Well, they suit you just the same." Charlotte sharply

denies that they, or by implication anything, might suit her, and rises to leave, saying, "The joke is far funnier than you think." That Jerry remains equal to the revelation, and follows Charlotte out of the dining room onto the deck, precipitates the ensuing sequence in which Charlotte shows the family photograph that marks her in the family's fixating way. (This longingly invites the question of the photographic basis of cinema, barely touched on in the present pages. Does, for example, the moving picture do its work by fixation or by metamorphosis? Here we need to think about change or difference in connection with concepts of identity and of repetition, in Kierkegaard's, Nietzsche's, and Freud's senses, invoked in *Pursuits of Happiness*.)

The story of *Now, Voyager* can be understood as a retelling of the fantasy of the ugly duckling. It is a recounting for grown-ups of the way a name can make you (count yourself) ugly, that tells how hard it is for a human being to find the way to her or his (legitimate?) name, the name of the kind to which one is kin. It is therewith a rebuke to our culture for its persistence in misunderstanding or mishearing the idiom, "an ugly duckling," refusing the fantasy, the irony in that description, a refusal expressed in the mother's corrupted phrase "my ugly duckling." We understand it too readily—as Charlotte, from her mother, seems to understand it, when we first encounter them—according to the paradigm "a black sheep." We take it, that is, as if the idiom "ugly duckling" described a certain duck. It is an understanding that precisely *denies* the fantasy that produces the fairy-tale idiomatic name for misnaming, namely the fantasy that one is—though mixed up with ducks—not a duck at all. Charlotte's anger, and her mother's anger, locked in each other, may be coded or abbreviated as expressing their repressed knowledge of the falseness of the name. Each has her use for the false name, so the situation has give in it. When Charlotte first doffs her name (with the help of a man), her mother becomes reconciled to a move to new ground with her. But when Charlotte later refuses to doff it (in favor of a man's name), she thereby causes, apparently, her mother's death. (Does Charlotte cause her mother's death? Parents sometimes create the impression, call it, that claiming one's own existence will be the ending of theirs. We might say that the birth of freedom may require taking such a chance; but this is only to say that independence cannot be gained without declaring it. Are, therefore, liberties always to be *taken*? But not *from* anyone, since no one [else] *has* yours.) This suggests a study for the question posed in remarriage comedy as to the absence of the woman's mother.[7]

Charlotte, in losing control early to Dr. Jaquith, refers to herself as "my mother's companion," "my mother's servant," and the place she is first shown to live in (where do people live?) is "my mother's room," and later her mother tells her that she is to occupy "your father's room." These are all names, I mean descriptions, carved in stone. There is no given way to erase the stone, no moment in this cinematic forest of symbols at which simply to unveil significance.

One symbolic description or depiction in the film for what I called the "appropriation" of symbols or names is just that they may be carved in stone—that is, they may be given the power to stamp and fix your identity, fix a relation to (a) truth. Irony is a contrary appropriation. Another antithetical procedure (contradictory to fixing) is to speak (of yourself, your desires) without "being afraid" ("I'm not afraid of you, Mother; I'm not afraid," Charlotte says, in dawning awe of herself); another is to speak in a mode of "voyaging," say "experimenting." In speaking of the happiness of the remarriage comedies I call this improvisation, or say living without fixation; remarriage comedy joins slapstick in laughing at human fixation. Emerson's word for fixation, the refusal of experimentation (in reading, in any walk of life), is "imbecility;" Whitman's word for the overcoming of fixation is "the open road." (The film's title is from Whitman, identified as such to Charlotte by Dr. Jaquith. Jaquith's claim, by the way, to leave scientific terms to "the fakers and the writers of books" is a gesture of warning in our appropriating theories of our work, for example our movies; a warning that theory, too, cannot magically escape our fixations, without work, but merely "reflect" our practice, but in more tractable, more hopeful form, one hopes. Did the makers of this movie know this? What makes movies?)

The main relation that I have left unconsidered in my account (apart from leaving out that of Jerry with his wife, the other obviously unknown woman of the film) is Charlotte's relation to Jerry's daughter Tina. How one comes to terms with that relation will determine how one understands the byplay of naming that goes on in Charlotte's calling her Tina and in Tina's coming to call Charlotte Camille, Jerry's names for each of them. Charlotte's relationship with Tina may be regarded either as the most disturbed or as

This is Jerry's child.

the most therapeutic of all we are shown; as the one in which the conditions of unhappiness in this world are perfectly synthesized and reproduced for another generation, or in which they are specifically relieved, or modified. If we cannot tell which is the case from what we see of that relationship so far, it is because, so I would like to take it, we are to understand that this matter is specifically in question, unsettled; that the worth of these transformations lies in how they are taken on, in their appropriation.

What is at stake here is brought forward if we ask whose child Tina is, if we ask who has fathered her—that is, within the fantasy that she is Charlotte's. Jerry gallantly gives her to Charlotte at the end, and Charlotte thanks him, but this is all to be taken within the air of the man's face-saving stupefaction. That Charlotte has taken the child as something precious given to her by Jerry may be what the extraordinary sequence betokens at Dr. Jaquith's Cascades the night Charlotte responds to Tina's sobbing in her sleep and comforts her by giving her another way to think about social truths such as good or bad looks, and suggests that when she feels nobody likes her she ask herself whether she ever expresses liking for anybody, then holds her spooned against her body to take her back to sleep, saying to herself, "This is Jerry's child." This may be a fantasy of giving birth, but it may contain a fantasy of the gift Freud says women demand as a compensation for their reduced stake in the Oedipus complex, a child signifying a penis. But if it is a birth fantasy, the fantasied father may be Dr. Jaquith, since before Jerry's gift Jaquith "gave" the child to Charlotte (to care for, to nurse, saying, "I'm crazy to do it," meaning perhaps, in its transgressions, crazy with desire). There are further possibilities. If Charlotte undergoes a fantasmic "delivery" then she can have produced a deferred understanding of her fatness as (fantasied) pregnancy. Since she declares to Dr. Jaquith in their first interview that her fatness is her mother's doing ("My mother doesn't approve of dieting") then something her mother had put into her has now come out of her. (Someone might prefer to say that something the mother has enclosed her in, perhaps to keep her for herself, has been removed from her, or she from it. Dr. Jaquith seems to take her eyeglasses in this way, as if to say they serve no other purpose, which is to say, to ask what [secondary] purpose they serve.) Further evidence for the mother as the cause of the pregnancy will suggest itself. And finally, Tina is blatantly and repeatedly identified by Charlotte as herself young. I assume that both men and women are capable of tracking desire in a fantasy of parthenogenesis.

Are any or all of these accepted appropriations of the relation between Charlotte and Tina? I have in effect said that the health or illness of their position can only be assessed in imagining a continuation of their lives. My claim about the importance of a political stance toward such a film is, accordingly, a claim that to rest assured that Charlotte's appropriation of Tina works against herself, harmful both to her and to Tina, that she is trapped in a deepening of her hysteria and of fragmentary identifications, not mapping a terrain affording the satisfactions there are in this culture for her erotic nature, is to treat her as Jerry does, as her mother did so long as she was uncontested, that is, to deprive her of an understanding and heartening of herself independent of ours. It is a decision at once about the nature of human pleasures, and about the worth and possibility of pleasures derivable in this culture, and, while we are at it, about the seriousness of the pleasures derivable from the medium of the culture's public entertainment called movies.

Another word about names as titles. Dr. Jaquith hadn't wanted to be called "Doctor" on being introduced to Charlotte; but her mother brutally refuses to go along with anything but the explicit.

And in the flashback on shipboard with the young Charlotte the
mother will say, "Could we try to remember that we're hardly
commercial travelers. It's bad enough that we have to associate
with these tourists on board"; then "tourist" is a title Charlotte
consequently will defiantly adopt on meeting Jerry, a title he helps,
along with Dr. Jaquith, instruct her to welcome. Then there is Jerry
and Charlotte's early exchange: "I don't even know whether it's
Miss or Mrs." "It's Aunt." Again, after her transformation into
Camille, the essential question—the question of essence—is not
the title but one's relation to the title, whether it turns one to stone.
I might characterize my view of the film (indeed of the films generally with which *Now, Voyager* is in generic argument) as studying
what the mysterious name "marriage" legitimately applies to, to
which changes of names, or refusals of change, it belongs. When
Charlotte informs her mother that she has broken her engagement
to Elliot somebody-or-other, her mother lashes out at her with
death-dealing violence: "Here you have the chance to join our
name, Vale, with one of the finest families in the city, Livingston
[living stone?], and you come in here and tell me that you're not in
love [*that* name!]! . . . I should think you'd be ashamed to be born
and to live all your life as Charlotte Vale. *Miss* Charlotte Vale." Do
we trust a mere Hollywood movie with the idea that a mother, in
however distraught a mood, is suggesting to her daughter that she
should be ashamed to be born, and that she is stone, unchanging
in that mode of being? And isn't there the suggestion that this
parent is as much a father as mother, hence as much a fantasmic
candidate to father her child? (The mother had told Dr. Jaquith
as they awaited Charlotte that first morning and marked her as
her late ugly duckling—"late" is a kind of name for the recently
dead—that Charlotte's father died shortly after she was born. He
was doubly replaced.) The suggestion comes my way, I feel sure, as
part of my feeling that Dr. Jaquith in this film is the mother for
whom, in the melodrama of the unknown woman, the woman can
be understood as in search.

This is as far as I will take what you might call my readings of
this film; and here another philosophical shoe should drop, which
I place in the ensuing second coda, or philosophical epilogue.

Say that I have brought the story of Charlotte Vale to a certain
open Freudian crossroads, to Freud's apparent drastic underplay-
ing, for most of his journey, of the female child's pre-Oedipal rela-

tion to the mother. But in my studies of *Letter from an Unknown Woman* and of *Gaslight* I have found that the philosophical question of skepticism with respect to self-existence—the issue that produces the origin of so much of modern philosophy in René Descartes's *cogito* argument, that I know I exist because I cannot doubt that I think—that in these films the question of skepticism is under investigation. If *Now, Voyager* is an equal member of the genre of the unknown woman it too must participate in this investigation. In *Letter from an Unknown Woman*, the woman undertakes on her own to ratify or prove the man's existence to him, to create him for himself by, as she virtually puts it, creating herself for him. That he fails to recognize her when she returns to him deals death all around, as if to say: no one can perform the *cogito* for you (a reason I put this film in the orbit of Henry James's "The Beast in the Jungle"). In *Gaslight* the man finds the woman's existence to be incompatible with his and he attempts to steal her life for himself by driving her mad; I call it a study of vampirism, one in which her declaration of her *cogito* is taken in madness and defeats the husband, as if to say: better an isolation amounting to, or risking, madness than the certainty of nonexistence in wishing to fill another's emptiness.

But in *Now, Voyager*, Jerry, the male candidate for villainy, is not enough of a villain to require an opposition to the death (his existence is sufficiently attested through guilt, as it were, by association), and the other man's existence seems acquired through sublimation, to say the least, of sexual demand. Does therefore the woman's unknownness in this film signify much more than that the second-rateness of the world—anyway of the choice of men in it—consists in its leaving sexual satisfaction illicit?

Let us go back to the long aria—I have said that some such aria (of denunciation or renunciation) is obligatory in each of the unknown woman melodramas—in which the woman names her mother a tyrant ("If that is what motherhood means, I want none of it"), succeeding which her mother passes away. (In *Gaslight* and in *Blonde Venus* such an aria is directed to a husband; in *Letter from an Unknown Woman* it is as if the entire letter (the film) is the aria, directed to the lover-father.) After this the daughter is shattered and it seems as if she will attempt to capitulate to the protection of Dr. Jaquith. She is spared this by the discovery of the young girl— Jerry's daughter—which gives her a chance to recreate herself through saving, let us say, the child. It is a relation of creation that, however equivocal, in her world nothing called marriage can replace.

Her speech beginning with the line about tyranny expressing itself as the maternal instinct (continuing Jaquith's angry remark in the opening sequence of the film, "A mother's rights, twaddle; a child has rights") is a fairly direct specification of John Locke's *Second Treatise of Government*, the central document of our tradition that identifies the existence of parental tyranny, that specifies mothers as well as fathers as responsible parents, and that argues for consent as the basis of legitimate power, that is of political authority (not of parental authority, since this comes to an end with the end of the need for parental protection, a moment whose desperate lateness occupies much of *Now, Voyager*). What may seem remarkable is that the argument in this film is enacted by one woman using it against another woman. The significance of this circumstance underscores Locke's presence in the encounter, since Locke's *First Treatise of Government* is a sustained argument against a book that had linked political with paternal authority and based both on Divine Right—Robert Filmer's classical vision of patriarchal culture, *Patriarcha*.

Now the significance I draw from the way this grown daughter contests the authority over her—a woman who has everything money can buy and that position can secure—is that the legitimacy of the social order in which she is to participate is determined (to the extent to which it can be determined) by her consent, by whether she, in her state of freedom, finds that she wants the balance of renunciation and security the present constitution of society affords her. The price is madly high: the life of desire (outside the price of marriage) is one of irony, of enforced transcendence, and of romance as creating "cads," a name Charlotte and Jerry each claim for themselves. It turns out in Locke's *Second Treatise* that the existence of consent, hence of the social order, may be no easier to be clear about and establish than, as in Descartes's *Meditations*, the existence of a finite other proved to be. In linking the position of a woman's voice (hence her individual existence) with the constitution of consent (hence the existence of the social order), the film offers a sort of explanation about why we remain studiedly unclear about both.

That Charlotte consents in the moments we conclude with—

and for her own reasons—is clear enough. That she would consent under altered conditions is unknowable. A good enough or just enough society—one that recognizes her say in it—will recognize this fact of, this threat in, or measure by, the woman's unknownness.

*Just a personal
idiosyncrasy.*

4

Postscript:
To Whom It May
Concern

> The untold want by life and land ne'er granted,
> Now voyager sail thou forth to seek and find.
>
> WALT WHITMAN, "*The Untold Want*," 1871

COMING AWAY from a first reading of Eve Kosofsky Sedgwick's "The Beast in the Closet: James and the Writing of Homosexual Panic," my sense of its pertinence to what I have written on film melodrama is so urgent that I find myself unwilling to make public the foregoing latest installment of my thoughts on the subject without including some initial responses, however hurried and improvisatory they must be now, to the material she has so remarkably brought together. Her work, among other matters, proposes an understanding of James's "The Beast in the Jungle" that to my mind cannot sensibly be passed by in thinking further about James's achievement. Since in readdressing James's text in my preceding remarks about *Now, Voyager*, and specifying my reason in having adduced it at the end of my earlier account of *Letter from an Unknown Woman* by describing that film's philosophical design—which relates the melodrama of the unknown woman to the woman's assignment (by whom?) to prove the man's existence, or preservation, to him, or for him, hence impossibly to attempt to perform his *cogito*, the taking on of his subjectivity, overcoming his skepticism by accepting that subjectivity as undeniable—I

NOTE.—The following abbreviations are used in this chapter: "BC" = "The Beast in the Closet"; "BJ" = "The Beast in the Jungle"; "DOC" = "Dissolution of the Oedipus Complex"; *PI* = *Philosophical Investigations;* "TD" = "Time and Desire in the Woman's Film."

am understandably interested, to begin with, in tracing out the connection between things Sedgwick says about John Marcher's "two secrets" and things I have said about secrecy as a cover for the idea of "privacy" in Ludwig Wittgenstein's (skeptical) fantasy of a private language.

Sedgwick writes: "Marcher feels that he knows, but has never told anyone but May Bartram (secret number one) that he is reserved for some very particular, uniquely rending fate in the future, whose nature is (secret number two) unknown to himself."[1] These formulations about unknownness resemble ones I have worried myself over from the beginning of my writing in characterizing skepticism as philosophy's inevitable shadow (as if the skeptic routinizes or depersonalizes Socrates' attestations of his sense that he knows that he does not know), claiming to know that we do not know what we think we know, interpreting this as the discovery that we cannot be *certain* of what we think we can be certain of, and producing other things to satisfy our requirement of certainty (for example, essences, sense-data, surfaces of things, and so on). I have surely brought James's text on myself both because of my adducings of it and because of my insistence elsewhere and often that skepticism is not philosophy's exclusive province but is its interpretation, or conformation, of an issue that "literature," for example, has its other interpretations of.

Sedgwick's interpretation of "The Beast in the Jungle" proceeds by working out an argument that "to the extent that Marcher's secret has *a* content, that content is homosexual" ("BC," p. 201), an argument no less concerned with defining the homosexual (or, in her understanding, the homosocial) provenance of the content than with refusing two explanations of the content of the "secret": the fictional one of the ending of the story to the effect that its content is logically empty ("He had been the man of his time, *the* man, to whom nothing on earth was to have happened" [quoted in "BC" p. 201]), and a theoretical one to the effect that the content is definitely or specifically (or metaphysically?) a unity, namely that Marcher is a well-known thing to be, call it homosexual. It is fundamental to Sedgwick's account that what she perceives and defines, backed by a theory of social formation, as "homosexual panic" is endemic to all and only heterosexual males (since particular developments in the nineteenth century). I will not contest this perception exactly, but I am in effect trying it out on myself. Sedgwick's

reading gives ample concrete opportunities for trying it in her high-
lighting of the vocabulary and rhetoric of James's text, while always
maintaining its, let us say, equivocality: for example, isolating a
moment of James's speaking for May Bartram:

> The rest of the world of course thought him *queer,* but she, she only,
> knew how, and above all why, *queer;* which was precisely what enabled
> her to dispose the concealing veil in the right folds. She took his *gaiety*
> from him—since it had to pass with them for gaiety—as she took
> everything else. . . .She traced his unhappy *perversion* through reaches
> of its course into which he could scarce follow it. (Quoted in "BC",
> p. 203; Sedgwick's emphases)

And Sedgwick goes on to mark occurrences of "periphrasis and
preterition" in James's use of terms such as "the catastrophe," "his
predicament," "horrors," "monstrosities," "all the loss and all the
shame that are thinkable," and Marcher's knowledge that he is,
unnameably, "exposed" (in "BC," p. 203). Marcher's "readiness to
organize the whole course of his life around the preparation for
it"—for his hidden fate—is what Sedgwick finds, hypothesizing
his sense of fate as "the possibility of something homosexual," to
produce "the reifying, totalizing, and blinding effect" of Marcher's
sense of the Unspeakable, the unified, worst thing that his panic
presents to him as "the superstition of the Beast" (quoted in "BC,"
p. 205). One of her virtuoso phrasings of the connection between
the unifying thing, the Beast, and the Unsayable, is that

> the outer secret, the secret of having a secret, functions, in Marcher's
> life, precisely as *the closet.* It is not a closet in which there is a homo-
> sexual man, for Marcher is not a homosexual man. Instead, however,
> it is the closet of, simply, the homosexual secret—the closet of imag-
> ining *a* homosexual secret. Yet it is unmistakable that Marcher lives as
> one who is *in the closet.* His angle on daily existence and intercourse
> is that of the closeted person. ("BC," p. 205)

Thinking in association with the modern philosophical encounter
with skepticism, as in the work of Descartes and of David Hume,
I think of apparently other closets, anyway of private chambers,
representing secrets in at least this sense, that outside them something tremendous cannot be spoken. Neither Descartes nor Hume
exhibit what one may recognize straight off as panic (sexually
identifiable), but Descartes, "seated by the fire, wearing a winter

dressing gown" —it seems we are in a private chamber—entertains a thought about "these" hands and "this" body, namely the
thought of denying that they are his, that he is defined by means
of his bodily configuration, which would, taken as it were seriously,
threaten his sanity. In order to press on with his investigation of the
certainty of his existence and identity, that is, in order to bypass the
threat of psychosis, Descartes raises the undismissable possibility
that there is no conclusive telling of the difference between sleep
and waking life, hence the possibility that he may now be asleep
dreaming his present waking life, a possibility he introduces by
saying, "Nevertheless, I must remember that I am a man," which
is, come to think of it, an extraordinary injunction to himself: how
might he have forgotten, or not borne sufficiently in mind, that he
is a man?[2]

Sedgwick, illustrating her impression of Marcher as unmistakably a "closeted person," cites this passage:

> The secret of the difference between the forms he went through—those
> of his little office under government, those of caring for his modest
> patrimony, for his library, for his garden in the country, for the people
> in London whose invitations he accepted and repaid—and the detach-
> ment that reigned beneath them and that made of all behaviour, all
> that could in the least be called behaviour, a long act of dissimulation.
> What it had come to was that he wore a mask painted with the social
> simper, out of the eye-holes of which there looked eyes of an expression
> not in the least matching the other features. This the stupid world, even
> after years, had never more than half-discovered. (Quoted in "BC,"
> p. 205)

Hume does not describe his chamber even to the extent that
Descartes appoints his; and we are told how little we know about
the details of Marcher's private living quarters. But Hume's treatment of his secrets from outside the closet of his panic—or rather
of some hypothesizable panic inside based on his elation in leaving
it in favor of the, let us say, ordinary world—is from our present
perspective shot with ponderable details:

> Another advantage of this philosophical system is its similarity to the
> vulgar one; by which means we can humour our reason for a moment,
> when it becomes troublesome and solicitous; and yet upon its least
> negligence or inattention, can easily return to our vulgar and natural

notions. Accordingly we find, that philosophers neglect not this advantage; but immediately upon leaving their closets, mingle with the rest of mankind in those exploded opinions.

The *intense* view of these manifold contradictions and imperfections in human reason has so wrought upon me, and heated my brain, that I . . . can look upon no opinion even as more probable or likely than another. Where am I or what? From what causes do I derive my existence, and to what condition shall I return? Whose favour shall I court, and whose anger must I dread? What beings surround me? and on whom have I any influence, or who have any influence on me? I am confounded with all these questions, and begin to fancy myself in the most deplorable condition imaginable, inviron'd with the deepest darkness, and utterly depriv'd of the use of every member and faculty.

Most fortunately it happens, that since reason is incapable of dispelling these clouds, nature herself suffices to that purpose, and cures me of this philosophical melancholy and delirium. . . .I dine, I play a game of back-gammon, I converse, and am merry with my friends; and when after three of four hour's amusement, I wou'd return to these speculations, they appear so cold, and strain'd, and ridiculous, that I cannot find in my heart to enter into them any farther.

Here then I find myself absolutely and necessarily determin'd to live, and talk, and act like other people in the common affairs of life.[3]

I note Hume's detail about being deprived of the use of every member, but we have little background against which to make much of that now. In commenting on Marcher's "dissimulation" and his consequent judgment that the world is "stupid" for never more than half-discovering "the secret of the difference" of his forms and "expression," Sedgwick says that "whatever the content of the inner secret, too, it is one whose protection requires, for him [Marcher], a playacting of heterosexuality that is conscious of being only window dressing. 'You help me,' he tells May Bartram, 'to pass for a man like another'" ("BC," p. 206). The philosophers seem not to be trying to avoid discovery; after all, they are publishing the findings of their closets, having "indulged a *reverie* in my chamber"[4]—unless we as their interested readers are to think of ourselves as in conspiracy with them, having a use for them, harboring hopes for them. Yet it is striking that when Hume depicts himself "determined to live, and talk, and act like other people," dining and playing and conversing with them, he depicts no effort to tell *them* of his discovery in his closet that "reason is incapable of dispelling these clouds"—namely of the deplorable condition that reflections refined and metaphysical have "inviron'd" him with —but rather he describes his use of their company to distract himself from his clouds of doubt, his "delirium." Does he remain therefore—is philosophy, so far as it is represented in Hume— consigned to a false, or theatrical, position? (If in its pleasures, how not in its gravities?)

Two obvious points suggest themselves with respect to Hume's scene in public. He makes no effort to tell his "friends" because, presumably (being capable of merriment with and for him), they are not philosophers; they are not in a position to know what he knows in knowing that he does not know. Hence his "deepest darkness" as he interprets it philosophically is precisely protected, and hence apparently there is, as it were, no room for the panic Sedgwick describes, one associated "monolithically" with scandal ("BC," p. 205). Alternatively, Hume's silence to them about the darkness of philosophy is a protection of them from him, from philosophy, since his discovery is about the human senses, about human reason and understanding, so about human nature and society, so about them. Why protect them? (It would not deflect the point at this stage to specify that he is protecting them from philosophy represented in, expressed by, a Western adult male, since I assume that in his merry scene the Western adult male is at most what he has in view).

It is Wittgenstein's *Philosophical Investigations* that more than any other work brings home to me questions of the inside and the outside of philosophical thinking. No issue has swirled around the *Investigations* more fervently than its denial of the possibility of a private language. My way with this controversy has been fairly long and reticular, beginning in effect by suggesting that philosophers who deny what they take Wittgenstein's denial of a private language, or of privacy, to amount to are thinking of the private realm as one of something like secrecy; and that those who affirm what they take Wittgenstein's denial of privacy to amount to are thinking of the public realm (as contrasted with what?) as one of something like a set of conventions. I find my way in this by suggesting that Wittgenstein's descriptions of what is called (not by him) the private language argument are his attempt to release a fantasy, one that philosophy may be thought to be the expression of, perhaps the cause, perhaps the cure. This material occurs in my *Claim of Reason*, which contains this provisional sense of the matter: "The fantasy of a private language, underlying the wish to deny the publicness of language, turns out, so far, to be a fantasy, or fear, either of inexpressiveness, one in which I am not merely unknown, but in which I am powerless to make myself known [on the following page I include in the fantasy the impossibility of making myself known to myself]; or one in which what I express is beyond my control [which I go on to describe as betraying myself, and as involving fears of attracting suspicion and of being under indictment, which may well suggest scandal]"[5]—so a fantasy of suffocation or of exposure. It sounds like the inside and outside of the closet to me; now.

And now moments rush to mind in my discussions of skepticism as a "threat" to which Wittgenstein's "return to the ordinary" is everywhere meant in response; together with my emphasis on Wittgenstein's showing the "emptiness" of assertions we are led to in philosophy as precisely ones on which we are most insistent; together with Wittgenstein's saying: "What is *hidden* . . . is of no interest to us"[6] which is a lead into the recurrent strand in my thinking about philosophy—especially, paradoxically it seems, in relation to the ordinary—as (the) esoteric, as if the ordinary is the perfectly open secret.[7] Sedgwick speaks of "the totalizing, insidiously symmetrical view that the 'nothing' that is Marcher's unspeakable fate is necessarily a mirror image of the 'everything' he could and should have had" ("BC," p. 202); which is a formulation of her perception that the conventional, insidious reading of "The Beast in the Jungle" makes May Bartram a figure for "the single creature in the world who is most perfectly fashioned to be caused the most exquisite pain and intimate destruction by him and him only," the "creature bred for sexual sacrifice" ("BC," pp. 198–99). (The woman of the unknown woman melodramas is beginning to loom—as a figure subjected to, produced by, a mode of reading, or nonreading.)

Sedgwick's formulation of "the totalizing, insidiously symmetrical view" of Marcher's "nothing" and "everything" puts me in mind of certain of Wittgenstein's striking formulations concerning the insidious symmetry or seesaw of the assertions of "nothing" and "something" that appear when we have stripped from ourselves the criteria that sketch out our attunements with one another, the

bonds or bounds of our common humanity, and hence are driven
to ask for the grounding of our knowledge of the other as though
there is a *thing* we need to divine in ourselves and others to insure
our humanity (or our "possession" of sentience "like" one
another's, "on analogy" with one another's, as it gets put in philosophy, or used to get). It is from such a state that I can find myself
insisting, for example, that "there is *something* there all the same
accompanying my cry of pain" (*PI*, §296)—something! in exactly
the crisis of (imagining myself as) crying out in pain!—quite as if
it might then and there turn out that I am an automaton, or that
if you take me so I may not be able to prove you wrong. To which
one of Wittgenstein's various responses is, "It is not a *something*
[that which is in me when I cry out], but not a *nothing* either!" (*PI*,
§304). (What I am calling the Wittgensteinian "seesaw" is less a
conflict of "views" than of something Wittgenstein calls "pictures,"
which are rather nonviews, antithoughts, like fantasies.) The idea
that there are things on the inside of us that determine our differences and our connections is, here as elsewhere, subject to the
Shakespearean sexualization of "thing" and "nothing." It is, in this
area where false unities or monoliths abound, notable that even so
apparently unsexy a writer as Thoreau is moved to remark, in
speaking of what adventurous, improvisatory life should be, in place
of its present self-tortures and fixated desperations (you can call
what it should be the life of the mind): "We should live quite laxly
and undefined in front."[8] He means, whatever else—I might say
that his words say—that we should not take a thing in front, say
on the outside of us, to define the essence of our sexual differences
and connections.

This is an especially poor moment for coyness. Am I in all seriousness considering that these coincidences of Wittgenstein's and
James's language suggest, granted the truth of the open secret that
Wittgenstein's sexual existence is to be identified in relation to
homosexuality, that this identification may be philosophy's business, that Wittgenstein's writing is to be found internally related to
that existence? I wonder. I mean I wonder whether I could pose the
question seriously enough. Nothing less pressing, no less difference,
could keep together the air of seductiveness in his writing (a quality
I characterized in *The World Viewed* as philosophy's aspiration to
exchange intimacy without taking it personally; as opposed to
vanity's demand to take every attention personally and none inti-

mately) with the famous and mysterious "fervor" in every passage
of his work (a matter that guides my essay on Wittgenstein in *This
New Yet Unapproachable America*), and these with the endlessly and
seemingly disproportionately trivial details of the ordinary and
everyday he devotes himself to, the level of existence Edgar Allan
Poe calls "mere household events," which in that opposite world
turn out ironically to be acts of horror.⁹ The idea of the ordinary,
its radical importance to Wittgenstein, is the point, touched on a
moment ago, of esotericism in his philosophy, that to which, to
see its importance, something like conversion seems required, a
putting aside of competing ideas of the important. (This conversion traces a stance of thinking that Emerson calls aversion, one
Poe calls perversion, and I believe, the absence of which Hegel calls
the inversion of the world.)—I do not imagine that it would help
protect my question about Wittgenstein's mode of existence from
the charge that it would reduce the question of a major intellectual
achievement of the century to that of a personal concern, for me to
claim that what it asks is how certain human beings can take their
private torments (for example, by intimacies scandalously greeted
as scandalous) as the means of providing humanity with a further
perspective on itself (for example, with its wish to escape itself, to
become inhuman in order not to be a scandal to itself). But I do
claim it. Would it make the claim more credible if one thinks of
this as a historical or human scandal exemplifying itself in a mind
of extreme expressiveness? In the face of the currently interlocked
views that Wittgenstein's sexuality is obviously impertinent and
that it is obviously pertinent to his philosophizing, I will simply
express my sense that no decorous philosopher could have anticipated the ferocity of intellectual drive, the unceremonious reach,
and yet the aristocratic fastidiousness of Wittgenstein's desire to
track down at once the human desire to elude the ordinariness
of the human and the counterdesire to be captured by it, by its
squalor ("our investigation . . . seems only to destroy . . . all that is
great and important") and by its glamour ("What we are destroying is nothing but houses of cards" [*PI*, §118]). I suppose that
what I am expressing here is the fact that I am from time to time
haunted—I rather take it for granted that this is quite generally true
of male heterosexual philosophers—by the origin of philosophy (in
ancient Greece) in an environment of homosexual intimacy.

Think further of the closet as the store in which each human hides the wish for exemption from the human—beginning with, and competing with, current constructions of the human and of the idea of the human—manifested as a craving to be exceptional. Freud investigates the creation of this store, if I understand, as narcissism, which is a reason I begin and end part 4 of *The Claim of Reason* with interpretations of skepticism as narcissism, in the closing case by way of a reading of Othello's sense of his perfection. Marcher says, or rather May Bartram says for him; "You had from your earliest time, as the deepest thing within you, the sense of being kept for something rare and strange, possibly prodigious and terrible, that was sooner or later to happen" (quoted in "BC," p. 201). The craving to be exceptional, thinking of Descartes and of Hume, can seem an invitation to madness; and in Wittgenstein's privacy there are, also, bouts of madness ("But what if one insisted on saying that there must also be something boiling in the picture of the pot" [*PI,* §297]). This parable is taken up in *The Claim of Reason* where the focus is on "insistence," which is either too much (*of course* in a picture of a pot boiling something is boiling in the pictured pot) or too little (why imagine anything is boiling in the materials that make up a *picture,* and, what is more, in preestablished harmony with just the spot at which the pot is depicted?).[10]

These bouts are associated in the *Investigations* with cravings for purity ("The more narrowly we examine actual language, the sharper becomes the conflict between it and our requirement. . . . The conflict becomes intolerable; the requirement is now in danger of becoming empty.—We have got on to slippery ice where there is no friction and so in a certain sense the conditions are ideal, but also, just because of that, we are unable to walk" [*PI,* §107]); and with a tortured darkness ("We feel as if we had to repair a torn spider's web with our fingers"; "we rack our brains" [*PI,* §106, 105]; "Philosophy is a battle against the bewitchment of our intelligence" [*PI,* §109]; "What we are destroying is nothing but houses of cards" [*PI,* §118]); and with self-questioning ("The real discovery is the one that makes me capable of stopping doing philosophy when I want to.—The one that gives philosophy peace, so that it is no longer tormented by questions which bring *itself* in question" [*PI,* §133]). Wittgenstein's philosophical prose is extraordinary in many ways, perhaps most characteristically, as I was suggesting, in its oscillation of urgency or fatefulness with punctual returns of familiarity and ease, an uncanny rhythm in which everything and nothing is shown to be at stake, in which questions are posed for which neither yes nor no are answers. That not everyone will enjoy this treatment goes by now without saying. But I mention here the price of Wittgenstein's prose in its extraordinary demand for conviction in its every word, the price of its containing (or its view of philosophy as having to contain) no theses, nothing to believe, to take another's word for; and no theory, nothing for which evidence is deferred. So a failure (on the reader's part) to find conviction in Wittgenstein's order of words results not in a degree of disbelief but in a state of bafflement, impatience, anger, contempt. It is a measure of the demand for conviction that the "houses of cards" Wittgenstein recognizes himself to be destroying, and to be calling "nothing," are ones that have seemed to us the houses of our greatness, as Plato's house, and Descartes's, and Kant's, and Bertrand Russell's. The demand may be thought of as the continuous refusal, hence offer, of irony.

My recent specifications of privacy's associations in the *Investigations*—threats or fears of madness, cravings for purity, tortured darkness, tormented self-questioning—are to be seen in the figure of the closet as produced by the fantasy of privacy that covers the terror at once of inexpressiveness and of (because of) expressiveness, self-betrayal. These now seem, to glance again at a direction that made an appearance a moment ago, staples of Poe's scenes of immurements and suffocation, in which the "tell-tale" heart turns out to be mine: being penned is why we write, and what we tell of, and which is untellable precisely, on Wittgenstein's grounds, because no one who could understand, no other, is in any position to understand, since any relevant position is no different from mine, the penned one. ("Only whom are we informing of this?"; "How is *telling* done?" [*PI*, §296, 363]). Intuitive differences between the untellable and the unspeakable, let alone the ineffable, should alert us to different causes for wordlessness, different relations to (in)expressiveness. In "Loss of Breath," Poe depicts a man trying to conceal from his wife, his bride of one night's standing, that he has lost his breath (soul? life?), trying to pass off this inexpressible condition (the condition of inexpressibility) as an expression of fervor: the story opens with his railing in his wife's ear in a "comic" panic of foul names, and the scene (I do not expect, or want, my word to be taken here; it should be checked) is one of orgasm, or its failure. I merely note in passing the complex interac-

tion of ideas in the opening of Poe's tale—of the human incapacity
to prove that one is either alive or dead (an obsessional parody of
the *cogito* argument); of the state of ecstasy as the transition from
being the one to being the other; of the intertwining of hatred
and love that expresses gratification, and gratitude, as fear and
contempt—all in some parody of Gothic romance, in which the
inexpressible is endlessly expressed, as though we have come to fear
for the survival of language itself, the human voice. If Poe had, as
it were, written something like "The Beast in the Jungle" he would
have made it derivable that the Beast is Marcher, that is, it is his
human body, which to express itself must submit itself to desire,
hence death, and by way of the "perversion" of biological instincts
into human drives.[11] (That I am a rational animal is something I
may indeed have to remember.) But the Beast as Marcher, or
perhaps his self-image, seems fairly clearly derivable from James's
narrative, in which at the close "he saw the Jungle of his life"—
which is the view from the Beast's perspective, as he is on the verge
of discloseting himself.[12] Then "the Jungle" is a contrary of whatever
face we attribute to the Beast: socially, it may be the straight world
of family discipline; politically, an interpretation of this world as
the state of nature; religiously, as the profane; philosophically, it
may be anything from the discipline of philosophical system to a
perceived chaos and pounce of ordinary language. But perhaps, in
my present state, I am imagining Bette Davis camping the words
"beast" and "jungle" to give these casts.

I am, I see, courting a confusion that is no joke, or eliding something I know I do not see my way through clearly, an old preoccupation of mine with philosophy's uninsistence, unassertiveness, the
impertinence to it of what Wittgenstein calls "theses," its being
unpossessable privately, so to speak. The perpetual denial of (this
condition of) philosophy, the perpetual wish to take private
authority over philosophy (something not just individuals but
states will wish), is emblematized in the foreword to *Must We
Mean What We Say?* as the habitual (mis)interpretation of Hamlet's
phrase to Horatio about what exceeds the dreams of "your philosophy," to mean what exceeds *Horatio's* philosophy, instead of, let us
say, the general state of philosophy. I have begun looking anew at
this issue of the authority of philosophy, call it, I mean its existence
as unauthorizable, as unfranchisable, in *Conditions Handsome and
Unhandsome,* under the title of "the argument of the ordinary." The

title covers the conflict between "two voices" in the *Investigations* (the voices of correctness and of temptation I called them early, in "The Availability of Wittgenstein's Later Philosophy") taken in conjunction with a perspective on these voices, a perspective from which to refuse to take either of the "sides" of their fixated, seesaw conflict, a perspective I say does not present itself to me as a further voice.[13] Now when I said, just now, that in Wittgenstein's closet there are bouts or fears of madness and cited his purple remarks about spider's webs and bewitchment and destruction of importance and unrelieved torment, I meant those citations as depictions of the closet, not as instances of what is expressed there. Those purple or "excessive" expressions are possible only from one who knows the closet, that is, knows the philosophical door, hence wall, between the ordinary and something that sides against it. But the perspective that refuses sides is neither on the inside nor on the outside. Where then?

Wittgenstein's *Investigations* is not, I have found, very helpful in understanding why we are, through what mechanisms we become in philosophy focused, fixated on telling what cannot be told, on speaking in emptiness, on saying what is untellable not because it is a secret but because it *could not* be a *secret*—like my being human. But no work of philosophy I know is better at divining that this is what we do, that this is what philosophy has wished, that the wish is a deep aspect of our lives, something one might imagine *gives* them depth, as if otherwise our depth might be taken from us.[14] It is something like imagining that psychoanalytic therapy, in depriving you of certain "conflicts," will deprive you of just what it is that you imagine makes you interesting.—Why doesn't May Bartram perish of boredom? Perhaps in the end she does. I gather this is roughly a version of Sedgwick's idea of her. Then I am, a bit, universalizing it.

Two immediate differences of Wittgenstein's closet (of what is expressed there, the voice of temptation; and of what depicts it but cannot be expressed there, the perspective that refuses sides, voices), from that of Descartes and that of Hume, are notable: (1) Wittgenstein's return to everyday, nonmad, nonpure, nontortured life, is one made everyday, not in distraction, yet not in imaginative isolation, but methodically, any time one finds oneself lost, fixated, spinning philosophy (imagining perhaps that one is repairing a spider's web); (2) what the philosopher returns to, in the merry din of his friends, is not to a class or status of human beings different from his philosophical class or status, but to, after all, his (human) kind. (This may well be taken as a political claim or consequence of Wittgensteinianism.) Plato is the one who gave us to think, or the means to think, that there is a return to the cave. But that is a myth. The cave is in us. To, as Emerson says things, hazard the contradiction: philosophy's return to the everyday is not a return but a turn; not an arrival but a coming to, a process of coming to, taking steps; a movement that presents itself sometimes as peace and sometimes as destruction. The voices inside and outside are made for one another, like a cursed marriage, or an ancient family quarrel (as Emerson describes marriage, in "Fate," when he perceives marriage as itself adultery: "they are ripe to be each other's victim").[15] I might cast the voices along the following lines: "Of course I can be certain that the world exists, and I and others in it!"; "Of course you cannot be certain of any such thing— and don't you dare kick me again; kick a stone instead, since you seem to imagine that kicking is a sensation that gets you closer to the world than sensations of seeing it or listening to it."

Let us hear another word or two from the region of the *Investigations* that refuses sides: "What gives the impression that we want to deny anything?" (*PI*, §305); "Only of what behaves like a human being can one say that it *has* pains. For one has to say it of a body, or, if you like of a soul which some body *has*. And how can a body *have* a soul?" (*PI*, §283). Am I to *remember* that *others* have pains? have a body? have a soul? "If I have exhausted the justifications . . . [t]hen I am inclined to say: 'This is simply what I do'" (*PI*, §217). Since I am interpreting a certain philosophical refusal of voice, call it silence, as a refusal of sides, this is apt to seem a refusal of argumentation, and many, most, of my philosophical colleagues are apt to take this as amounting to a refusal of philosophy. How can I deny it? It is not my *thesis* that philosophy does not debate theses.

In my Introduction, near the end of section 1, I cite a passage from "Being Odd, Getting Even" in which certain of these matters came together for me in the following way: "If some image of marriage, as an interpretation of domestication, in these writers [Poe and Hawthorne] is the fictional equivalent of what these philosophers [most of the ones in question here] understand to be the ordinary, or the everyday, then the threat to the ordinary named skepticism should show up in fiction's favorite threat to forms of

marriage, namely, in forms of melodrama." I hypothesize that
something causing the outthrow of imagery binding the homosexual panic of heterosexual maleness to a familiar philosophical
skepticism, the philosophical denial of the certainty that the world
exists, and I and others in it, is that both take the cursed marriage
as (the image of) the threat to the intimacy of one soul's examina-
tion of and by another promised in philosophy. I do not say what
marriage may be cursed by—whether by the excuse of romance, or
by precapitalist institutional (pre)arrangements, or more specifically by bourgeois social construction. I have noted that the avoidance of marriage is already in full expression in Shakespeare's
retelling of Antony's story in *Antony and Cleopatra*. It is in the
context of such questions that I wrote out my first description of
Now, Voyager.[16] I assume that Nietzsche is invoking philosophy's
origins, in his way, in announcing his observation that one cannot
imagine the great philosophers married and his proposition that
"a married philosopher belongs *in comedy*." And given the extent to
which what we recognize as philosophy, and as marriage and as
family and friend and society, high and low, public and private,
have modified themselves since ancient Greece, the empirical
implication of Nietzsche's observation (he prefaces his proposition
with the question, "What great philosopher hitherto has been
married?") holds until remarkably late.[17] (Here I mention among
so many topics I am racing past in Sedgwick's essay her way of
bringing to attention the transitional or marginal figure in
nineteenth-century fiction called "the bachelor.")

The haunting of later philosophy by philosophy's cultural
beginnings have intensified for me, in a sense it has stabilized, over
the past two years in the work I have begun on the subject of moral
or Emersonian perfectionism, the classical forms of which are
Platonic and Aristotelian friendship. It is a dimension of moral life
rather occluded in academic moral philosophy's concentration on
the struggle between utilitarianism and Kantianism,[18] and I have
said that my investment in understanding the Hollywood comedy
of remarriage is based on my claim that the central pairs in them
are achieving, desire the achieving more than of anything else, of
a structure of relationship that seems intuitively to satisfy features
of moral perfectionism—in their willingness and capacity for
mutual education, for transformation, for conversation, intellectual adventure, improvisation, devotedness, for a certain perversity

or incestuousness, and for presenting and being the cause of presenting, in unpredictable circumstances, the lineaments of satisfied desire, say happiness. Which is to raise the question, under late conditions, not of course whether philosophers can marry—that is apparently settled—but how it comes about that they can; or, remembering that philosophers are no longer a kind apart, how it is that marriage has become (imaginable as) an intellectual adventure. Nietzsche's crack about the married philosopher belonging in comedy finds, of course, its literal realization in Socrates' appearance in Aristophanes' *The Clouds*. Less literally, its realization might be a sense of hilarity in the supposition that truth can be pursued in the presence of a commitment to help another (with oneself) sustain illusions, for example, that marriage is a sacrament, that in it two are one, that these are metaphysical assureds, not human tasks, and so on. (And I suppose that this comedy bears on groups larger than pairs.) Yet I rather fancy that Nietzsche would have seen the point of the comedies of remarriage, that he leaves it open to the future that a philosopher—granted that his or her marriage belongs in comedy—might be realizable as plighting a troth with someone who also sees the humor of the situation, that the sharing of laughter between friends is an increase not only of laughter but of philosophy, laughter for example at the spiritual ambitiousness (as for a contest in which defeat is as happy as victory) of such a thing as marriage and friendship.

While I am not denying Sedgwick's reading of "The Beast in the Jungle," I should perhaps add here, in light of the claims I make about the role of a certain mode of conversation, or say responsiveness, in remarriage comedy, that I more or less understand John Marcher and May Bartram to be married (they even satisfy the feature of those comedies according to which marriage requires the fantasy that the pair have known one another with unique intimacy in the all-but-forgotten past). (More accurately, for him it had been forgotten, for her not; so perhaps it makes better sense, if it makes sense at all, to say of their case that she is married to him, but that he is not married to her, until the final lines, on her grave.) It is a state of cursed marriage, a nightmare parody of what marriage might be, though in the common world the awful vigil, consisting in compulsively imagining that what is happening has yet to happen (the negation of adventure and improvisation), will mostly go on without the talk, constituting a nightmare parody of philosophical silence, not merely a state of unresponsiveness, but of a negation of responsiveness.

Now given the differences I note in Wittgenstein's air of privacy from that in Descartes and in Hume—summarized by saying that in Wittgenstein the philosophical return to the everyday is not a return but a turn, a coming to, which is open to common humanity, implying that inhabitants of the inside and the outside of the closet are of a kind—the clarity of two of Sedgwick's main distinctions seems brought into question: that between homosexuality and heterosexuality (a clarity of distinction necessitated by the clarity Sedgwick wants in the claim that "*only* the homosexual-identified man" [one of "the historically small group of consciously and self-acceptingly homosexual men"] "is at all exempt" from "endemic male homosexual panic" ["BC," pp. 185–86, 188]); and hence the distinction between this panic and, let us say, castration anxiety. Sedgwick speaks of the transition she describes in James's story from Marcher's "being the suffering object of a Law or judgment . . . to being the embodiment of that Law" as "in certain respects, familiarly Oedipal" ("BC," p. 208), that is, a transition to the latency ("peace") and respectability gained in what Freud calls "The Dissolution of the Oedipus Complex."[19] To speak of the clarity of main distinctions of Sedgwick's as brought into question is not in itself to deny her account, since I understand her to be saying that the life of these distinctions is to bring themselves into question.

But it may be that I am moved in the wrong way here by something Sedgwick deplores and wishes to alleviate, a desire to show "The Beast in the Jungle" to be "universally applicable (for example, about 'the artist')" ("BC," p. 198)—in my case, about "the philosopher." My desire, I trust, is not to moralize James's story but on something like the contrary to continue bringing the claims of Emersonian perfectionism into more specific view, an essential feature of which is a fear and hatred of rule-struck moralism in moral life and theory. It goes with my desire, in taking it for granted that, like psychoanalysis, philosophy is, let us say, psychologically motivated (though the psychology may not yet exist that understands it)—perhaps worth saying to those who conceive either that philosophy's motivation is solely political (and that the politics exists), or who deny that any so-called motivation is philosophically pertinent—to continue specifying the work of philosophy.

Someone interested in understanding philosophy's motivation should not take it for granted that this amounts to understanding, say, a passion for argument (though it may require the patience for argument), or the need for religion, or that philosophy's quest for intellectual fastidiousness, or lucidity of consciousness, depends on an independently conceived and formed state of purity. (A question that should come up here is the relation of homosexual panic to male hysteria, and whether these are restricted to males.)

However the general question of philosophical motivation stands, I want now, as a transition to aligning my remarks on *Now, Voyager*—specifically my adducing them in connection with "The Beast in the Jungle"—with Sedgwick's "The Beast in the Closet," to say how more familiarly Oedipal considerations work themselves out in related structures.

I do this, with the merest of summary lines at the moment, by acknowledging the receipt of an offprint, given me in response to my presentation of material on *Gaslight*, of Tania Modleski's "Time and Desire in the Woman's Film,"[20] with the request to me, which I took not as unfriendly but also not as encouraging, to say how I would relate its view of "the woman's film" to the view I had been proposing. Reading it through, I of course see its pertinence. Modleski's and my readings of *Letter from an Unknown Woman* do, evidently, indeed strikingly share certain features: (1) they invoke a theory of hysteria and (2) cite "the talking cure"; (3) they define "the feminine man"; (4) they note two kinds of time; and (5) they mention a connection with "The Beast in the Jungle." And Modleski cites passages from Hélène Cixous and from Julia Kristeva which I find admirable. Our rather systematic differences of reading are fairly clearly not to be attributed to Modleski's siding with the woman and my siding with the man. This seems sufficiently indicated by, for example, her thinking rather better of Stefan in *Letter* than I do (or perhaps I am more threatened by him). A general cause of our systematic differences must be a function, on my side, of my work on the Hollywood comedy of remarriage, in which three of the five features I note as shared by us—the talking cure; a version of the feminine man; two kinds of time— are features shaped and reshaped as I go at defining remarriage comedy in *Pursuits of Happiness*. And each undergoes a transfiguration in characterizing the melodrama of the unknown woman.

I will note my view of these things only far enough to give the suggestion of a coherent alternative view of the pair in *Letter* to that given in Modleski's paper. The importance for me is not that her view may be wrong but that it is internal to these structures to invite competing interpretations (and of course of interpreation itself). Melodrama, in its negations of communication, of what I call conversation, may be said to be about interpretation, about the fact that an interpretation, being a way of seeing or taking something, contains as part of its grammar (in Wittgenstein's way of speaking) that there is a competing way, a way this way eclipses. This is one reason that Wittgenstein's duck-rabbit is a figure for interpretation. (Another reason is that competing interpretations may not see different things but may see a totality of things differently.) Shakespeare's melodramatic invitations to the competition of meaning is the fabulous case. *Gaslight* is the member of the genre of the melodrama of the unknown woman that makes the competition of interpretation its explicit narrative theme, a man's efforts to drive a woman mad by demonstrating to her that she is incapable of a voice in her self-interpretation. Competing interpretation is, redescribed, the feature of irony I assign the genre, and it seems to me a neglect of this feature that allows Modleski to be confident in speaking of "Lisa's letter [as performing] . . . the 'talking cure' for Stefan" ("TD," p. 24).

"Stefan [is] cured when after reading Lisa's letter, he looks back at her image behind the glass door, and looks back again to find that the picture has vanished" ("TD," p. 25). This is a strong, plausible observation about a crucial or crossroads moment. Modleski bases her claim of cure on Freud's saying that "the hysteric is a visual type of person whose cure consists in making a '"picture" vanish "like a ghost that has been laid to rest," . . . getting rid of it by turning it into words'" ("TD," p. 25). (Modleski cites Freud from another citation of it; since I do not at the moment place the Freud citation, I am not sure which are his exact words.) But the remark as from Freud does not quite fit the events (of the film's ending) to which Modleski applies it, in two respects. First, Stefan does not turn the image into words; after finishing reading the letter he is, except for a question to his servant ("You knew her?"), without words, in a sense unresponsive, so the image must vanish by other means. Second, taking up my reading of *Letter* in Chapter 3, the effect of Stefan's reading of Lisa's letter is at once to cause a

different visualization from the one Modleski refers to, a melodramatic cadence of returning images of grown Lisa that, looking up
from his reading, he is assaulted by, covering his eyes in a traditional
depiction of being horror-struck. I call these images death-dealing.
The image of a young Lisa behind the glass door comes a few
minutes later, as Stefan leaves for his duel. While similarly banal
this later image differs notably from the earlier sequence of images
in being located in the same space with Stefan, as if he is taking
some present part in this quasi-hallucinatory image. In view of this
juxtaposition of two modes of returning images, I do not respond
to the vanishing of young Lisa's image as signaling Stefan's cure but
rather as suggesting that he has internalized the image, appropriated it nostagically, a fixated image of his past, of what might
have been, to take with him to his fatal appointment.

Nor need we assume that this means that her image fixates what
might have been for him together with her; it may well mean
singly, for him, what might have come of his lost promise. Her
image reflects the place and the time he first encountered her, on,
for her, that thrilling day he moved into the building she lived
in and dreamed in (a final moment of narrative in retrograde
motion, neatly winding back the yarn into a tidy ball, for those,
for that part of us, who must have it so). Stefan's reactions to the
image's presencing and then to its vanishing are quite mysterious.
But their feel, to me, is not that of major insight, not a cry of loss,
as in the closing, interrupted, words of Lisa's letter: "If only . . . "
His mood is wistful, already past something, as if it is he who
haunts the world. Seeing the image of the young Lisa in place,
beyond time, the feel of his thought is as of letting the story play
itself out, all passion all but spent: Of course that is who she was;
I remember; I must have seen her all the time. He turns to go
through the gate, then looks back to see the image vanished; and I
can imagine a further thought: Even I was young then; I wonder
when it became too late to find my way; it is touching that, unlike
the others, she imagined it could be cured; I wonder. There is a
certain bravery my formulation for him, while denying that he is
cured, grants him; it allows him to recognize that he had not sought
rescue but enjoyed acting it out, so that there was between him
and Lisa no "if only"; his whole point (in acting) was *not* to remember what was his to remember, and in that Lisa was a perfect
companion, bringing him into her childhood travels with her

wistful, imaginative, trapped father. The idea that his fate was bound with hers, that he missed his in missing hers, was her construction. Or rather, to imagine her desire *returned* was her compulsion, a *compulsion to be desired*—a formulation that accepts and turns around Sedgwick's cardinal claim concerning the male compulsion to desire women. It will come back.

Calling the initial onslaught of grown Lisa's images (the melodramatic cadence of images) death-dealing alludes of course to the film's narrative surface in making the consequence of her (letter's) narration Stefan's distraction from his intention not to fight the duel; I might accordingly call the image of young Lisa death-enhancing. Both modes of returning images raise the question of how desires, and their images, are of death; of the relation of film as such, always coming after, immortalizing events, to death. In the talking cure, as figured in Freud's study of *Gradiva*,[21] or, in *Now, Voyager*, in the man's initial encounters with Charlotte, one person is enabled to enter into the fixated, paralyzed fantasy of another and to guide a liberating modification of it. But Lisa from beginning to end claims already to know Stefan's inner life. Her letter says she consciously "prepared" herself for him, meaning from a time before she was a candidate for him, young Lisa. And ironies of Ophuls's camera manner cross Lisa's steps throughout, as when, famously, a complex, fascinating movement of the camera, an autograph movement of fascination, which had witnessed young Lisa's crushed witnessing of another woman entering Stefan's apartment with him (as it were instead of her) literally, or mechanically, repeats itself as we witness grown Lisa enter with him: she has mechanically stepped into her fantasy. Since each of us has such a place of substitution, we are offered hers to share; but neither she nor we have reason to believe that the man shares it, that she is anything more to him than one more number in that train of women she has witnessed enter his prepared apartment throughout her youth of witnessing. *Perhaps*—such is Ophuls's mastery of glamour, such is mastery by fantasy—the man had received an uncanny access of insight and sincerity and meant *her* in his final appeal to "her" at the opera. How would he have known? How would she have known? She characterizes herself at that fateful encounter as having been hypnotized ("Your eyes were out there"). But his state is not the issue for her; doubt is not part of her system. When she returns to his apartment at the end, she does not listen to his effort to describe his sense of "not being Mozart" and hence turning to other "talents," or to his fantasy of the rescuing goddess—doubtless these narratives are not worth listening to for anything special in them about *her*, since no one knows better than she that he has already said whatever it is he says to each in his train of women—but is lost in agony within her own thwarted fantasy of what this time was to be. (Given the power of transference to published revised editions of old fantasies [Freud's image], where is the instant of difference to come from that makes repetition a new step, a path, a circle with a little larger diameter?) At the end she prepares herself and him (and her son and her husband) for sacrifice, and Stefan picks up his cue to keep an appointment— not one to step toward a life to call his but as sent to his fate, call it his disappointment.

Passing by the critical issue of kinds of time (in *Pursuits of Happiness* I locate the issue as the effort to transform linear or fixed succession by, let us say, eternal recurrence, invoking Nietzsche's reflections on our vengefulness as a revenge against time's "It was," a transformation, the transformation neither Lisa nor Stefan manage; they are not alone), I take up Modleski's and my attention to the "feminine man" as the maleness that attracts the woman in view in these films. (To open up an understanding of this [these] path[s] of attraction is part of Sedgwick's achievement.) Here is where, generally, I feel Modleski's account is forced by a certain indiscriminateness in the accepted concept of "the woman's film," one which has to include, along with *Letter* and *Stella Dallas,* films such as *Back Street, Madame X,* and *Dark Victory,* in which the enormity of the woman's hidden, anonymous sacrifice is made sublimely large by the stupendous uninterestingness of the man, expertly figured, for example, in the acting of John Boles in *Stella;* an account formed in isolation from (remarriage) comedies, which also feature a "feminine man," a man, anyway, who is also out to transfigure patriarchal power, in and with whom the transformation of time is possible: the two kinds of time, repetitive or recurrent, fixed or open, suffered or revised, are related as the tragic and the comic. There are accordingly two (at least) types of males in search of women in these films who are contrary to the law-laying father: in the melodramas, the reactively "sensitive" male who is another face of the reactively masculine male; in the comedies, the improvisatory, somewhat unsocialized male, with a readiness for education that makes him awkward, prone to fall all over himself (bless his heart); a late adolescent one may say, without fixed appointments, or struggling against them, reaching for joy in place of melancholy, who always seems *to have time.* (His leisure for love and adventure in the Hollywood remarriage comedies is often symbolized by money, a symbol Thoreau and Emerson read as such, and plenty more, a reading essential to what I think is to treasure in these films.) This male of remarriage comedy is, unlike the victorious males of classical comedy, favored by the woman's father, if he is present (and if he is present he is, as I put it, always "on the side of the woman's desire," even helping to lay aside the law), and is shown to be nurturant, either literally cooking for the woman, or cooking with her, never cooked for, somehow assured of sustenance. (This suggests another look at the late bleak moment, on Lisa's final return to Stefan's apartment, at which he sends his mute servant out to bring in a late supper from the local restaurant.) Evidently I must learn what it is Kristeva has said about "the pre-oedipal, imaginary father," cited by Modleski as from a 1982 lecture given by Kristeva (see "TD," p. 30n.22).

Glancing now at the question I wish to pursue of a psychoanalytic understanding "alternative" to the idea as proposed by Sedgwick of homosexual panic endemic to, and confined to, heterosexual males—the alternative of castration anxiety that she has herself indicated, where what constitutes, or motivates, an alternative is part of the question—let us take up moments from the Cixous passage Modleski helpfully adduces:

> "Man cannot live without resigning himself to loss. He has to mourn. It's his way of withstanding castration. He goes through castration, that is, and by sublimation incorporates the lost object. . . . But I believe women *do not mourn,* and this is where the pain lies. . . . She basically *takes up the challenge of loss* . . . , seizing it, living it." (Quoted in "TD," p. 28)

This is important and is to be thought through. Take Modleski's application of this passage in her perception that Stefan, "at the end of the film, [resigns] himself to his loss and the fate which consequently awaits him" ("TD," p. 28). My impression of him is rather of one incapable of mourning, of resigning himself;[22] he instead discovers in himself his "other talents" (with women) for passing or killing time, eventually assigning himself a fate in which a literal

The death-dealing set (continued on facing page)

The death-enhancing set (continued on facing page)

loss presents itself as gain (call this self-sacrifice); it is a (sad and
satisfying) farewell to his old fantasy of rescue, or redemption, or
exemption (by "genius"). Then take Modleski's perception that
Lisa "refuses to hold on to a man who has forgotten her, and what's
more important, refuses to *hold him to* an obligation . . . she will
not make him pay. So she takes up the challenge of loss and lives
it" ("TD," p. 28). What obligation? I have said that she casts herself
privately into a role in which she must know she will not so much
as be forgotten (barring a miracle; I hope it is not me who bars it),
but merely compulsively succeeded, as she was preceded. And what
about an obligation to tell him of their son? What is the sense of
timing that waits to tell him only of the son's death (the one that

bears his name—the son, the death)? And not make him pay? She sees that every male connected with her, who can speak, pays in this revenge against time's "It was." Her way of not holding on is to consign Stefan (the father) to her husband's mode of honor, a fate she enacts by receiving her husband's threat (promise), surrounded by images of weapons, in their house, that he will not give her up, having given her all she has asked in marrying him, and by then in effect leading him to her entrance into Stefan's apartment. All have a use—set assignments—for the fantasy acted out.

Other women in the genre of the unknown woman, reconceiving time, for whom revenge is impertinent—Davis as Charlotte Vale, Stanwyck as Stella Dallas, Dietrich in *Blonde*

Venus—can be understood to take up the challenge of pain in the conscious exploration of their lives. (The failure to overcome revenge gives *Letter* a special place in the genre of the unknown woman, rather as the darkness and anarchy of *His Girl Friday* gives it a special place in remarriage comedy. Each shows in a rawer state, yet not less sophisticated, the magnitude of the forces arrayed against the woman's chances of exercising her judgment.) But to show this one has to conceive how these women conceive the promise of their lives. Modleski finds that in *Stella Dallas* "Stephen [Stella's husband] proves to be more domineering than Stella can bear. So she relinquishes her desire for men altogether and trans- fers it exclusively to her daughter" ("TD," p. 26). But Stephen Dallas is not domineering, he makes nothing of interest happen but is merely very respectable, with educated manners, something Stella, before she knew, and from her sense of the enclosed squalor of her family's existence, interpreted as glamour. But never for a moment, so far as I can see, is he, personally, the "object of Stella's desirous gaze" ("TD," p. 26). And if she has transferred her desire exclusively to her daughter, what is the cause of her giving the daughter up, or turning her over, to another mother? The formulation "transfer- ring her desire" is not one to leave unexamined. It is, to begin with, more or less the excuse Stella offers her accepting, amusing, but boorish male friend for lacking erotic interest in him (the other masculine choice in the way Stella's life has played out so far). It seems that we are invited by Modleski's formulation to accede to the view shared, I gather, by viewers who partake gladly, or popu- larly, of American popular culture as well as by many others who sophisticatedly deplore the culture's efforts to help reproduce its repression of women by creating the "woman's film," to read Stella as sacrificing her (total) investment in her daughter for the daugh- ter's good, that is, for a rich, respectable life for the daughter with her father and his new family. If we grant that there is such a genre as "the woman's film" and that some of its members convey a deplorable message, may we not consider further the possibility of a countergenre such as that of the unknown woman, which contests that message, whose details instead declare that the women left alone with their own judgment in spaces defined by *Stella Dallas,* and *Now, Voyager,* and *Blonde Venus* are capable of judging the goodness of the "good" world, and contain untold reserves of desire, which may or may not find worthwhile investment? (Couldn't this thought itself be their more sophisticated trap? Doubtless, but that is nothing new. The question is whether it could be their step.)

Consider together with Cixous's formulations a text in which (something else I know I need to know more of) Jacques Lacan takes up "a formulation that doesn't come out in Freud's text but whose pertinence is everywhere indicated: the Oedipus complex goes into its decline insofar as the subject must mourn the phallus."[23] Looking back at Freud's text against Lacan's, I note that Freud gives three answers to the question of what brings about the dissolution of the Oedipus complex: (1) what Freud calls an onto-genetic one and describes as "painful disappointments"; (2) what he calls a phylogenetic one and describes by saying "the time has come"; and (3) the threat of castration. It is my impression that the usual reading of Freud's text (I speak for myself) rather passes by the first two of Freud's suggestions—understandably, since Freud himself seems to move past them as accounts of the destruction of "the child's phallic genital organization" (which he locates as "contemporaneous with" the Oedipus complex ["DOC," pp. 175, 174]), that is, as accounts of the repression of the complex, its presence in the unconscious, which Freud understands as happening only with the threat of castration. But Lacan, guided by Freud's text, organizes his remarks on *Hamlet* precisely around theories of "appointments," or missed appointments, say disappointment, and the time's having (not) come, which Lacan writes variously as "the hour of the Other," that is, one not of one's own. The idea, I gather, is that it is through the tracing of these missed times that "the humanization of sexuality," the means or cues through which "we are accustomed by our experience to make the accidents of the evolution of desire fall into place," is to be assessed in the individual case.[24] One line of division within the woman's film is between structures in which appointments and disappointments (are inter-preted to) happen by accident, and those in which there are no accidents (and perhaps combinations of both, or competitions over the question of what an accident is). *Back Street* and *Love Affair* are examples that promote the accident; that is a principal reason they are not members of the genre I define of the unknown woman. And I have said, in effect, that *Letter* ends with the man keeping an appointment that is not his, or rather by accepting an appointment as his that at the beginning of the film he had denied was his—no doubt he was mistaken both times, which means right both times, but never exactly in his favor.

"The Dissolution of the Oedipus Complex" contains another insistence whose implication may initiate the alternative account of closeting I sense. When Freud introduces the threat of castration he notes at once that "usually it is from women that the threat emanates" (p. 174), and he goes on to specify the medium of that threat, as well as of the symbolic mitigation of the threat (substituting the hand for the original member that "is to be removed"), as the work of the woman's voice: it is the woman who *says* what "the father or the doctor" will do, and who *says* how the punishment may be "mitigated"; her overwhelming threat, accordingly, is *to tell*. However this division of legal labor—between telling and executing—gets encoded, it emerges that the one responsible for maintaining and affirming the child's existence is the one whose voice can negate it, mar it, give it away. Then the key to one's (male) preservation is to control the woman's voice, contradictorily to stop it from speaking (from reporting) and to make it speak (to promise a further mitigation or intercession). Some control.—I am not prepared to say that all the reasons men have for controlling the woman's voice come down to this contradictory pair: Lear has his reasons, Othello his, Coriolanus his, Petruchio his, Tamora and her sons theirs, a particular legal system its, various religions theirs. What I am so far suggesting is that a certain frenzy in the effort of control is the expression of the wish not singly for the woman's silence but, at the same time, for her voice, say her confidence.

Then an indicated alternative way to understand closeting is as the maintaining not of the place the man cannot leave, the space of what it is not his to say, but (also, before that) the place he cannot let the woman leave, the space of what he does not want, and wants, her to say. This identification of the source of the ratification of his existence, of the answer to his life, suggests that it is in force only so long as his powers of seduction and suggestibility are in force, which supplies (an alternative) motive for Sedgwick's "compulsion to love women." In retaining the more "familiar," Oedipal interpretation of what Marcher senses "is to happen"— his appointment—and what May Bartram tells him "has happened," we have, I find, a cause of her assertion of the thing's happening as precisely what he cannot take from her (neither remove nor accept). What it more familiarly means is that she is not in control of what will happen or will not happen to him, of whether fathers and doctors will force him outside, into the open execution of competition and the rest; that his trust in her, or alliance with her, is well-placed, well-based (she is to be trusted to think well of his life and not to harm it), and it is ill-placed, ill-based (there is nothing of the kind he imagines in her *to be trusted*). His life is based on hoping otherwise, on trusting hope. (It's been coming to mind: "Georgie Porgie, pudding and pie, / Kissed the girls and made them cry. / When the boys came out to play / Georgie Porgie ran away." Apart from reading Sedgwick, I don't know when I would have seen that Georgie can be taken to run not from his fear of the boys but from his unsecured love of them. But surely I would have always seen that the distinction is insecure?) And the familiar alternative brings to the fore James's implied answer to Marcher's tormented question, ending the third paragraph from the end, about the encountered man's face that brings Marcher to and will see him thrown down at the close: "What had the man *had* to make him, by the loss of it, so bleed and yet live?" ("BJ," p. 400). The implied answer is that the question misses something. The question is not as to what, but as to how the capacity for "mourning" (specified in the preceding paragraph) comes, let us say the capacity to let yourself matter to another, one you have found for yourself. The positive answer, that mourning comes with the dissolution of the Oedipus complex, with the threat of the appointment or happening of castration, is going around in circles. If the necessity to mourn implies an incapacity to challenge pain, to live it, it at least shows the capacity to let pain terminate, if it will, not interminably to kill time—yours and others—by humoring it; wry sadness is not mourning. (As we learn to distrust our attribution to women of depth and mystery, seeing its uses in denying their reality, we seem to get awfully attached to asserting the superficiality of men. I share something of this attachment, as my views of Jerry and Stefan and Mr. Dallas attest.)

If my sketch of an alternative interpretation of closeting, along perhaps more familiar lines, does its work, it should begin specifying the connection between the way I have read *Now, Voyager* and James's "The Beast in the Jungle" as well as why my response to Sedgwick's reading of the James story has made this postscript urgent.

Begin with Sedgwick's observation that a "hammeringly tendentious blur" in virtually all the James criticism is its failure to connect its connections of James's life and his narratives "to the specificity of James's—or of any—sexuality" results in its assuming "without any space for doubt that the moral point of the story is not only that May Bartram desired John Marcher but that John Marcher *should have desired* May Bartram" ("BC," p. 198). It may be that the assumption might require further formulation or conditioning. (For example: *given his acceptance* of her presence on his terms, he should have . . . ; that is, he should not have accepted it otherwise. This is still fairly "nonsensical as a moral judgment" ("BC," p. 165) since it amounts to saying, as Marcher puts it, "The real form it [the "friendship"] should have taken on the basis that stood out large was the form of their marrying" [quoted in "BC," pp. 176, 206]. Marcher gives a moralistic reason for avoiding this "form," one that blurs the fact that if they could have married there would have been no problem to which not marrying was the solution.) This aside, Sedgwick's charge of tendentiousness seems to me to match my exasperation at the shared critical responses to *Now, Voyager* that I have come across, mostly heard in conversation (part of my life is shaped by bemusement at the lack of a body of film criticism to exist in the same world with "the James criticism"), specifically at what I felt was being taken as the moral of the story—one that assumes, roughly, that Charlotte should, was right to, have sacrificed sexual encounter with this man (hence apparently to renounce any further sexual encounter altogether) if she is to "have" "his"/"their" child; and that Jerry should, is right to, stick to his punishing marriage. One then has a choice of reactions—tears with her tears of "sacrifice," or (more recently) scorn for the society that requires it. In taking Jerry to be muddled but relieved (masochistically from his guilt, but also, I can now say, from his derivative compulsion to desire) and Charlotte to have grown beyond the reach of that provenance or offer of desire, I am denying, what Sedgwick denies of May Bartram, that Charlotte was "bred for sexual sacrifice."

The idea of Jerry's "compulsion to desire" carries, I find, less illumination than it does in the cases of Marcher or of Stefan, for, I think, various reasons: because Charlotte has a closet of her own; because Jerry is genuinely interested in her closet and does her good; because Jerry already has someone in his closet, a demanding/rejecting wife whose limitations on Jerry are evidently necessary to him, suggesting that they make possible his straying as far into freedom as he does; and because one feels no compulsion in him to repeat his rescue fantasy elsewhere, that he and Charlotte, in discovering matching fantasies, took a step, without paradox or torture, but with a shared wistfulness toward his limitation, a lucky confluence of inner theaters. Still, Jerry does say something like "if I were free I would spend my life proving that you are not immune to happiness," which suggests that he would, in another world, play the sacrificing woman to this woman's compulsion to desire, but that in the present world he would just as soon retire from the erotic game while he's ahead.

But what are Charlotte's possibilities? Let me follow up my intuition in having just now worded her valence as a "compulsion to desire," thus giving it a male direction, as opposed to my having attributed to Lisa an interlocking, sacrificial "compulsion to be desired," which in turn I implicitly attributed to Jerry as the source of his compulsion to desire. I go back to my insistence on Bette Davis's invitation to camp; and back to Charlotte's secrets, and her announcement of her "idiosyncrasy," and to her later sudden expression of the wish for a passionate existence, as reasons for refusing a man's offer of marriage (and therewith turning away the possibility of "a man of my own, a house of my own, a child of my own")—the refusal that seems to kill her mother (who may well have had a further understanding of what Charlotte means in saying she turned the man down because she "doesn't love him"; and her mother might have taken that as a perfect reason for going ahead with the "marriage"). And I go back to the rebuke in my turning aside the conventional understanding of "ugly duckling" and describing Charlotte as "mixed up with ducks but not a duck at all"; and perhaps above all to my insistence that Charlotte has transcended this man's realm. Collecting these thoughts, it is worth making explicit the question whether my idea is that she is contemplating, perhaps refusing, a homosexual possibility, hence perhaps for that reason all future erotic possibility. It is worth making explicit not because these films, and their genre, contain explicit evidence for an answer, but because they contain material to show the lack of symmetry between, for example, this woman's saying yes or no to the possibility and, for example, John Marcher's saying either. The underlying idea is that women (in our culture) are, with catastrophic price, not socially compelled to desire men but only to show, say theatricalize, subjection to them (perhaps because their relations with other women are not publicly much monitored, perhaps thought to be unthinkable rather than unnameable).

Questions between women are worked out through the feature of the melodrama of the unknown woman that I have called "the world of women" (something absent from the comedy of remarriage) and "the woman's search for the mother" (thus pairing it with the more famous male search for the father). The question is posed in *Letter from an Unknown Woman* in the cinematic "replacement" or "transfiguration" of Lisa by or into a nun, raising the speculation, among others, of a religious dimension of (her) sexuality, or say of its transcendental, fanatical dimension, as well as, contrariwise, invoking the erotic dimension of the (enclosed, closeted) religious life; and further, since the depicted letter is written, or completed, authorized, autographed, dispatched, by the "Sister-in-charge," and its effect is identified (through the further signing by the mute servant, a figure for the film's director) as the work of (this) film, the speculation continues with the idea that the film's erotic life contains its particular order of the religious (repetitively invoked visually by the imagery of crosses in the erotically charged mysteries of Ophuls's camera placement and movement) in the transcendental presencing of, as said, its death-dealing and death-enhancing images, as from outside the world, "beyond" it. The world of women is more elaborated in the thematic surface of *Gaslight*, where the social array of women's roles holds no place for the woman who is, as if consequently, abandoned to madness, but where redemption, or possibility, comes from the region of her dead "Aunt"; and of *Stella Dallas*, where Stella's mutual recognition—almost—with the mother to whom she discovers she can entrust her daughter, nominates the woman at the same time as the mother Stella never had, from whom she receives, so I read here a mutuality of gifts, authorization to try the world on her own terms; from which it follows that Stella's gift of and for her daughter, painful as the challenge is, is not precisely, or is precisely not, self-sacrifice, while the other woman does not, ironically, quite know what she herself is giving.[25]

The question of homosexual possibility poses itself differently in the cases of the colossal cinematic figures of Marlene Dietrich and Greta Garbo. In place of any word now about the narrative structures and thematic lines they each motivate, I adduce a text of Freud's that I was led to adduce in *Pursuits of Happiness,* together with the way I placed it there:

> The recent theme of ambivalence, of the pair's revolving positive and negative charges, together with the theme of activeness and passiveness touched upon before, must also require placement for us in certain texts of Freud—for example, in this juxtaposition from *Civilization and Its Discontents,* footnoting some factors that contribute to civilization's dampening of [in Freud's words] "the importance of sexuality as a source of pleasurable sensations, that is, as a means of fulfilling the purpose of life." Freud's note ends section IV:
>
> "If we assume it to be a fact that each individual has both male and female desires which need satisfaction in his [or her?] sexual life, we shall be prepared for the possibility that these needs will not both be gratified on the same object, and that they will interfere with each other, if they cannot be kept apart so that each impulse flows into a special channel suited for it. Another difficulty arises from the circumstance that so often a measure of direct aggressiveness is coupled with an erotic relationship, over and above its inherent sadistic components. The love-object does not always view these complications with the degree of understanding and tolerance manifested by the peasant woman who complained that her husband did not love her any more, because he had not beaten her for a week."[26]

The value—if any—of the idea that masculine/feminine oscillation may be studied by mapping it onto active/passive oscillation is of course a function of how good a map you have of the active and the passive. Anyone with civilization enough to be reading Freud has all but inescapably been amply prepared for what Freud suavely phrases as the "possibility" that our male and female desires will *not* be thus satisfied ("on the same object"). What Freud evidently imagines will do us good is to think, to prepare ourselves to discover, or rediscover, the experience, the "possibility," that they *can* be satisfied on the same object, which is to say, the same body; perhaps even that "normally" they are. Then Dietrich's and Garbo's cross-dressing (for example, Dietrich's white tails and top hat in *Blonde Venus,* or Garbo's riding habit, her face all but covered by the matching wide-brimmed hat in the dashing opening horseback ride of *Queen Christina*) may be read—is read, I think, by audiences of the films of theirs I know—as their demand to gratify both tracks of impulse on the same body, a male body (I do not judge whether exclusively). Their male dress would accordingly declare that they have, among others, the same tastes in bodies that the male they will choose has, and they wish his gratification as well as, so to speak, their own, as if their own bodies are an instance of what they desire. (This speaks to Freud's puzzling, not unintuitive—but did he theorize it?—attribution of narcissism particularly to female sexuality.)

Does the fact that men mostly cannot, in our culture, cross-dress openly, mean that they cannot cross-dress to the same effect as women can? It seems, for example, essential to Dietrich's effect that the singing act that "justifies" her male dress is for a mixed audience; when she sings solely for men she dresses straight. (So I seem to recall.) For the equivalent region of remarriage comedy, "role reversal" does a lot of work, together with something at some point being or seeming or going wrong with the man's clothes— Cary Grant can actually go so far as to dress in a negligee in the somewhat special *Bringing Up Baby;* Spencer Tracy has to be content, except for a sequence in which he wears an apron, to have his pants almost fall down and to wear his hat to bed; and Henry Fonda to soil one dinner jacket after another at the same meal; all of these under sexual pressure. And what seems to be going on in the comedies, to pair with masochistic sublimation in the melodramas, is a containment of sadism ("the taint of villainy") in which it is altogether essential, for example, to have a shared sense, as in *Adam's Rib,* of "the difference between a slap and a slug."

Then perhaps Charlotte's homosexual possibility was already what was working out in her union with Jerry, that his air of the feminine (carried by various versions of outsideness or exoticism: a European of some kind, an artist [specifically an "architect," ambiguous as between science and art], game but insufficiently appreciated, unfinished with his life) made him a feminine object for her. In which case this relation was constituted as . . . what? Homosexual or heterosexual? One within the other? And the answer will be a function of what Jerry takes Charlotte for (and of what she fantasizes he takes her for). It needn't be that she is, say because rich and destined for familial power, a masculine object for him. Here, rather, her morbidity must come into question, that is, how he interprets her morbid sense of herself. ("I've been ill," she cries out in the scene of self-identification as the fat lady, "and I'm still not well.") I have emphasized that he is devoted to this morbidity. The suggestion is that he takes her as homosexual. (That the film's title, and the epitome of the therapeutic narrative offered Charlotte for her life, are words of Walt Whitman, all at once takes on new resonance.)[27]

But now, thinking of the shared privacies and the ironic isolation in the generic pair of remarriage comedy and unknown woman melodrama, I go back for an instant to my suggestion that the epistemological closet is alternatively interpretable as the place not of the man's keeping of his unknown secret but of his containing of the woman's secret knowledge of him. Doesn't this suggest that the intuition is doomed that initiated my interest in Sedgwick's closet as a figure for the philosopher's (epistemological, to say the least) closet, and hence in the weight of an alternative interpretation of the compulsion to desire, since too obviously there is no woman closeted with the philosophical skeptic? Certainly it suggests that we have yet to locate, or to know we have (re)located— if it is present—the feminine voice that the male philosopher is refusing to let out, say acknowledge.

Before giving the answer I have to this question of location, a suggestion is in order about whether the closet of the unknowable secret of homosexual panic could in principle be the one led to by the apparently all-too-knowable secret of castration anxiety, the one the woman both is not to tell and is to tell again, to recount. That secret, on Freud's account, is of masturbation. ("It happens particularly often that the little boy is threatened with castration, not because he plays with his penis with his hand, but because he wets his bed every night and cannot be got to be clean. Those in charge of him behave as if this nocturnal incontinence was the result and the proof of his being unduly concerned with his penis, and they are probably right" ["DOC," p. 175].) Is this just a different closet? Is one behind or within the other? Are both within a third? There are connections, communications (whether they are more direct than the various transfigurations or symbolic transformations of instincts are bound to be in constituting human sexuality, I leave open):

First, like the concept of homosexual panic, the concept of castration anxiety, tied to masturbation, constructs into a "monolith" or scenario, for one closeted by it, by taking it as a fate.

Sedgwick writes: "In [Marcher's] view [the monolith is of] the inseparability of homosexual desire, yielding, discovery, scandal, shame, annihilation" ("BC," p. 205). The masturbation monolith or scenario inflects most of these scenes, differing in ending not with annihilation but with castration, and including reverie and insanity. One might say that the scandal in the one closet is of the human subjection to privacy, in the other of the human subjection to publicity (under various historical configurations). It is not clear what is open to consciousness and what is not. Second, the sense of one's unknownness to oneself has a double origin in the anxiety associated with the phenomenon of masturbation. As in homosexual panic, there is a sense of the mystery of one's sexual identification (Will I be a different sex if I am castrated? What sex is my mother?) and a sense of theater in dissimulating how your desires are satisfied—or in suggesting that they do not require (normal?) satisfaction. But masturbation is early recognized as taking place within a conscious fantasy, and I think it plausible to assume that human beings knew before Freud discovered it of them, that this conscious fantasy screened an unconscious one, unknowable by ordinary lights. And third, the concept of homosexuality (within homosexual panic) and of masturbation (within castration anxiety) are joined in histories of disputes concerning morbidity.[28] Possible connections suggest themselves with philosophy's quest for purity.

The issue of tracing the differences and the samenesses of the closets will depend on how seriously one wishes to follow out the underlying suggestion of both, that philosophy takes on, under either formation, the burden of privacy. As a general connection this is not new. Remember Socrates, at the end of Book IX of *The Republic*, contemplating the construction of "our city of words": "For him who wishes to look upon, and as he looks, set up the government of his soul it makes no difference whether it exists anywhere or will exist. He would take part in the public affairs of that city only, not of any other."[29] But if philosophy in its origins takes on the burden, or government, of privacy, this burden becomes representable as one of inexpressiveness, or voicelessness, or spiritual suffocation, only when the voice has publicly been called for—that is, after consent becomes a political reality. But then philosophy also becomes democratized (and hence sophistry becomes each person's prerogative); anyone may be forced to

philosophize since no one (no male?) is exempt from the closet
of privacy. Apart from this democratization, I would require
authority for speaking in the name of philosophy. It is the (historical) fact of the absence of philosophical authority, beyond the
burden of the self, that, if I understand, causes Nietzsche to
demonstrate his arrogation of the subject, which may be taken for
arrogance. (One may object to my reading the scene of the Socratic
discussion of justice in terms of "the government of privacy" on
the ground that the privacy is shared by these depicted friends, and
moreover, in being written, is open to others. Then we might say:
philosophy's conversation takes on responsibility for the absent,
the possible, the desired.)

Even in the absence of a good account of the relation of castration anxiety and homosexual panic as representations of the closet
of privacy, construed as the site(s) of unknowable secrets; without,
for example, an account of their relations as expressions of the
secret of childhood sexuality, of the basis of human existence as
such in human sexuality, which the human race keeps (or at some
stage found it needed to keep) from itself; I have a fairly definite
thought about the obvious difference between Marcher's closet
and the closets of Descartes and of Hume, that is, about the absence
of the woman in the space of the philosopher (as that has been
published). The thought concerns, as I was formulating the issue,
the location of the feminine voice the philosopher is (has been)
bound not to let out.

I would like to say that this voice is the man's own, his to own,
one of its tones, his voice of response and of satisfaction, as
opposed to his voice of debts (accounts, consequences) and of
orders (demands, compulsions). Does someone imagine that one
set of tones is confined to one sex or gender? Or that tones may not
be modified in moving from sex to sex or gender to gender? As
Spencer Tracy puts it in *Adam's Rib:* "There ain't any of us hasn't
got our little tricks," meaning particularly in that setting that he
can cry and wear a hat to bed just as well as any woman can. The
setting is the closing sequence of the film, before a four-poster
bed, behind the curtains of which the pair are about to take their
marriage, where, in discussing "the difference" between men and
women, this man reveals that the tears he had earlier shed were
put on by him ("they got me what I wanted, they got me you
back"); real tears of course, but cultivated for the occasion.—

Suppose we grant that his present declaration of control then was true then. Then is there, even here, still here, an implication that this man is taking tears as streaks of theatricality distinctive of women, inherently inaccurate, excessive, manipulative? Here is another opportunity for testing how seriously we are to take (this, any) film. I would begin an answer as follows.

The man is saying that men have been and are manipulable by a woman's tears; and that he is prepared to contest, with her, the structure that thus produces, or say manufactures, tears, that values them by devaluing them. So the implication of his showing her that he knows how tears are produced—knows the trick, or recipe, of their manufacture—*may* be taken as meant to discount her tears. But does something suggest—beyond theory—that this man has an impulse, even in anger, to belittle this woman? If not—I think not—then his putting tears on, as a trick, is to be taken to invoke a history and structure in which men are trained *not* to shed tears; *that* is his symmetrical little "trick" of (in)expressiveness, no less nor more worthy than any other part of the history and structure of expression, of the representation of suffering.

Still the ground is treacherous; even this man may be—something he once accused this woman of doing—having *too* much fun. So let us go further. His surprising her by producing tears shows her that he is something of an unknown woman himself, even to her, from whom he has no secrets; he has his privacy, let us say, which he remains prepared to partake of with her. It is this fact of revelation that, if anything does, has the effect for which he took the conversation back to tears: "You wouldn't," he says to her when she suggests that she might oppose him in the election for a judgeship, might take as it were their marriage into an explicitly wider political arena, having won in a court. She asks why not, and he replies: "Because I'd cry, and then you wouldn't." Then follows his demonstration of tears. So we should also see that the demonstration of his being trained not to cry means precisely that he has not gone on (many men seem to have) to learn the trick of not feeling, of becoming invulnerable; that she has the power to slug him, so that she must exercise her power not to (too much), call it her tact; and that she may need the show of his flair for theater, for the melodramatic, to be reminded of this fact—even she, even about him—the fact that expression is to be read, responded to, even when there is, on the surface so to speak, nothing to require responding to, the fact that a response other than that of (manipulative) tears might alter, refigure, that surface. Remembering that language—or let's say culture—can deflect—Jean Laplanche says pervert—an expression from its impulse so far as to deny that there is anything (to be) expressed, we have then to remember that inexpressiveness or unintelligibility is the natural drag of culture, or drift (it is not a risk, any more than having a body is a risk); that without culture's transfigurations (conversions, aversions, perversions, inversions, subversions) of the biological there would be no (human) expression, no human sexuality.

The man's refusal of his woman's voice, to let it out (not to speak in it, necessarily, however that might sound, but to listen to it, to know how it sounds), creates the sense that his words, his appeals to the outside, are not *answered*. To compensate for this arid silence, you might wish to construct a theory of language that explains that language "must" lack, or is by nature thwarted from—at least an ironic half of the time—the power of reference. Or you might view science as the drafting of "laws" that nature "obeys" (listens to), like it or not, and then identify philosophy's desire with science's. But it is really not the same, is it? Not, at any rate, now.

This withdrawal of the world (a formulation that recurs in my various reformulations or replacements of skepticism), or this withholding of a voice before it, is an alternative understanding of that late phase of John Marcher's progress that he experiences, from the strange man's grief-stricken face that came at him in the graveyard, as the wonder "what wrong, what wound it expressed, what injury not to be healed."

> What had the man *had* to make him, by the loss of it, so bleed and yet live?
>
> Something—and this reached him with a pang—that *he*, John Marcher, hadn't. . . . No passion had ever touched him, for this was what passion meant. . . . What he had missed made these things a train of fire. . . . He had seen *outside* of his life, not learned it within, the way a woman was mourned when she had been loved for herself.
> ("BJ," pp. 400–401)

In place of the capacity to mourn, to experience loss, there is found eternal disappointment.

Sedgwick finds that at the end "James and Marcher are presented as coming together"—a daring idea—"Marcher's revelation underwritten by James's rhetorical authority" ("BC," p. 200). I do not seem to see this, yet I seem to see that the final paragraphs of "The Beast in the Jungle" are about James's "underwriting":

> The creature beneath the sod *knew* of his rare experience, so that, strangely now, the place had lost for him its mere blankness of expression. . . . This garden of death gave him the few square feet of earth on which he could still most live . . . by clear right of the register that he could scan like an open page. The open page was the tomb of his friend. . . . He had before him in sharper incision than ever the open page of his story. ("BJ," pp. 397–98, 401)

James is openly declaring, in the open page of his writing, the cause of writing to be the power of losing the place of one's inexpressiveness and finding the right to read death. I do not deny that this is linked to a mechanism that turns, as Sedgwick articulates it, the "desire for the male face into an envious identification with male loss," which is how "Marcher finally comes into *any* relation to a woman" ("BC," p. 212); but this is compatible with the idea of a "forgotten," misplaced feminine voice, letting it out, uttering it; and compatible with Marcher's words—though he misses their insight—"that *she* was what he had missed" ("BJ," p. 401). But if the "she" is his buried feminine voice, then the answer, and gratification, of that voice, released, might be sought on the body of a female as well as of a male. We do not know specifically the ingredients of such a choice in Marcher's case, but since we are speaking of what comes first I note that in the paragraph before "the shock of the [male] face" ("BJ," p. 399), James describes, after identifying the open page of Marcher's life with the tomb of his friend, his seeming to wander "through the old years with his hand in the arm of a companion who was, in the most extraordinary manner, his other, his younger self; and to wander, which was more extraordinary yet, round and round a third presence—not wandering she, but stationary . . . his point, so to speak, of orientation" ("BJ," p. 398). If the "third presence" is the condition of, the appearance to him of the grief-stricken male face, then it is "she" whose orientation has brought into view the male face "before" the male face brings him into relation with her. If his "desire for the male face," which turns into "envious identification with male loss," is readable as desire for the father, which turns into envious identification with

his possessions—then this instability is the cost of keeping the
woman (from) talking, keeping her between.

I cite a last case by which to measure James's text, especially the
idea that he comes together with Marcher and relegates May
Bartram to the cause of "a stylish and 'satisfyingly' Jamesian formal
gesture . . . 'He had been the man of his time, *the* man, to whom
nothing on earth was to have happened'" (see "BC," p. 200). The
text is Emerson's "Experience," of which "The Beast in the Jungle"
appears to me as a kind of Jamesian rewriting. James's formal
gesture is matched by Emerson's apparent paradox: "I grieve that
grief can teach me nothing, nor carry me one step into real nature,"
sealed in closeness by such sentences as, speaking of his son's death,
"I cannot get it nearer to me" and "Nothing is left us now but
death."[30] The texture of "Experience" is woven of a father's/
writer's/founder's need to mourn and his incapacity to mourn; and
of a transfiguration or conversion of the philosophers' concepts of
"experience" and "ideas" and "impressions" as fixed or metaphysical substitutes for the withdrawal of the world, its deadness to our
approach; all set in an intricate play between activity and passivity
that is driven to reraise the question how it is, and whether it is,
that thinking makes anything happen (whether and how the will is
practical), often in the key of the question of what constitutes
success and succession, in Kant's, in Shakespeare's, and in America's
senses[31]—worth comparing with Marcher's final sense of his
reverse, his fate to have "failed, with the last exactitude, of all he
was to fail of" ("BJ," p. 402). Thinking who James's famous male
kin were, I find the possibility open that James is identifying his
formal gesture ("*the* man to whom nothing was to happen") as a
philosophical one, and Marcher as the philosopher, not coming
together with James, who is rather enacting the philosophizing of
our lives, our compulsion to turn human life, as Nietzsche put the
matter, into a riddle, and expressing the harder riddle of getting
ourselves to stop. The philosophizing happens top and bottom,
by vulgarizing one's life, conforming it, unconsciously; and by
refining or subliming it, averting or inverting it, in a falsely found
consciousness. (Emerson's idea of success [hence of failure] in
"Experience" is worked out in terms of the figure of taking steps,
and lasting; and I do not find it impossible that James meant the
name "Marcher" in allusion to Emerson's essay.) I have only heard
T. S. Eliot's excessively famous crack about James having a mind so

fine no idea could violate it cited in its vulgar interpretation, to mean that James's fineness was not to admit ideas. But recognizing in James's mind, his writing, the power to anticipate and trace the source and consequences of ideas (as in reading such as Sedgwick's), so that their force is more for good than for harm (a matter the Enlightenment or, in a term inflected for "The Beast in the Jungle," the awakening, took too much for granted), we may understand Eliot's remark to perceive that it is the philosophical mind that, in violating ideas, is violated by them. (And as usual a criticism of philosophy moving in close enough to matter to philosophy, becomes philosophy. Violation by, because to, ideas is a formulation of Kant's teaching and, differently, of Locke's.) The philosophical here includes the religious mind. On a religious view burdensome still to Emerson's and to James's America, the unknowable something that has or has not happened to the human being, that has or has not always already happened, is election to salvation, causing its own cursed compulsion to desire. This compulsion may be seen as an interpretation of, or as interpreted by, what in following out the manifestation of skepticism in *The Winter's Tale* I call the fanaticism of love, which I take as violently negating the violence of skeptical doubt, and as relating to it as feminine to masculine.[32] In this light, James's story is again of a private encounter assigned the weight of an answer to a religious question. From here, James's prose is awake with the knowledge that the moral life does not exist, and life devours itself, except to the extent that one has (and the world has) let oneself happen to the world, hence the world to oneself, in its own strangeness; a condition philosophy discovers and denies.

The evidence that Stella knows her effect at the
resort hotel turns simply on her massively authenticated knowledge
of clothes, that she is an expert at their construction and,
if you like, at their deconstruction.

5

Stella's Taste:
Reading Stella Dallas

I T IS, AS I HAVE SAID, only with this final installment or experiment
in broaching the characterization of a public genre of film melodrama—one with intellectual properties of interest to me in
thinking, for example, about philosophical skepticism in relation
to gender difference, and in questioning the idea of film, especially
the Hollywood film, as a homogeneous, and transparently popular art—that I explicitly and somewhat consecutively join issue
with an instance of thematically feminist writing on film, Linda
Williams's "'Something Else Besides a Mother': *Stella Dallas* and
the Maternal Melodrama."[1] And, as I also said, it is the film *Stella
Dallas* itself, so to speak, that made further postponement, from
my side of things, more impertinent than continuing to go on
waiting (I'm not sure for what better preparation, or for what reas-
suring invitation). A presiding question of the texts I have produced
on the particular film comedies and melodramas I have been moved
to read through is whether a male voice, constructed out of a history such as mine, is well taken into a conversation with women
on the issues I find raised in such films. But this question is a way
precisely of articulating the subject of *Stella Dallas*.

Like the women in the companion members of this film's genre
of melodrama, its featured woman's subjectivity is manifested by
her isolation ("unknownness"). (This condition is not absent from
remarriage comedy, but there the woman's subjectivity is equally
manifested by circumstances in which she can exercise her capacity
for play [in private], and sometimes her capacity for work [in

public].) The women whose story is sought in these narratives is at some stage shown to be at a loss—not simply over the conflicting desires or demands between, as it is put, being a mother and being a woman, but over questions of what a mother does (about which Charlotte Vale is most explicit: "If that's what motherhood is, I want none of it!") and what a woman is (when the man asks Charlotte, "Is it Miss or Mrs.?" she replies, "It's Aunt"), about what a mother has to teach, what a woman has to learn, whether her talent is for work or rather for the appreciation of work, whether romance is agreeable or marriage is refusable, how far idiosyncracy is manageable. In finding herself, or finding somewhere to turn, she is helped by certain women; but the world of women, as it stands, is shown here not in general to hold a sufficient answer for her, and no man she knows can name it. For a man (like me) even to notice this lack of, or in, the men available to this woman, is something that periodically feels impertinent to me, ignorantly expansive, something rather going beyond the affront that criticism inherently courts. But it is internal to the idea of a genre that I am working with that a subject deemed significant for one member must be found significant—or its absence compensated for—in each of the others. So when I notice that the male's explicit limitation in *Stella* is manifested as perceptual incompetence, in one man's affable crudeness and in another man's dulled conventionality, I have to go on to notice that in *Letter* it is manifested as a man's virtuosic self-absorption and compulsive seductiveness, and in *Now, Voyager* as his courteous but advancing irrelevance, and in *Gaslight* as old-fashioned, fixated menace.

The reading I propose of *Stella Dallas* is one I began preparing in the fall of 1983 and presented in my lecture class on film in the spring of 1984. At that time William Rothman had just published a long review essay on the film in which he concentrates on its concluding sequence and contests the apparently uncontested opinion that Stella—in her concluding, isolating departure from the viewing of her daughter's wedding—is, let's say, vacating her existence in favor of her daughter's. I agreed with Rothman's resistance to such a perception of Stella, if not with his account of her prior obliviousness of the effect of her existence, hence of the transformations required to reach the concluding state in which we see her. This resistance and consequent transformations fit the mood in which I was then working out readings of *Now, Voyager* and of *Letter from an Unknown Woman* for the same course of lectures.

The essay of Linda Williams I take up here appeared, I learned some years later, also in 1984. It explicitly challenges the arguments, at several points, of Ann Kaplan's article "The Case of the Missing Mother," and exempts it from her judgment that *Stella Dallas,* though "it keeps coming up in the context of melodrama, sentiment, motherhood and female spectatorship, . . . has not been given the full scrutiny it deserves" (p. 322n.10). I have read Kaplan's reply to Williams, and I have read Mary Ann Doane's pages on the film in her book *The Desire to Desire* in which she names the Williams and the Kaplan articles as "two other feminist analyses of *Stella Dallas* with somewhat different overall emphases" (p. 191n.15). I have no standing, and no motive, from which to attempt to place these different emphases nor to seek out others. My project, through its origin in an effort to bring into play, and relate, a small number of comedies and a smaller number of melodramas, is shaped by a set of preoccupations of mine with intersections between cinema and philosophical skepticism, between skepticism and tragedy and melodrama, hence (it turned out) between skepticism and gender, and between the two main traditions and institutional formations of Western philosophy, and between each of these traditions and psychoanalysis. (These matters, and my sense for a long time of intellectual isolation in pursuing them, is something I touch upon in my response to Tania Modleski's Letter to the Editors of *Critical Inquiry,* cited in the Introduction. I hope that my use of Linda Williams's text shows, for all my disagreements with it, my sense of its seriousness and pertinence to what I call "my project." I am relieved to have come across it in good time. This sort of thing should go without saying, but even I, for all my overlaps yet asynchronies with the interests of my culture, have had to recognize that the expression of intellectual indebtedness or helpfulness is no longer dischargeable on exactly intellectual grounds. No doubt it never was. But it is as if a current preoccupation with an [anti]metaphysics of citationality and of authorship have come to mask a politics of who is citable by whom and who not.)

Running headlong, in working through *Stella Dallas,* into the question of the pertinence of the male voice, was not exactly a surprise (I go into the matter explicitly in the essay on *Now,*

Voyager, questioning my right to, as it seemed I might be wishing to do, speak for Charlotte Vale, but I did not find it there to be an unanswerable charge); nor is it unwelcome (since it must be an issue raised throughout the genre, I must have been trying to get it to the surface). Why it was only in 1991, writing the first full draft of the present essay, that I found myself willing to confront more systematically the provenance and pertinence of my own voice in these precincts (willing as it were to run headlong into them), is something I attribute to my willingness for taking further steps in autobiographical expression, the mode in which, increasingly, I am convinced that my encounter with feminism must take place. As I now turn to my reading of *Stella Dallas* with some consecutiveness, my opening paragraph of the reading will attest to this conviction. I do not say that it is because I was beginning to write autobiographically that I begin my thoughts on *Stella* with a moment of autobiography; it is exactly as true to say that it is because I began this opening with a moment of autobiography that I have subsequently gone on (in the first chapter of *A Pitch of Philosophy*) to take autobiographical expression distinctly further than I have ever done before. I trust this impulse will not be lost.

WHEN MY MOTHER asked for an opinion from my father and me about a new garment or ornament she had on, a characteristic form she gave her question was, "Too Stella Dallas?" The most frequent scene of the question was our getting ready to leave our apartment for the Friday night movies, by far the most important, and reliable, source of common pleasure for the three of us. I knew even then, so I seem always to have remembered it, that my mother's reference to Stella Dallas was not to a figure from whom she was entirely dissociating herself. Her question was concerned to ward off a certain obviousness of display, not to deny the demand to be noticed.

I have found *Stella Dallas* to be the most harrowing of the four melodramas to view again and again in the course of trying to formulate my experiences of the set. Let me therefore begin by saying what the thought was that allowed me, or forced me, to overcome the distress of witnessing over and over the events depicted in this film and to feel that the knowledge gained from its experience might be worth the price of the experience.

The enabling thought concerns the famous sequence—one of

the most famous, or unforgettable, I dare say, in the history of American cinema—in which Stella's excessive costume at a fancy resort hotel makes her an object of ridicule to refined society and—so the accepted view goes, unchallenged so far as I know—precipitates her plan to separate from her daughter, the act all but universally understood as Stella's "self-sacrifice." This understanding is based on the assumption, as expressed in the essay I have cited by Linda Williams, that Stella is "as oblivious as ever to the shocking effect of her appearance" when at the hotel she makes "a 'Christmas tree' spectacle of herself" (p. 312). My thought is that the pressure of this interpretation is excessive, too insistent, that there is massive evidence in the film that Stella knows exactly what her effect is there, that her spectacle is *part* of her strategy for separating Laurel from her, not the catastrophe of misunderstanding that causes her afterward to form her strategy (though a kind of supplementary strategy afterward also turns out to be necessary).

I say that the evidence for her knowledge of her effect is massive. But it need not, for my argument, have been stronger than is necessary to form a plausible alternative interpretation to the accepted one of Stella's oblivion at the hotel and her eradication at the end. For even a plausible alternative interpretation suggests the fixed, forced quality of the accepted response to her film. That response aligns itself too readily with the ironic misinterpretations that Stella is subject to by the march of respectable figures through her life—by her husband, whose rigorous self-pity, or disappointment, snatches at nourishment for itself; by the school teachers on the train, whom somehow we know to be childless, observing Stella's loud laughter and agreeing that "women like that shouldn't be allowed to have children"; by their cohort and its progeny at the resort hotel; arguably by Laurel at the end, unwilling where her father is unable to "read between those pitiful lines" of Stella's letter to her (we will come back to this); and even by Mrs. Morrison, though she is surely closer to Stella's event.

The evidence that Stella knows her effect at the resort hotel turns simply on her massively authenticated knowledge of clothes, that she is an expert at their construction and, if you like, deconstruction. The principle authentication is given in the sequence in which Mrs. Morrison, the highest and most humane judge of propriety in this depicted world, helping Laurel unpack her suitcases on her first visit, is impressed, even moved, to learn that

Laurel's mother has herself made all of Laurel's beautiful and, what's more, exactly appropriate clothes. But this might be taken to mean only that Stella is expert at "copying" clothes, for others to wear and in which to make their effect, not that she knows their effect when she herself wears them. But her sure knowledge of her own effect is separately authenticated in the sequence in which we see her hurriedly and surely alter a black dress in which to receive her husband Stephen, who has unexpectedly shown up to take Laurel away, this time for a Christmas vacation at Mrs. Morrison's house.

The resulting, not quite basic black dress is not exactly Stella's taste (though her alteration has demonstrated that it is just a rip and a stitch away from her taste), but it certainly satisfies Stephen's. He even goes so far as to suggest, as if in response, that he and Laurel might take a later train in order to stay and have dinner with her. But when Ed Munn barges in drunk, in a virtuosically destructive sequence, brilliantly played on all sides, Stephen reverts to the appetite of his disappointment and takes Laurel away at once, and Stella learns the futility of appealing to the taste of those who have no taste for her. This represents an unforeseen answer to the education she had asked Stephen for at the beginning of the film. Here he shows how effective a teacher he is.

It is this learning—on the way of looking at things I am following—that precipitates the scandal in the resort hotel in which Stella appeals, as it were, to the distaste of those for whom she knows she is distasteful. Why take it as certain that her overstatement in clothes in this sequence exactly expresses her own taste, any more than her understatement in the black dress exactly expressed her own taste? After all, we are shown—in the hotel as at home in the case of the black dress—the details of her preparation, as she piles on the jewelry and the perfume and the fur piece. On those occasions on which she is oblivious to her effect, there specifically is no preparation on her part, as on the occasion of the practical joke with the itch powder. Must the Christmas tree spectacle be conceived as expressing her taste because she must be conceived, as on the occasion of Stephen's sudden visit, to be seeking approval? But suppose, as I am suggesting, she has concluded from that visit that that strategy is hopeless and that what she seeks now, at the hotel, is disapproval. What is the benefit of public disapproval?

Stella learns the futility of appealing to the taste of those who have no taste for her.

On my theory of the film, Stella's plan for Laurel begins much earlier than in her raising it on her visit to Mrs. Morrison at home to ask her if she will take Laurel to live there when she and Stephen are married. I take the mark of its beginning to be precisely the close of the sequence of her final lesson from Stephen as he reneges on his expansively thoughtful suggestion that he and Laurel take a later train. Stella stands in that black dress, her back to the camera, watching the closed door behind which Stephen and Laurel have disappeared. The shot is held somewhat longer than one might expect, calling attention to itself. (Of course I cannot prove this. It can only be tested for oneself, like taste.) As elsewhere, a figure on film turned away from us tends to signal a state of self-absorption, of self-assessment, a sense of thoughts under collection in privacy.

It is a kind of further confirmation of this theory of the earliness of Stella's plan that when the initial attempt to send Laurel away backfires and Laurel is drawn all the closer to her mother in per-ceiving her as self-sacrificing ("Oh, my poor mother! My wonderful mother! She did hear what they said! I must go to her!") Stella repeats the strategy—and again we are shown the elaborate details of its preparation. Again she scandalizes the respectable, now in the form of appealing to the distaste of her daughter, excessively and differently enacting the part of a woman with common desires of her own. I do not claim that this repetition of strategy can be demonstrated, taken alone, to be a stronger interpretation of Stella than one which takes her to have been oblivious or passive in her public disgrace but aware and active in her subsequent private disgrace. What makes the interpretation of repetition strong to my mind—beyond confirming the fact, and importance of the fact, that Stella is capable of, and gifted for, theater—is precisely that it does not require the fixation on oblivion as characteristic of Stella.

That the attribution of this characteristic to her does require fixation or insistence is suggested by a conflict of perceptions expressed by Linda Williams when she speaks of Stella at the resort hotel being as "oblivious as ever to the shocking effect of her appearance." This seems somewhat at odds with Williams's description on the previous page of Stella as "increasingly flaunting an exaggeratedly feminine presence that the offended community prefers not to see. . . . But the more ruffles, feathers, furs, and clanking jewelry that Stella dons, the more she emphasizes her pathetic inadequacy. . . . 'Style' is the warpaint she applies with each new assault on her legitimacy as a woman and a mother" (p. 311). I do not say that flaunting a feminine presence and applying war paint cannot be managed obliviously, but I find a certain unacknowledged tension or ambivalence in this registering of Stella's consciousness, between wanting to see her as active and as passive, as triumphant and as pathetic. Someone may well feel that a struggle between triumph and pathos precisely fits the case of Stella Dallas. Without exactly denying that, I am attributing the cause of ambivalence not to Stella's struggle but to ours in perceiving it. This is by no means to deny that Stella's struggle can include more pain than we might imagine.

I see no linear build-up of feathers and furs and clanking jewelry. Stella's taste in her presentation is, unarguably, more flamboyant, say "louder," than it is refined; but only once, at the resort hotel, is it egregious to the point of scandal.

I count six events in which the community (or one or two of its representatives) takes offense at Stella's behavior (apart from, or later than, Stella's father giving orders for her to leave the house when he discovers she hasn't slept in her room): (1) Stephen's reaction to Stella's fun and earrings at the River Club; (2) Stephen's shock coming in upon a scene of liquor and song in which Ed Munn and Stella seem to be sharing the care, or ignoring the care, of infant Laurel; (3) the school teachers' contempt for Stella's laughter as she and Ed Munn, having left the train car in which Ed spreads around his itch powder, lurch raucously into the parlor car; (4) Stephen's revulsion as Ed Munn returns to Stella's apartment, having earlier deposited his Christmas turkey, as Stephen is phoning about a later train; (5) the chorus of reactions of the older generation, but most vocally and individually of the younger, at the resort hotel; and (6) Laurel's horror at her mother's cliché expression of desire by listening to jazz, smoking a cigarette, and reading a cheap woman's magazine—it is a scene from such a magazine, or from a movie.

Stephen retains enough human intelligence early in his and Stella's history to recognize that "the earrings don't matter." And his later two revulsions at Ed Munn's presence are caused by episodes not merely not of Stella's flaunting but by ones she herself has no taste for and is in the act of trying to stop. Neither is the event of itch powder her idea, and her participation in it to the point of loud laughter may be understood otherwise than as her flaunting or battling anything: to evince appreciation, even perhaps overappreciation, for Ed's practical joke is one of the few routes open to her to return Ed's good feeling for her and friendship for her—she does not gamble or drink, so she cannot keep him company there, and he is of no erotic interest to her, to say the least. Far from her flaunting her feminine, reactive laughter before an offended community, this laughter depends on her feeling invisible to that community, as Ed's itch powder joke itself depends upon its invisibility; this complex event forms the single instance of Stella's obliviousness to her giving offense. As for Stella's painful flaunting before Laurel, this involves no general increase of furs, feathers, etc.; it is the enacting of a specific setting designed as if for an assignation (we accompany her to Ed Munn's squalid, anonymous rooming house from which, having failed to rouse him, she takes a photograph of him to set up on her mantle at home) with which Laurel's presence is specifically incompatible. This leaves the

Christmas tree spectacle at the resort hotel as the only event, among the six events of Stella's giving offense, in which she scandalously flaunts the excessive piling on of ornamentation.

What then is the source of the fixation on Stella's self-oblivion, hence on her "pathetic inadequacy"? (p. 311). And how then are we to think about her plan to send Laurel away? If these questions put in question the perception that "the final moment of the film 'resolves' the contradiction of Stella's attempt to be a woman *and* a mother by eradicating both" (p. 314), then how are we to take Stella's ecstatic walk toward us at the film's close? Are we to think of her as having a future?

Something like the idea of the pathetic is named once in the film, in reference to an act of Stella's, when Mrs. Morrison tellingly asks Stephen, "Can't you read between those pitiful lines?" She is in the narrative referring to Stella's letter to Laurel beginning, "By the time you read this" (a fateful phrase); the letter continues by saying that its author will be Mrs. Ed. Munn. But I cannot doubt that Mrs. Morrison, or someone, is simultaneously referring to the lines of this film as such, hence asking their addressee—us—to read, to interpret, for example, her own line, and not alone as warning us to get beyond the film's lines to its silences and its images, which are equally to be contended with; but as asking us to get quite beyond an interpretation of the pitiful as pathos for the film's lines and its silences and its images more generally. Mrs. Morrison instructs Stephen, "Laurel is here. Who has accomplished this?"

To accomplish something is the reverse of being pathetic. What does Stella accomplish in placing Laurel there? Where is there? Who is Mrs. Morrison?

It seems generally recognized that her place may be located by the brilliantly lit, horizontally rectangular window, hardly avoidable as a figure for a film screen, through which, in the film's final sequence, Stella views Laurel's wedding. (Hardly avoidable now, yet doubtless on the whole avoided for four-and-a-half of the five decades since the film was made. Has our repression of film's power of significance all at once been overcome?) The general idea seems to be that Stella has placed Laurel into the fantasied film world that we had seen her absorbed in when we were first shown her and Stephen out together, at the movies. Walking out of that film, whose ending is with a kiss at a fancy ball, Stella thoughtfully nibbles the brim of the hat still in her hand as they reach the public sidewalk. Then on the sidewalk at the end of her, or Laurel's, film Stella famously clenches her handkerchief between her teeth as if in a kind of apotheosis, and contesting, of the expected reaction to tearjerkers. On the walk home from the early film Stella says to Stephen something like, "I don't want to be like me. I want to learn to do things refined, like the people in the movie, like the people you're around." Hence, many people find it easiest to think that at the end Stella gets her wish and, eradicating herself, and seeing her daughter as a publicly unapproachable star, identifies herself as her creator, to her own infinite but private, necessarily mute, satisfaction.

This may account generally for the sense of Stella's obliviousness and pathos; and it specifically registers a sense of substitution or transformation. But is this surely to be tuned in a negative key, taking the substitution to be a denial of something; and not in a positive, taking the transformation to be an affirmation of something? Can we have this both ways?

Denial seems confirmed in certain stretches of feminist film theory's adoption or adaptation of Freud's theory of fetishism, according to which in patriarchal society men in general—not merely individual males with a particular choice of neurotic symptoms—undertake to reassure themselves of their own intactness by a mechanism of substitution which allows them to disavow (with half of the mind) the woman's horrifying lack of intactness. Linda Williams proposes a way of going beyond "the psychoanalytic model of cinematic pleasure based on fetishistic disavowal" (p. 318) by taking the contradiction between believing and knowing to be directed not to the question of the woman's biological givens, as it were, but to her "socially constructed position under patriarchy" (p. 319). A contradiction between believing and knowing is a way of characterizing the problematic of philosophical skepticism, and its occurence in understanding the phenomenon of film is something that has marked my thoughts about film from their outset. This is not the time to go into Williams's proposal about psychoanalytic disavowal, so I simply note my impression that fetishism tends to be used at a phase of film theory to cover just about every Freudian mechanism of disavowal or denial, which is roughly to say, to cover just about every Freudian mechanism. Film seems to be the perfect agent for generalizing the Freudian fetishistic process, extending it to the masculine gender as such—a generalizing rati-

fied somehow by taking on at the same time a Marxian development of the idea of the universal commodification (in capitalist
society) of women. But if these mechanisms or schematisms *deter-*
mine men's perception and representation of women—namely as
Freudian monsters and/or Marxian objects, hence without human
subjectivity, say without the complexity and reversals of human
sexuality (but what does "human" mean now?)—then it is a
wonder, a nightmare (a miracle, as Nora says at the end of *A Doll's*
House), that women should converse with men at all about serious
matters. ("Serious?" replies Nora's husband when she observes to
him that they have never had a serious talk. "What do you mean
by that?")

The melodrama of the unknown woman raises this wonder of
conversation between women and men thematically in showing
repeatedly the defeat of conversation by circling densities of irony.
What could be clearer in *Stella Dallas,* in which the line "Can't you
read between those pitiful lines?" is said—courteously, and who
knows with what depth of resignation and despair—by a woman
to a man; a man, Stephen Dallas, known to us by then to be incapable of reading anything serious whatever, if that means seeing how
something might be taken. He merely takes, without question;
merely suffers from what he sees, in perfect oblivion of further
possibility. Is *this* the figure, occupying the, so to speak, dominant
masculine position in the film, with whom I am offered identification?—as if I am to read his masculine melancholy and his femi-
nized subjection to the wishes, or say voices, of women (he is
essentially speechless before other men) as expressing my own
sense of being misunderstood.

Or am I to try to exempt myself from the charges against the
masculine brought in such films, as in its representation by them
in such a figure as Stephen Dallas? How can I try to exempt myself
apart from going on with saying what these films are to me? And
how can I go on with this without contesting the mechanisms that
seem to show conversation with a man to be pointless on these
subjects?

I would like it to be considered that the theory of fetishism is
not an explanation for a victimization and self-oblivion of the
woman of these melodramas and for a generalization of this process
that confirms an essentially male stake in viewing these films: first
because the film *Stella Dallas* itself contests a fixed view of the

woman's victimization; and second because the details of Freud's description of fetishization do not account for what becomes of things and persons on film, say for the relation between a photographic image and what it is an image of.

The second of these claims amounts, intuitively, to the idea that film assaults human perception at a more primitive level than the work of fetishizing suggests; that film's enforcement of passiveness, or say victimization, together with its animation of the world, entertains a region not of invitation or fascination primarily to the masculine nor even, yet perhaps closer, to the feminine, but primarily to the infantile, before the establishment of human gender, that is, before the choices of identification and objectification of female and male, call them mama and papa, have settled themselves, to the extent that they will be settled. And if it turns out that the theory of fetishism does not account for the experience of film, and if the theory thereby serves to disavow something about film, then it will follow, according to that theory, that the theory has been fetishized.

Why stay with Hollywood's self-perception about, or its intentions for, what it named "women's pictures," adopt its position that they are made essentially, and appeal essentially, for and to women? This self-perception goes together in my mind with a fantasm repeated remarkably often in my hearing, of women crying through these films alone, on "wet, wasted afternoons." I do not share this fantasm, I suppose because my mother went to work each day I was growing up and hence was no more free to sit in a movie theater afternoons than men who had jobs were, and because for a long time (as Proust's narrator says) I went to the movies with my mother and father both Friday nights and Sunday afternoons (rain or shine), where *Stella Dallas* or *Mildred Pierce* or *Mrs. Miniver* were as likely to be playing as *Stagecoach* or *Citizen Kane* or *His Girl Friday*.

I assume that films such as *Stella Dallas* and *Gaslight* and *Letter from an Unknown Woman* and *Now, Voyager* could not attain their power—which I am not interested now to distinguish from the power of works in the other great arts in Western culture—apart from their discovery of one or more of the great subjects, or possibilities, of the medium of film. I claim of remarriage comedy that its subject, or a way of putting one of its principle subjects, is the creation of the woman with and by means of a man, something I describe further as a search for the new creation of the human, say of human relationship, which implies that friendship and mutual education between the sexes is still a happy possibility, that our experience, and voices, are still to be owned by each of us and shared between us, say by dispossessing those who would dispossess us of them. I have formulated the subject of the melodrama of the unknown woman as the irony of human identity. And I have formulated the narrative drive of the genre as a woman's search for the mother. And now, having come to insist on the dimension of infantalization in the viewing of film (cutting across cultures, races, genders, generations)—something I have mentioned more than once in what I have written about film, without insisting on it—I will articulate this subject further as the search for the mother's gaze—the responsiveness of her face—in view of its loss, or of threatened separation from it.

That film gazes at us (or glares or glances) aligns it with the great arts, though its specific way of animating the world—unlike poetry's, or painting's, or theater's—is unprecedented, still being absorbed, worked through. We will doubtless think of animation as something that must be brought to works of art, say in terms of the powers of each of the arts to produce psychological transference, or as Emerson puts it, to return our thoughts to us with a certain alienated majesty.

The formulation in terms of the search for the mother's gaze should take us at once to Stella at the end of what we are shown of her existence, placed before, barred at a distance from, the shining rectangle of her daughter's departure into marriage, replying to a policeman's demand for her to disperse with the rest of the viewers by saying, "I want to see her face . . . "

May we read between her lines? There is another notation, early in the film, of Stella's revelation on seeing Laurel's face. She has succeeded in getting Stephen to take her to the River Club the first night she is home from her confinement in the hospital, in part by asking, "Why do husbands and doctors and nurses think they know more about having babies than mothers do?"; then on their return from the club, where she has met Ed Munn, she says to Stephen that she is ready to take her lecture but that while he can correct her grammar he is not to tell her how to dress; and she tells him to go to New York, for his better position, without her, saying, "I'm not leaving, just when we've gotten in with the right crowd." The notation I have in mind comes now, as Stella walks into the next room, starts unloosening the top of her evening gown, looks into a crib and exclaims, "Can you beat that? Laying here wide awake waiting for her dinner and not a squawk out of her!"—as if what she sees in Laurel's infant face ratifies her decision to send Stephen away. We never, for example, hear another word about the crowd at the River Club.

What did she see? Visiting a seminar of mine in which *Stella Dallas* and its related melodramas were discussed, Anita Sokolsky replied, in effect, that Stella sees that she must teach Laurel to cry. That is a wonderful thing to say, but it got swamped in the ensuing discussion and I lost the chance to respond to it then. I felt two directions in the proposed teaching of tears. One direction—I felt the one meant—is the teaching of a daughter to raise the cry for justice, to demand a voice in her history. But another direction is the learning from a daughter to bear and express the pain of separation, that is, not to deny the need for satisfaction, say the right to define happiness. In imagining Stella's astonishment at the infant Laurel's silence in her hunger as an imperative to herself to learn about happiness, I put this together with her having just refused to learn this at the hands of her husband. My feeling, not surprisingly, is that she recognizes the question, resting with Laurel's satisfaction, not as decided but as posed: How can one be so certain that one's needs are appreciated as not to have to squawk about them? Can it be that the providing of happiness might yet be happiness enough, having just ruled out that version of mutuality with a man?

Before pressing further what Stella's ruling out this man betokens, let us ponder the end of the events we witness—Stella's witnessing of her daughter's wedding, her satisfying herself of Laurel's state of satisfaction, and her walking away from the world of the transparent and reflective screen. How we imagine her walk there is fateful. It is the completion of her education: she learns that the world of the screen, whose education in the world of refinement had at the beginning made her cry with longing, is not for her. But "not for her" is perfectly ambiguous, its interpretations melodramatically opposed. What I have called the accepted view (the perception of Stella at the end sacrificed as a mother and as a woman) takes Stella to accept her own barring from that world, and, still convinced of its incalculable desirability, to taste her belonging to it through her gift of it to and from her daughter.

My opposed view takes Stella to learn that the world Laurel apparently desires—of law, church, exclusiveness, belonging—is not to her own taste. (I say apparently. Laurel seems in a trance. Has she seen through her mother's strategy, and is she assessing her participation in the world to which her mother consigns her, resigning herself to a happiness her mother must not know? Would this constitute satisfaction for her?) Stella walks away from the world she had longed for, and from the only person she has loved, continues to love. She turns her back to that screen. But in favor— if she is not eradicated—of what? What is that screen? What, walk- ing away, does she walk toward? Why almost straight toward us? May we imagine that we have here some Emersonian/Thoreauvian image of what Nietzsche will call the pain of individuation, of the passion Thoreau builds *Walden* to find, expressed as his scandalous pun on mo(u)rning, the transfiguration of mourning as grief into morning as dawning and ecstasy? And if just possibly so, wouldn't this be just one more proof—as if we needed more—that meta- physical speculation about freedom or self-creation is a cover for social injustice? Needless to say, such a speculation may be appro- priated in this retrogressive way—as may the work of Emerson and Thoreau in general. They seem indeed, as steadily as these films, readily to permit, if not quite to invite, such a way of appropriation. My heart is set in the one case as in the other on making out another way.

We have just begun considering the closing sequence of *Stella Dallas*. Before following it further, I note that the interpretation of Stella's perception of the wedding image as her substitute, or reflected satisfaction in seeing her delegate enter the higher world to which she herself can never belong, fits a fact of American life more blatantly on the public mind during the period in which this film was made than issues of feminism were (though the issues must socially and psychologically be entangled)—namely the issue of immigrancy, particularly its consequences for the rising waves of children of immigrants, for whom belonging to proper, educated society had become a standing possibility. It is a possibility laced with the perils (the comedies and the tragedies) of correcting speech and manners and dress, and democratically colored by the fact that no one exactly knows what in America proper is nor how important it is, so that what Emerson and Mill call the demand for conformity becomes withering, both absolute and obscure.

Such a child—I speak from experience—recognizes subjection to the familiar double bind. If I am not different from them (my parents) and do not enter into a society to which they cannot belong, thus justifying their sacrifices, how can they love me? If I am different from them and do enter where they cannot belong, how can they love me? I would like to see this anxiety compared with the experience of women that Linda Williams invokes as fitting Bertholt Brecht's description of the exile as one who "lives the tension of two different cultures" (as on p. 317). But the position of women is neither that of exiles nor of immigrants: unlike the immigrant, the woman's problem is not one of not belonging but one of belonging, only on the wrong terms; unlike the exile, the woman is not between two different cultures but is at odds with the one in which she was born and is roughly in the process of transfiguring into one that does not exist, one as it were still in confinement. Hence the pertinence of some logic being worked out at the end of *The Awful Truth* in which one of the central pair says to the other, and receives a reply in kind, "You're wrong about things being different because they're not the same. Things are different except in a different way. . . . So, as long as I'm different, don't you think things could be the same again? Only a little different."

How did Stella get to her position in front of the rectangle of the wedding ceremony? Perhaps we imagine she read the announcement of the wedding in the society pages of a newspaper. But how does she find that window? Does this bear explanation? The explanation for that window being open to view is given a little sequence of its own as Mrs. Morrison says to a butler, "I told you those curtains weren't to be drawn. Open them please." After they are opened and the butler withdraws, she walks to the window, gazes out, and says to herself, "Yes." Is this to be understood as Mrs. Morrison making available to Stella what place she can have in the wedding? Or as proving to Stella that her wishes have faithfully been met? Or perhaps as offering to Stella a view that she is free to interpret in her own—unknown—terms?

Before any decision is made among these possibilities, supposing one is to be made, we should consider that, in Mrs. Morrison's knowledge that Stella will appear at that window, the film screen is being identified as a field of communication between women.—But isn't this simply obvious, simply a function of the

We have repeatedly seen Laurel mothering Stella, typically in scenes of rejection.

obvious fact that in a woman's film women speak to one another,
mostly to one another? But this is not what I mean. Each way the
film screen (or camera, or projector, or any of a film's conditions
of existence) is acknowledged and identified in a significant film,
enters into some as yet unassessed interaction with every other
way—in the case of the screen, with, for example, the censoring
blanket in *It Happened One Night,* and with the compact mirror
held in the hand of a woman con artist in *The Lady Eve;* in the case
of the camera, with the man's impenetrable gaze at the dreaming,
aroused woman in *The Marquise of O—,* and with a home movie
in *Adam's Rib;* in the case of the projector with a bright twirling
object inducing suggestion and, in the case of the running strip of
film, with the iterated elements of an archeological reconstruction
in *Bringing Up Baby;* in the case of, let us say, the film itself, as an
artifact, with the letter from the woman in *Letter from an Unknown
Woman.* . . . I have formulated the field of feminine communication

I have formulated the field of feminine communication affected by the film screen, as allegorized by the lit window at the end of *Stella Dallas*, as a search for the mother's gaze.

effected by the film screen, as allegorized by the lit window at the end of *Stella Dallas,* as a search for the mother's gaze.

How can that be what Stella is drawn to before the window screen? Isn't Stella the mother, the source of the desired gaze, not its desirous object? But how is this distinction to be understood? Does the fact or position of motherhood negate the fact or position of daughterhood? I do not mean merely that every mother is a daughter. I mean that we have repeatedly seen Laurel mothering Stella, typically in scenes of rejection—at the unattended birthday party (where was Stephen on that occasion?), and peroxiding Stella's hair, and preparing to leave the resort hotel while Stella cries like a child being treated unfairly, and on the train after the voices recount Stella's spectacle earlier that day at the hotel. (Linda Williams finely characterizes the mutuality of mothering between Stella and Laurel. Nancy Chodorow's work on mothering is of particular pertinence here.) When the daughter is motherly to her mother both may be comforted (they may, for example, do what Laurel calls cuddle together); and mothering may be transmitted so. Fathering, for us, is not. When the son is fatherly to his father, the father is transcended. It seems the daughter's pain in transcending the mother is, in turn, not so dramatically, if ever, ended. Laurel, at the end, is prepared, for the time being, to imagine that her mother does not know about the wedding. (Here is a place from which to think about why, in remarriage comedy, the principal woman's mother does not, except carefully displaced, appear, as if not both can pursue happiness at the same time in the same environment.)

So it does not follow from Stella's wanting to see Laurel's face through the window that she wants to gaze motheringly upon it more than to be gazed upon by it. And recollect the extended sequence between Stella and Mrs. Morrison, the feeling of which is present in Mrs. Morrison's responsibility for communication by the shining window. I remarked that Stella is childish at the end of the resort hotel sequence; then on the train back home she is essentially silent, only recovering her voice again in the subsequent sequence, at Mrs. Morrison's house. I find that Stella presents herself there, and is received, no more as a mother than as a child, with her hesitant questions about whether this fine lady and Stella's husband, as it were, are going to, or would plan to, get married, and with motives disguised in a way that mothers are bound to see through. Mrs. Morrison, as the interview is closing, and the two women rise, cannot keep her hands off Stella. I do not say that this clinging is as to a daughter more than as to a mother; it seems rather that the blurring between these positions continues. So it is also Mrs. Morrison's gaze, real or imagined, coming to Stella from the screen she gazes at.

In the infantine basis of our position as viewers, Stella's gaze before the window, as the camera gives it to us, is the mother's, backed by mothers; and as Stella turns to walk toward us, her gaze, transforming itself, looms toward us, as if the screen is looming, its gaze *just* turned away, always to be searched for. (For what it grants; for what it wants.)

I have asked whether we are to imagine a future for Stella, since I deny that she is eradicated as a woman and as a mother. What is her walking (almost) toward us? Where is she walking? Let us ask again: What is she walking away from?

As Stella walks toward us, her gaze, transforming itself, looms toward us, as if the screen is looming, its gaze just turned away, always to be searched for.

The question arose: What does it betoken that Stella tells her husband she will not be instructed by him? In remarriage comedy and, it turns out, in the derived melodrama of the unknown woman, what it betokens is that the man is not her husband, that there is no marriage between them. In no other member of these sets of films is the feature of the woman's demand for education and its transformations more explicit and emphatic than in the early sequences of *Stella Dallas*. What Stella learns from the late gaze of the screen—from the ratification by Mrs. Morrison's acceptance of her terms and by Laurel's satisfaction perhaps not in those terms, including her willingness for the time being not to know that Stella knows—is that Stella has the right not to share their tastes, that she is free to leave not just the man of the marriage but the consequences of a marriage she allowed herself to believe would transform her.

We know that Stella has no taste for men in general. This is evident not only from her excuse to Ed Munn for her lack of interest in him ("I don't think there's a man on earth that could get me going again") but from the opening sequence among the primitive sequences with her family as her brother teases and tries to kiss her and she pushes him away saying, "Take your filthy hands off me," and from their ensuing exchange about whether any mill hand's hand is good enough to touch her. Laurel's taking after her father is emphasized several times in the film, a matter to be contrasted with Stella's emphasis on education; but she takes after her mother in her distaste for the ordinary run of men. That Stella has given up the idea of partaking of life with a man, however, does not mean that she is asking Laurel to fill that lack (though there are indications that she is tempted to), that is, not asking Laurel to imagine her mother as for that reason lacking something. Laurel's readiness to imagine Stella so is expressed in her outcry when she returns to live with her father and Mrs. Morrison, handing the letter with its pathetic lines to them, saying, "I thought she did it [that is, sent me away] for me! But she chose *him!*" Laurel had left Mrs. Morrison's house saying, "My home will be with my mother for as long as I live." Stella undertakes to teach Laurel otherwise, to cause her to cry over separation, as for a solace preceding one's own happiness, not replacing it. But has Laurel learned this? What can we tell from the window?

I note that in speaking just now of the early sequences of Stella's family as "primitive" I did not mean that they were cinematically or artistically unsophisticated but that their apparent archaism of cinematic means is in service of the infantalization of perception, provides abbreviated perceptual clues of confusion and emotional violence—I recall the wooden, shadowy father delivering ugly orders; the monosyllabic, helpless mother; the noisy, nervous brother, the filthiness of whose hands is ambiguous as being caused by his work in the mill, or by his maleness, or by his incestuousness; and Stella primping before the cheap mirror, as if always knowing that, wherever else she finds to be, she does not belong, she from the beginning does not belong, here, at what the world calls home.

The striking source I know for the connection between a woman's leaving husband and children on the ground that there is no marriage between them because he is not the man to educate her, and setting out on her own to find that education, is Nora's exit and closing of the door to conclude *A Doll's House*. In leaving the doll's house Nora is explicitly leaving a house of illusion, of moralistic sadism and anxious pleasures. I do not feel that any future I might imagine for her is as important as the sense that she has one, beginning with her saying in effect that the taste for the world she has known is not hers.

In fancying Stella walking away as one continuation of Nora walking out, there is the additional moment to consider of her walking toward us. Again a house is turned away from, one that for a woman contains (self-)destructive illusion, or a way of illusory perception she had taken as reality, a way allegorized as a perception of the film screen. The mother's gaze she has received from such a screen replaces that of the screen she had identified with the world of the man she married. The ratifying of her insistence on her own taste, that is, of her taking on the thinking of her own existence, the announcing of her *cogito ergo sum,* happened without—as in Descartes's presenting of it, it happens without— yet knowing who she is who is proving her existence. Her walk toward us, as if the screen becomes her gaze, is allegorized as the presenting or creating of a star, or as the interpretation of stardom. It is the negation, in advance so to speak, of a theory of the star as fetish. This star, call her Barbara Stanwyck, is without obvious beauty or glamour, first parodying them by excessive ornamenta- tion, then taking over the screen stripped of ornament, in a nonde- script hat and cloth overcoat. But she has a future. Not just because now we know—we soon knew—that this woman is the star of *The Lady Eve* and *Double Indemnity* and *Ball of Fire,* all women, it happens, on the wrong side of the law; but because she is presented *here* as a star (the camera showing her that particular insatiable interest in her every action and reaction), which entails the promise of return, of unpredictable reincarnation.

MY STAKE in the way of looking at *Stella Dallas* I have sketched out here is not alone in providing an alternative to an accepted account of the film but in providing *this* account, marked by the suggestion that its principle figure puts herself in the way of a transfiguration or conversion of her life that I associate with the teaching of Emer- son and of Thoreau and that I claim is common to the members of both the genre of the comedy of remarriage and of the melodrama of the unknown woman. I came up against this transfiguration in my preceding remarks as I was led to speak of the pain of individuation and of Thoreau's pivotal pun between mourning as grieving and morning as dawning or ecstasy.

The acceptance of such an idea (of the woman's transfiguration) would provide a certain verification of this philosophy, hence of philosophy as such, as I care most about it. To propose the idea may also be seen as part of my effort to preserve that philosophy, or rather to show that it *is* preserved, is in existence, in effect, in works of lasting public power—world-famous, world-favored films—while the Emerson text itself, so to speak, is repressed in the public it helped to found. (Some might take such a strategy of presentation as dispersing philosophy past recall.)

The sense of preserving philosophy as I care about it most—together with this way of expressing the care—comes from a companion effort of mine, the first I have made, to see the price of preserving this mode of philosophizing in the face of Emerson's apparent silence about the institution of slavery in his essay "Fate," which is in practice an essay on Freedom. In that work I characterize my task as one of showing Emerson's effort to preserve philosophy in the face of conditions (those which preserve the institution of slavery) that deny or negate philosophy.[2]

I might characterize an essential feature of my task in the present instance as one of testing a manifestation or consequence of philosophizing, as I care about it most, against an interpretation of that manifestation (Stella as oblivious, her film as analogously oblivious) that would in my eyes negate its value, hence negate the value of that philosophizing. The Emersonianism of the films I have written about as genres depict human beings as on a kind of journey—using terms of Emerson as drastically overfamiliar as they are drastically underinterpreted—a journey from what he means by conformity to what he means by self-reliance; which comes to saying (so I have claimed) a journey, or path, or step, from haunting the world to existing in it; which may be expressed as the asserting of one's *cogito ergo sum,* one's own "I think, therefore I am," call it the power to think for oneself, to judge the world, to acquire—as Nora puts it at the end of *A Doll's House*—one's own experience of the world.

I have written as though the woman's demand for a voice, for a language, for attention to, and the power to enforce attention to, her own subjectivity, say to her difference of existence, is expressible as a response to an Emersonian demand for thinking. I suppose that what for me authorizes this supposition is my interpretation of Emerson's authorship as itself responding to his sense of the *right* to such a demand as already voiced on the feminine side, requiring a sense of thinking as reception (Emerson also says an "impressionableness"), and as a bearing of pain, which the masculine in philosophy would avoid. (That is not a straightforward empirical observation but a conceptual claim. If it is wrong it is not so much false as wrongheaded.) To overcome this avoidance is essential to Emerson's hopes for bringing an American difference to philosophy.

Does this idea of the feminine philosophical demand serve to prefigure, or does it serve once more to eradicate, the feminine difference?—to articulate or to blur the difference between the denial to woman of political expression and a man's melancholy sense of his own inexpressiveness? But my more particular question here is this: Is such a question of the relation of the Emersonian and the feminine demands for language of one's own a topic for a serious conversation between women and men? I answer the question here and now as follows. It is, to echo an introductory thought of this book, the logic of human intimacy, or separateness—call this the field of serious and playful conversation or exchange—that to exchange understanding with another is to share pain with that other, and that to take pleasure from another is to extend that pleasure. And what reason is there to enter this logic in a particular case? No reason.

IN DISCUSSION after essentially the forgoing text on *Stella Dallas* was given in May of 1991 as a lecture at Williams College, about a year after the seminar in which that version of the material had been introduced, it was again a late intervention of Anita Sokolsky's that bears repeating here. She commented that instead of characterizing the progression of Stella's concluding states as from mourning to ecstacy, she would rather say it is from melancholia to mourning. I find this a fruitful reformulation, to which I respond, I believe responded then, roughly by adding two complications to think about further. First, encoded in the idea of a Thoreauvian pun on morning and mourning is the idea that the ecstacy in question is still part of the *work* of mourning, not a sign that mourning is all at once over. Second, the "grief" of mourning is not one I am sure I understand here exactly as Freud's structure of melancholia (say with ideas of self-abandonment) but with an interlocking depression and rage. Now I am recapturing another of my mother's moods, somehow associated with the demand to be noticed (perhaps with its explicit failure, perhaps with the implicit failure of having to demand it). She named this state migraine— definable, I assumed, assume, through her therapy for it, which was to play the piano, in a darkened room (her eyes were evidently affected), alone. (I am interpreting the mood, after the fact, from the few times I came home from school late in the afternoon to enter such a scene.) What music she would play then (mostly Chopin, her favorite composer), and how she became a prominent pianist in Atlanta, then largely a culturally unprominent part of the country, and hence what her relation was to a certain stardom, and to her refusal of the chance for more, are pertinent matters. They must concern the relation between searching for the mother's gaze and being subjected to her moods. Hence they concern the question of what her moods are subjected to, to what scenes of inheritance. Was the music filling the loss or impoverishment of a self-abandoned ego (so speaking to melancholia), or was it remembering, say recounting, the origins, hence losses, of her reception of, her glamorous talent for, the world of music (so speaking of dispossession and nostalgia)? Music, moods, worlds, abandonment, subjection, dispossession—of course; we are speaking of melodrama.

Notes

Introduction

1. Catherine Clément, *Opera*, p. 100.
2. Julia Kristeva, *Tales of Love*, pp. 226, 227.

Chapter One

1. See, e.g., Charles Bernheimer and Claire Kahane, eds., *In Dora's Case: Freud—Hysteria—Feminism.*
2. Stanley Cavell. *The Claim of Reason: Wittgenstein, Skepticism, Morality, and Tragedy.*
3. Jacques Derrida, "Cogito and the History of Madness," in *Writing and Difference.* (Page references cited in text.)
4. Stanley Cavell. *Must We Mean What We Say? A Book of Essays.* (Page references cited in text).
5. J. L. Austin, "Other Minds," in *Philosophical Papers.*
6. Henry David Thoreau, *Walden*, chap. 3.
7. Ralph Waldo Emerson, "Experience," in *Emerson: Essays and Lectures*, pp. 469–92.
8. Ralph Waldo Emerson, "Fate," in *Emerson: Essays and Lectures*, pp. 941–68.

Chapter Two

1. See, e.g., Stanley Cavell, "An Emerson Mood," in *The Senses of Walden: An Expanded Edition*, pp. 142–43.
2. See Neil Hertz, "Dora's Secrets, Freud's Techniques," pp. 221–42; Shoshana Felman, "Turning the Screw of Interpretation," pp. 94–207; and Eve Kosofsky Sedgwick, "Homophobia, Misogyny, and Capital: The Example of *Our Mutual Friend*," pp. 126–51.

In this connection I want to reaffirm my continuing indebtedness to the work and friendship of Michael Fried. His extraordinary book, *Realism, Writing, Disfiguration: On Thomas Eakins and Stephen Crane*, also more explicitly relates itself to Freudian concepts than his past writing has done. I cannot forbear noting specifically, for those who will appreciate the kind of confirmation or ratification one may derive from simultaneous or crossing discoveries in writing that one admires, the light thrown by Fried's breakthrough discussion of Stephen Crane on the passage from James's "The Beast in the Jungle" on which the present essay closes.

3. Sigmund Freud, *The Interpretation of Dreams,* in *Standard Edition,* 4:144, 145.

4. See Harold Bloom, "Freud's Concepts of Defense and the Poetic Will" (lecture to Forum on Psychiatry and the Humanities, 1980), in Smith, ed., *The Literary Freud: Mechanisms of Defense and the Poetic Will,* pp. 1–28.

5. See Jacques Derrida, "Coming into One's Own," in Hartman, ed., *Psychoanalysis and the Question of the Text.* The translator, James Hulbert, warns that he has abridged a section from a much longer work in progress. The work has now appeared as "Freud's Legacy," in *The Postcard: From Socrates to Freud and Beyond.* Translated by Alan Bass (Chicago: University of Chicago Press [1987]).

6. Immanuel Kant, *The Critique of Pure Reason,* p. A109. In a set of editorial notes prepared for my use, Joseph H. Smith, in responding to my claim that Freud here takes on Kant's views exactly at a point at which he wishes to distinguish the psychoanalytic idea of the unconscious from "the unconscious of the philosophers," finds that "it is inconceivable to me that Freud was unaware of being Kantian here." I am grateful, first of all, for the confirmation that the Kantian provenance of Freud's thought seems so patent. But further, as to whether Freud could in that case have been "unaware" of the provenance, I would like to propose the following: if Freud was aware of it, then his omitting of Kant's name just here, where he is explicitly dissociating himself from philosophy, is motivated, deliberate, showing an awareness that his claim to dissociation is from the beginning compromised, say ambivalent; but if, on the contrary, Freud was not aware of his Kantianism just here, say unconscious of it, then he was repressing this fact of his origin. Either of these possibilities, suppression or repression, I am regarding as fateful to the development of psychoanalysis as a field of investigation (supposing this more distinct from psychoanalysis as a therapy than it perhaps can be) and rather in support of my claim that Freud's self-interpretation of his relation to philosophy is suspicious and, contrary to what I know of its reception by later psychoanalysts, ought to be treated.

I cite one piece of positive evidence here to indicate Freud's ambivalent awareness or resistant understanding of the depth of his intellectual debt to Kant (one may press this evidence to the point of suppression or repression). Of the dozen or so references to Kant listed in the general index of the *Standard Edition,* one bears directly on whether Freud saw the Kantianism of his view of the proof and the place of the unconscious. At the end of the first section of "The Unconscious" Freud says this:

> The psycho-analytic assumption of unconscious mental activity appears
> to us . . . as an extension of the corrections undertaken by Kant of our
> views on external perception. Just as Kant warned us not to overlook the
> fact that our perceptions are subjectively conditioned and must not be
> regarded as identical with what is perceived though unknowable, so
> psycho-analysis warns us not to equate perceptions by means of con-
> sciousness with the unconscious mental processes which are their object.
> Like the physical, the psychical is not necessarily in reality what it ap-
> pears to us to be. (14:171)

This expression of indebtedness to Kant precisely discounts the
debt, since Kant equally "warned us" not to equate the appearance
of the psychic with the reality of it, the warning Freud arrogates to
psychoanalysis as an "extension" of Kant's philosophical contribu-
tion to the study of knowledge. It is the *connection* of the study of
inner and outer that my paper claims is "pure Kant."

Now Freud might have meant something further in his arrogation. He might have been compressing, in his discounting of the
debt to Kant, a claim to the effect that Kant did not lay out the conditions of the appearance of the inner world with the systematicness
with which he laid out the conditions of the appearance of the outer
world, the world of objects; in short, that Kant lacked the tools with
which to elicit a system of categories of the understanding for the
psyche, or the subjective, comparable to the one he elicited for the
external, or the objective, world. These tools, unlike those of Aris-
totle that Kant deployed, came into the possession of Western
thought only with psychoanalysis. Something of this sort seems to
me correct. But if Freud had claimed this explicitly, hence taken on
the obligation to say whether, for example, his "categories" had the
same status as Kant's, then the awareness would have been inevitable that his quarrel with philosophy was necessary, was philosophy.
Unawareness of his inheritance of Kant would then indeed have
been inconceivable.

7. Ibid., p. A158, B197.

8. See Martin Heidegger, *What Is Called Thinking?* The quotation
from Kant is on p. 243; that from Schelling on pp. 90–91.

9. Ralph Waldo Emerson, "Circles," in *Essays: First Series*, pp. 404,
411–12.

10. Heidegger, *What Is Called Thinking?* p. 90.

11. After a conversation with Kurt Fischer, I realize that I should,
even in this opening sketch of the problem of inheriting philosophy,
be more cautious, or specific, in speaking of Freud's "inheritance"
of classical German philosophy. I do not mean that an Austrian student in the later nineteenth century would have had just the same
philosophical education as a German student of the period; nor
does my claim require that Freud read so much as a page in one

of Kant's works. It would have been enough for my (or Freud's) purposes for him to have received his Kant from the quotations of Kant he would have encountered in his reading of Schopenhauer. My focus, that is, in speaking here of Freud's inheritance of the German outburst, is rather on who Freud is, on what becomes of ideas in that mind, than on what, apart from a mind of that resourcefulness, German philosophy is thought to be. I assume that more or less the same ought to be said of the inheritance of German thought by that other Austrian student, Wittgenstein.

12. See Bloom, "Freud's Concepts of Defense and the Poetic Will," p. 7. Bloom means here to be speaking for Freud; as do I.

13. Emerson, "Self-Reliance," in *Essays: First Series,* p. 264.

14. Lacan, "God and the *Jouissance* of ~~The~~Woman," in Mitchell and Rose, eds., *Feminine Sexuality,* p. 144.

15. See n. 2 above.

16. Lacan, "A Love Letter," in Mitchell and Rose, eds., *Feminine Sexuality,* p. 154.

17. Ludwig Wittgenstein, *Philosophical Investigations,* trans. G. E. M. Anscombe, p. 178.

18. G. W. F. Hegel, *The Introduction to Hegel's Philosophy of Fine Art,* trans. Bernard Bosanquet (London, 1886), p. 150.

19. Emerson, "Behavior," in *Conduct of Life,* p. 1037a.

20. Freud, *Fragment of an Analysis of a Case of Hysteria,* in *Standard Edition,* 7:77–78.

21. Freud, "The Neuro-Psychoses of Defence," in *Standard Edition,* 3:50.

22. For the phrase "private theatre," see Breuer and Freud, *Studies on Hysteria,* in *Standard Edition,* 2:22.

23. See, for example, Freud, "The Neuro-Psychoses of Defence," in *Standard Edition,* 3:51.

24. Freud, "Notes Upon a Case of Obsessional Neurosis," in *Standard Edition,* 10:157.

25. Freud, "The Neuro-Psychoses of Defence," *Standard Edition,* 3:50.

26. Freud, "The 'Uncanny,'" in *Standard Edition,* 17:230.

27. Freud, "Analysis Terminable and Interminable," in *Standard Edition,* 23:252.

28. Emerson, "Self-Reliance," *Essays: First Series,* p. 262.

29. Cavell, "Politics as Opposed to What?" *Critical Inquiry* 9 (September 1982): 157–78.

30. Freud, "A Child Is Being Beaten," in *Standard Edition,* 17:179–204.

31. Henry James, "The Beast in the Jungle," in vol. 11 of *The Complete Tales of Henry James,* pp. 397–402.

Chapter Three

1. The relevant idea of two modes of film genre is worked out in Cavell, "The Fact of Television," in *Themes Out of School: Effects and Causes.*

2. An important early corrective to the dismissal of such films occurs in Molly Haskell, *From Reverence to Rape: The Treatment of Women in the Movies.* See also Charles Affron, *Star Acting: Gish, Garbo, Davis.* For the study of *Now, Voyager* there is the decisive help of the publication of its script: see Casey Robinson, *Now, Voyager.*

3. Freud's apparent first use of the phrase "somatic compliance" and a discussion of it appears in "Fragment of an Analysis of a Case of Hysteria," in *Standard Edition,* 7:40–42. See also Breuer and Freud, *Studies on Hysteria,* in *Standard Edition,* 2:164–68.

4. See Freud, "The Neuro-Psychoses of Defence," in *Standard Edition,* 3:157; and Chap. 2 of the present volume, pp. 105–7.

5. Ralph Waldo Emerson, "Self-Reliance," in *Essays: First Series,* p. 265.

6. At the reception following my presentation of this material at Chicago, I joined, a bit late, a wonderful exchange between Janel Mueller and James Chandler on, among other topics, the question whether the opening shot of a stone with VALE engraved on it is to be taken as a headstone, and whether those letters are meant to spell the Latin for "farewell," and, if so, who is saying farewell to what.

7. Naomi Scheman's "Missing Mothers/Desiring Daughters: Framing the Sight Women," pp. 62–83, is pertinent here as elsewhere.

Chapter Four

NOTE.—The following abbreviations are used in this chapter: "BC" = "The Beast in the Closet"; "BJ" = "The Beast in the Jungle"; "DOC" = "Dissolution of the Oedipus Complex"; *PI* = *Philosophical Investigations;* "TD" = "Time and Desire in the Woman's Film."

1. Eve Kosofsky Sedgwick, "The Beast in the Closet: James and the Writing of Homosexual Panic," in *Sex, Politics, and Science in the Nineteenth-Century Novel,* ed. Ruth Bernard Yeazell (Baltimore, 1986), p. 173; reprinted in *Speaking of Gender,* ed. Elaine Showalter (New York, 1989); and in Sedgwick, *Epistemology of the Closet,* pp. 204–5. (Page references in the text are from *Epistemology of the Closet.*)

2. René Descartes, *Meditations,* in *Philosophical Works of Descartes,* p. 145.

3. David Hume, *A Treatise of Human Nature,* ed. L. A. Selby-Bigge and P. H. Nidditch, Book 1, Part 4, Section 7, pp. 216, 268–69.

4. Ibid., p. 270.

5. Cavell, *The Claim of Reason: Wittgenstein, Skepticism, Morality, and Tragedy,* p. 351.

6. Ludwig Wittgenstein, *Philosophical Investigations,* para. 126, my emphasis.

7. See Cavell, "Foreword: An Audience for Philosophy," p. xxvii, and "The Politics of Interpretation (Politics as Opposed to What?)," p. 34.

8. Henry David Thoreau, "Conclusion," *Walden,* ed. J. Lyndon Shanley, p. 324.

9. Edgar Allan Poe, "The Black Cat," 3:849.

10. See Cavell, *The Claim of Reason,* p. 332.

11. I take this formulation about instincts into drives from Jean Laplanche, *Life and Death in Psychoanalysis.* Arnold Davidson's "How to Do the History of Psychoanalysis: A Reading of Freud's *Three Essays*" is particularly pertinent here.

12. Henry James, "The Beast in the Jungle," *The Complete Tales of Henry James,* 11:402.

13. See Cavell, *Must We Mean What We Say?* pp. xxvi, 44–72; and *Conditions Handsome and Unhandsome,* chap. 2.

14. James Conant's "Must We Show What We Cannot Say?" is particularly useful here, where it is so hard to be useful, arguing that the motivating issues of Wittgenstein's *Philosophical Investigations* are already at work in his *Tractatus.* Conant puts in play various mis-formations of Wittgenstein's ideas of, call it, the ineffable, of "what cannot be said, only shown" ("thereof must we be silent"); it is in this light that it would be useful to assess Sedgwick's play and placement of what she formulates as "the-articulated-denial-of-articulability" ("BC," p. 172).

15. Emerson, "Fate," in *The Conduct of Life,* p. 947.

16. See Cavell, "Two Cheers for Romance."

17. Friedrich Nietzsche, *On the Genealogy of Morals, Basic Writings of Nietzsche,* p. 543.

18. Emersonian perfectionism is the guiding subject of *Conditions Handsome and Unhandsome.* It contains references to the work of other philosophers contesting in related ways the current conformation of moral philosophy, for example that of G. E. M. Anscombe, Annette Baier, Cora Diamond, Philippa Foot, Alasdaire MacIntyre, Iris Murdoch, and Bernard Williams.

19. See Freud, "The Dissolution of the Oedipus Complex," in *Standard Edition,* 19:172–79.

20. See Tania Modleski, "Time and Desire in the Woman's Film," in Christine Gledhill, ed., *Home Is Where the Heart Is,* pp. 326–38.

21. See Freud, "Delusions and Dreams in Jensen's *Gradiva*," in *Standard Edition*, 9:3–95.

22. See Freud, "On Transcience," in *Standard Edition*, 14:303–7.

23. Jacques Lacan, "Desire and the Interpretation of Desire in *Hamlet*," in Felman, ed., *Literature and Psychoanalysis*, p. 46. Lacan is citing Freud's "The Dissolution of the Oedipus Complex."

24. Ibid., p. 43.

25. Again, see Rothman's "Pathos and Transfiguration in the Face of the Camera."

26. Cavell, *Pursuits of Happiness*, pp. 89–90.

27. But now I find something more needs to come out. In my epigraph to this Postscript I give the words of Whitman's that are actually cited in *Now, Voyager*. The theater of their presentation is carefully marked: in Dr. Jaquith's termination of Charlotte's treatment he hands her a slip of folded paper saying, "I've had it looked up and typed for you on a slip of paper. If old Walt didn't have you in mind when he wrote this, he had hundreds of others like you," whereupon he says "Bye" casually and leaves. Charlotte opens the slip and, in close-up, reads "The Untold Want." That, especially its title phrase, is good enough in our present context. But the phrase "Now Voyager" appears in a companion poem of Whitman's from the same year (1871), where "Voyager," unlike its appearance in "The Untold Want," is capitalized. This time the title is "Now Finalè to the Shore":

> Now finalè to the shore,
> Now, land and life finalè and farewell,
> Now Voyager depart, (much, much for thee is yet in store,)
> Often enough hast thou adventur'd o'er the seas,
> Cautiously cruising, studying the charts,
> Duly again to port and hawser's tie returning;
> But now obey thy cherish'd secret wish,
> Embrace thy friends, leave all in order,
> To port and hawser's tie no more returning,
> Depart upon thy endless cruise old Sailor.
>
> (*Leaves of Grass*, pp. 502–3)

Of course the capitalization of "Voyager" would in any case have been required in using it for the film's title; but my thought is not that this longer version of the idea is more the thread of the film than the shorter version, only that it is equally there, in a number of registers: not alone in the repeated idea of cruising, nor in the possible allusion to the name Vale in "farewell," especially in association with taking leave of life, but in the overall secret mythologizing of existence ("studying the charts"), as in Charlotte's "We have the stars," and her self-presentation of flowers. We can tell Charlotte's progress as from her early departure to find her "untold want," to her late knowledge, having now "adventur'd o'er the seas" and found some untold want, of departure itself, living untold, without titles.

28. On "the experience of sexuality," especially in relation to the complex history of what is categorized as morbid, and in relation, among many others, to Michel Foucault's work, see Arnold Davidson's "Sex and the Emergence of Sexuality."

29. Plato, *The Republic,* p. 238.

30. Emerson, "Experience," in *Essays: Second Series,* p. 473.

31. Such a way of seeing "Experience" is worked out in my "Finding as Founding," pp. 77–118.

32. See Cavell, *Disowning Knowledge in Six Plays of Shakespeare,* p. 17.

Chapter Five

1. All references to Williams's essay are to its occurrence in Gledhill (see Bibliography).

2. See "Emerson's Constitutional Amending," in Cavell, *Philosophical Passages.*

Bibliography

Affron, Charles. *Star Acting: Gish, Garbo, Davis.* New York: Dutton, 1977.

Aristophanes. *The Clouds.* Edited and with an introduction by K. J. Dover. Oxford: Clarendon Press, 1968.

Austin, J. L. "Other Minds." In *Philosophical Papers.*

———. *Philosophical Papers.* 3d ed. Edited by J. O. Urmson and G. J. Warnock. Oxford: Oxford University Press, 1961.

Beckett, Samuel. *Endgame.* New York: Grove Press, 1958.

Bernheimer, Charles, and Claire Kahane, eds. *In Dora's Case: Freud—Hysteria—Feminism.* New York: Columbia University Press, 1985.

Bloom, Harold. *The Anxiety of Influence: A Theory of Poetry.* Oxford: Oxford University Press, 1975.

———. "Freud's Concepts of Defense and the Poetic Will." In Smith ed., *The Literary Freud: Mechanisms of Defense and the Poetic Will.*

Breuer, Josef, and Sigmund Freud. *Studies on Hysteria.* In *Standard Edition,* vol. 2.

Brooks, Peter. *The Melodramatic Imagination: Balzac, Henry James, Melodrama and the Mode of Excess.* New Haven: Yale University Press, 1976.

Cavell, Stanley. "The Availability of Wittgenstein's Later Philosophy." In *Must We Mean What We Say?*

———. "Being Odd, Getting Even." In *In Quest of the Ordinary.*

———. *The Claim of Reason: Wittgenstein, Skepticism, Morality, and Tragedy.* Oxford: Oxford University Press, 1979.

———. *Conditions Handsome and Unhandsome: The Constitution of Emersonian Perfectionism.* Chicago: University of Chicago Press, 1990.

———. "Declining Decline: Wittgenstein as a Philosopher of Culture." In *This New Yet Unapproachable America.*

———. *Disowning Knowledge: In Six Plays of Shakespeare.* Cambridge: Cambridge University Press, 1987.

———. "An Emerson Mood." In *The Senses of Walden: An Expanded Edition.*

———. "Emerson's Constitutional Amending: Reading 'Fate.'" In *Philosophical Passages.*

———. "The Fact of Television." In *Themes Out of School: Effects and Causes.* Chicago: University of Chicago Press, 1988.

———. "Finding as Founding: Taking Steps in Emerson's 'Experience.'" In *This New Yet Unapproachable America.*

———. "Forward: An Audience for Philosophy." In *Must We Mean What We Say?*

———. "Macbeth Appalled." *Raritan* 12, nos. 2 and 3.

———. "Must We Mean What We Say?" In *Must We Mean What We Say?*

———. *Must We Mean What We Say? A Book of Essays.* Cambridge: Cambridge University Press, 1976 [1969].

———. "Othello and the Stake of the Other." In *Disowning Knowledge.*

———. *Philosophical Passages: Wittgenstein, Emerson, Austin, Derrida.* Cambridge, Mass.: Blackwell, 1995.

———. *A Pitch of Philosophy: Autobiographical Exercises.* Cambridge, Mass.: Harvard University Press, 1994.

———. "Politics as Opposed to What?" *Critical Inquiry* 9 (September 1982): 157–78. Reprinted as "The Politics of Interpretation (Politics as Opposed to What?)." In *Themes Out of School.*

———. *Pursuits of Happiness: The Hollywood Comedy of Remarriage.* Cambridge, Mass.: Harvard University Press, [1976] 1981.

———. *In Quest of the Ordinary: Lines of Skepticism and Romanticism.* Chicago: University of Chicago Press, 1988.

———. "Recounting Gains, Showing Losses: Reading *The Winters Tale.*" In *Disowning Knowledge.*

———. "Reply to Modleski." *Critical Inquiry* 16 (Autumn 1990).

———. *The Senses of Walden: An Expanded Edition.* Chicago: University of Chicago Press, 1981 [1972].

———. *Themes Out of School: Effects and Causes.* San Francisco: North Point Press, 1984.

———. *This New Yet Unapproachable America*. Albuquerque: Living Batch Press, 1988.

———. "Two Cheers for Romance." In Gaylin and Persons, eds., *Passionate Attachments: Thinking about Love*.

———. *The World Viewed: Reflections on the Ontology of Film*. Enlarged ed. Cambridge, Mass.: Harvard University Press, 1979 [1971].

Chodorow, Nancy. *The Reproduction of Mothering: Psychoanalysis and the Sociology of Gender*. Berkeley: University of California Press, 1978.

Clément, Catherine. *Opera: Or the Undoing of Women*. Translated by Betsy Wing. Minneapolis: University of Minnesota Press, 1988.

Coleridge, Samuel Taylor. *Aids to Reflection*. Edited by John Beer. Princeton: Princeton University Press, 1993.

Conant, James. "Must We Show What We Cannot Say?" In Fleming and Payne, eds., *The Senses of Stanley Cavell*.

Cowie, Elizabeth. "Fantasia." *m/f*, no. 9, (1984).

Davidson, Arnold. "How to Do the History of Psychoanalysis: A Reading of Freud's *Three Essays on the Theory of Sexuality.*" In Meltzer, ed., *The Trial(s) of Psychoanalysis*.

———. "Sex and the Emergence of Sexuality." *Critical Inquiry* 14 (Autumn 1987).

de Lauretis, Teresa. *The Practice of Love: Lesbian Sexuality and Perverse Desire*. Bloomington: Indiana University Press, 1994.

Derrida, Jacques. "Cogito and the History of Madness." In *Writing and Difference*. Translated by Alan Bass. Chicago: University of Chicago Press, 1978.

———. "Coming into One's Own." In Hartman, ed. *Psychoanalysis and the Question of the Text*.

———. "Signature Event Context." In *Margins of Philosophy*. Translated by Alan Bass. Chicago: University of Chicago Press, 1982.

Descartes, René. *Meditations on First Philosophy*. In *The Philosophical Works of Descartes*. 2 vols. Translated and edited by Elizabeth S. Haldane and G. R. T. Ross. Cambridge: Cambridge University Press, 1991.

Deutelbaum, Marshall, and Leland Poague, eds. *A Hitchcock Reader*. Ames, Iowa: Iowa State University Press, 1986.

Doane, Mary Ann. *The Desire to Desire: The Woman's Film of the 1940's*. Bloomington: University of Indiana Press, 1987.

Dumas, Alexandre. *La Dame aux Camilias.* Translated by Edmund Gross. Gloucester: Sutton, 1986.

Emerson, Ralph Waldo. "Behavior." In *The Conduct of Life, in Emerson: Essays and Lectures.*

———. "Circles." In *Essays: First Series, in Emerson: Essays and Lectures.*

———. *Emerson: Essays and Lectures.* Edited by Joel Porte. New York: Library of America, 1983.

———. "Experience." In *Essays: Second Series, in Emerson: Essays and Lectures.*

———. "Fate." In *The Conduct of Life. In Emerson: Essays and Lectures.*

———. "The Poet." In *Essays: Second Series, in Emerson: Essays and Lectures.*

———. "Politics." In *Essays: Second Series, in Emerson: Essays and Lectures.*

———. "Self-Reliance." In *Essays: First Series, in Emerson: Essays and Lectures.*

Felman, Shoshana, ed. *Literature and Psychoanalysis: The Question of Reading Otherwise.* Baltimore: Johns Hopkins University Press, 1982.

———. "Turning the Screw of Interpretation." *Yale French Studies* 55/56 (1977). Also in *Literature and Psychoanalysis: The Question of Reading Otherwise.*

Filmer, Robert Sir. *Patriarcha.* In *Patriarcha and Other Writings.* Edited by Johann P. Somerville. Cambridge: Cambridge University Press, 1991.

Flaubert, Gustave. *Madame Bovary.* Translated by Eleanor Marx. New York: Dutton, 1966.

Fleming, Richard, and Michael Payne, eds. *The Senses of Stanley Cavell. Bucknell Review* 32, no. 1. Lewisburg, Penn.: Bucknell University Press, 1989.

Foucault, Michel. *Madness and Civilization: A History of Insanity in the Age of Reason.* New York: Vintage Books, 1973.

Freud, Sigmund. "Analysis Terminable and Interminable." In *Standard Edition,* vol. 23.

———. *Beyond the Pleasure Principle.* In *Standard Edition,* vol. 18.

———. "A Child Is Being Beaten." In *Standard Edition,* vol. 17.

———. "Delusions and Dreams in Jensen's *Gradiva.*" In *Standard Edition,* vol. 9.

―――. "The Dissolution of the Oedipus Complex." In *Standard Edition*, vol. 19.

―――. "Female Sexuality." In *Standard Edition*, vol. 21.

―――. "Fragment of an Analysis of a Case of Hysteria." In *Standard Edition*, vol. 7.

―――. *The Interpretation of Dreams*. In *Standard Edition*, vols. 4 and 5.

―――. "Mourning and Melancholia." In *Standard Edition*, vol. 14.

―――. "The Neuro-Psychosis of Defence." In *Standard Edition*, vol. 3.

―――. "Notes upon a Case of Obsessional Neurosis." In *Standard Edition*, vol. 10.

―――. "Project for a Scientific Psychology." In *Standard Edition*, vol. 1.

―――. *The Standard Edition of the Complete Psychological Works of Sigmund Freud*. 24 vols. Edited and translated by James Strachey in collaboration with Anna Freud. London: Hogarth Press, 1966.

―――. "Three Essays on the Theory of Sexuality." In *Standard Edition*, vol. 7.

―――. "On Transcience." In *Standard Edition*, vol. 14.

―――. "The 'Uncanny.'" In *Standard Edition*, vol. 17.

―――. "The Unconscious." In *Standard Edition*, vol. 14.

Fried, Michael. *Realism, Writing, Disfiguration: On Thomas Eakins and Stephen Crane*. Chicago: University of Chicago Press, 1987.

Gaylin, Willard, and Ethil Persons, eds. *Passionate Attachments: Thinking about Love*. New York: Free Press, 1988.

Gledhill, Christine, ed. *Home Is Where the Heart Is: Studies in Melodrama and the Woman's Film*. London: British Film Institute Publishing, 1987.

Gould, Timothy. "Where the Action Is: Stanley Cavell and the Skeptic's Activity." In Fleming and Payne, eds., *The Senses of Stanley Cavell*.

Hanson, Karen. "Being Doubted, Being Assured." In Fleming and Payne, eds., *The Senses of Stanley Cavell*.

Hartman, Geoffrey H., ed. *Psychoanalysis and the Question of the Text*. Baltimore: Johns Hopkins University Press, 1978.

Haskell, Molly. *From Reverence to Rape: The Treatment of Women in the Movies*. 2d. ed. Chicago: University of Chicago Press, 1987.

Hegel, G. W. F. *The Introduction to Hegel's Philosophy of Fine Art*.

Translated by Bernard Bosanquet. London: Keagan Paul, 1905 [1886].

———. *The Phenomenology of the Spirit.* Translated by A. V. Miller with an analysis of the text by J. N. Findlay. Oxford: Oxford University Press, 1977.

Heidegger, Martin. *Being and Time.* Translated by J. Macquarrie and E. Robinson. New York: Harper Books, 1962.

———. *What Is Called Thinking?* Translated by J. Glenn Gray. New York: Harper and Row, 1964.

Hertz, Neil. "Dora's Secrets, Freud's Techniques." In Bernheimer and Kahane, eds., *In Dora's Case: Freud—Hysteria—Feminism.*

Hoffman, E. T. A. "The Sandman." In *Selected Writings of E. T. A. Hoffman.* Vol. 1. Edited and translated by Elizabeth C. Knight and Leonard J. Kent. Chicago: University of Chicago Press, 1969.

Hume, David. *A Treatise of Human Nature.* Edited by L. A. Selby-Bigge. Oxford: Clarendon Press, 1978.

Ibsen, Henrik. *Complete Major Prose Plays.* Translated and introduced by Rolf Fjelde. New York: New American Library, 1965.

———. "A Doll's House." In *Complete Major Prose Plays.*

———. "Ghosts." In *Complete Major Prose Plays.*

James, Henry. "The Beast in the Jungle." In vol. 11 of *The Complete Tales of Henry James.* 12 vols. Edited by Leon Edel. Philadelphia: Lippincott, 1962–64.

Kafka, Franz. "Josephine the Singer, or The Mouse Folk." In *The Penal Colony: Stories and Short Pieces.* Translated by Willa and Edwin Muir. New York: Shocken Books, 1963.

Kant, Immanuel. *The Critique of Pure Reason.* Translated by Norman Kemp Smith. New York: St. Martin's Press, 1965 [1950].

Kaplan, E. Ann. "The Case of the Missing Mother: Maternal Issues in Vidor's *Stella Dallas.*" *Heresies* 16 (1983).

Keane, Marian. "A Closer Look at Scopophilia." In Deutelbaum and Poague, eds., *A Hitchcock Reader.*

Kierkegaard, Soren. *Repetition.* Translated by Walter Lowrie. Princeton: Princeton University Press, 1941.

Kleist, Heinrich von. "The Marquise of O—." In *The Marquise of O— and Other Stories.* Translated and with an introduction by Martin Greenberg. New York: Criterion Books, 1960.

Kristeva, Julia. *Tales of Love.* Translated by Leon Roudiez. New York: Columbia University Press, 1987.

Lacan, Jacques. "Desire and the Interpretation of Desire in *Hamlet.*"

In Shoshana Felman, ed., *Literature and Psychoanalysis: The Question of Reading Otherwise.*

———. *Ecrits: A Selection.* Translated by Alan Sheridan. New York: W. W. Norton, 1977.

———. *Feminine Sexuality: Jacques Lacan and the Ecole Freudienne.* Edited by Juliet Michell and Jacqueline Rose, translated by Jacqueline Rose. New York: W. W. Norton, 1985.

———. "God and the *Jouissance* of The Woman." In Michell and Rose, eds., *Feminine Sexuality.*

———. "A Love Letter." In Michell and Rose, eds., *Feminine Sexuality.*

———. "The Signification of the Phallus." In *Ecrits.*

Laplanche, Jean. *Life and Death in Psychoanalysis.* Translated by Jeffrey Mehlman. Baltimore: Johns Hopkins University Press, 1985 [1976].

Leverenz, David. "The Politics of Emerson's Man-Making Words." *Publications of the Modern Language Association* 101, no. 1 (January 1986).

Locke, John. *Two Treatises of Government.* 2d ed. Edited by Peter Laslett. Cambridge: Cambridge University Press, 1970.

Lowith, Karl. *From Hegel to Nietzsche.* New York: Garland Publishing, 1984.

Marcus, Steven. "Freud and Dora: Story, History, Case History." In Bernheimer and Kahane, eds., *In Dora's Case.*

Meltzer, Françoise, ed. *The Trial(s) of Psychoanalysis.* Chicago: University of Chicago Press, 1987.

Mill, John Stuart. *On Liberty.* Edited by Elizabeth Rapaport. Indianapolis, Ind.: Hackett, 1978.

Milton, John. *The Doctrine and Discipline of Divorce.* In *The Complete Prose Works of John Milton.* General editor, Don M. Wolfe. New Haven: Yale University Press, 1980.

Modleski, Tania. *Feminism without Women: Culture and Criticism in a "Postfeminist" Age.* New York: Routledge, 1991.

———. "Reply to Cavell." *Critical Inquiry* 16 (Autumn 1990).

———. "Time and Desire in the Woman's Film." In Gledhill, ed., *Home Is Where the Heart Is.*

Mulvey, Laura. "Visual Pleasure and Narrative Cinema." *Screen* 16, no. 3 (Autumn 1975).

Nietzsche, Friedrich. *The Gay Science.* Translated by Walter Kaufman. New York: Vintage Press, 1974 [1968].

————. *On the Genealogy of Morals. In Basic Writings of Nietzsche.* Translated by Walter Kaufman and R. J. Hollingdale. New York: Random House, 1968.

————. *Thus Spoke Zarathustra.* Translated by Walter Kaufman. New York: Penguin Books, 1978.

Pagels, Elaine. *Adam, Eve, and The Serpent.* New York: Random House, 1988.

Plato. *The Republic.* Translated by G. M. A. Grube. Indianapolis, Ind.: Hackett Publishing, 1974.

Poe, Edgar Allan. "The Black Cat." In *Collected Works,* vol. 3.

————. *Collected Works: Tales and Sketches 1843–1849.* 3 vols. Edited by Thomas Ollive Mabbot. Cambridge, Mass.: Harvard University Press, 1978.

————. "Loss of Breath." In *Collected Works,* vol. 2.

Prouty, Olive Higgins. *Now Voyager.* Boston, Mass.: Houghton Mifflin, 1941.

Robinson, Casey. *Now, Voyager.* Edited by Jeanne Thomas Allen. Madison, Wis., 1984.

Rothman, William. *The "I" of the Camera: Essays in Film Criticism, History, and Aesthetics.* Cambridge: Cambridge University Press, 1988.

————. "Pathos and Transfiguration in the Face of the Camera: A Reading of *Stella Dallas.*" In *The "I" of the Camera.*

Sartre, John Paul. *Being and Nothingness: A Phenomenological Essay on Ontology.* Translated and with an introduction by Hazel E. Barnes. New York: Washington Square Press, 1966.

Scheman, Naomi. "Missing Mothers/Desiring Daughters: Framing the Sight Women," *Critical Inquiry* 15 (Autumn 1988).

Sedgwick, Eve Kosofsky. "The Beast in the Closet: James and the Writing of Homosexual Panic." In *The Epistemology of the Closet.* Berkeley: University of California Press, 1990.

————. "Homophobia, Mysogyny, and Capital: The Example of *Our Mutual Friend.*" *Raritan* 2 (Winter 1983). Also in *Between Men: English Literature and Male Homosocial Desire.* New York: Columbia University Press, 1985.

Shakespeare, William. *All's Well That Ends Well.* The Arden Shakespeare. Edited by G. K. Hunter. London: Methuen, 1969.

————. *Anthony and Cleopatra.* The Arden Shakespeare. Edited by M. R. Ridley. Cambridge, Mass.: Harvard University Press, 1956.

————. *Titus Andronicus*. The Arden Shakespeare. Edited by J. C. Maxwell. London: Methuen, 1968.

————. *The Winter's Tale*. The Arden Shakespeare. Edited by J. H. P. Pafford. London: Methuen, 1978.

Smith, Joseph H., ed. *The Literary Freud: Mechanisms of Defense and the Poetic Will*. New Haven: Yale University Press, 1980.

Thoreau, Henry David. *Walden*. Edited by J. Lyndon Shanley. Princeton: Princeton University Press, 1974.

Tolstoy, Leo. *Anna Karenina*. Edited and with an introduction by Harold Bloom. New York: Chelsea House, 1987.

Whitman, Walt. *Leaves of Grass*. Edited by Scully Bradley and Harold W. Blodgett (New York: W. W. Norton, 1973).

————. "Now Finalè to the Shore." In *Leaves of Grass*.

————. "Song of the Open Road." In *Leaves of Grass*.

————. "The Untold Want." In *Leaves of Grass*.

Williams, Linda. "'Something Else Besides A Mother': *Stella Dallas* and the Maternal Melodrama." In Gledhill, ed., *Home Is Where the Heart Is*.

Wittgenstein, Ludwig. *Philosophical Investigations*. Translated by G. E. M. Anscombe. New York: Macmillan, 1968.

————. *Tractatus Logico-Philosophicus*. Translated by Pears and McGuiness. London: Routledge, 1961.

Zweig, Stefan. *Letter from an Unknown Woman*. New York: Viking Press, 1932.

Filmography

Adam's Rib (1949). Directed by George Cukor, with Katharine Hepburn and Spencer Tracy.

Affair to Remember, An (1957). Directed by Leo McCarey, with Cary Grant and Deborah Kerr.

Awful Truth, The (1937). Directed by Leo McCarey, with Cary Grant, Irene Dunne, and Ralph Bellamy.

Back Street (1961). Directed by David Miller, with Susan Hayward, John Gavin, and Vera Miles.

Ball of Fire (1941). Directed by Howard Hawks, with Gary Cooper and Barbara Stanwyck.

Bill of Divorcement, A (1932). Directed by George Cukor, with John Barrymore, Billie Burke, and Katharine Hepburn.

Blonde Venus (1932). Directed by Josef von Sternberg, with Marlene Dietrich, Herbert Marshall, and Cary Grant.

Bringing Up Baby (1938). Directed by Howard Hawks, with Cary Grant and Katharine Hepburn.

Camille (1936). Directed by George Cukor, with Greta Garbo, Robert Taylor, and Lionel Barrymore.

City Lights (1931). Directed by Charles Chaplin, with Charlie Chaplin.

Dark Victory (1939). Directed by Edmund Goulding, with Bette Davis, George Brent, Humphrey Bogart, and Ronald Reagan.

Double Indemnity (1944). Directed by Billy Wilder, with Fred MacMurray, Barbara Stanwyck, and Edward G. Robinson.

Dr. Jekyll and Mr. Hyde (1941). Directed by Victor Fleming, with Spencer Tracy, Ingrid Bergman, and Lana Turner.

Gaslight (1944). Directed by George Cukor, with Ingrid Bergman and Charles Boyer.

His Girl Friday (1940). Directed by Howard Hawks, with Cary Grant, Rosalind Russell, and Ralph Bellamy.

It Happened One Night (1934). Directed by Frank Capra, with Clark Gable and Claudette Colbert.

Lady Eve, The (1941). Directed by Preston Sturges, with Barbara Stanwyck, Henry Fonda, and Charles Coburn.

Letter from an Unknown Woman (1948). Directed by Max Ophuls, with Joan Fontaine and Louis Jourdan.

Little Foxes, The (1941). Directed by William Wyler, with Bette Davis and Herbert Marshall.

Love Affair (1939). Directed by Leo McCarey, with Irene Dunne and Charles Boyer.

Madame X (1966). Directed by David Lowell Rich, with Lana Turner and John Forsythe.

Marquise of O— (1976). Directed by Eric Rohmer.

Mildred Pierce (1945). Directed by Michael Curtiz, with Joan Crawford, Jack Carson, and Zachary Scott.

Mrs. Miniver (1942). Directed by William Wyler, with Greer Garson, Walter Pidgeon, and May Whitty.

Ninotchka (1939). Directed by Ernst Lubitsch, with Greta Garbo, Melvyn Douglas, and Bela Lugosi.

Now, Voyager (1942). Directed by Irving Rapper, with Bette Davis, Paul Henreid, and Claude Rains.

Old Acquaintance (1943). Directed by Victor Sherman, with Bette Davis and Miriam Hopkins.

Philadelphia Story, The (1940). Directed by George Cukor, with Cary Grant, Katharine Hepburn, and James Stewart.

Queen Christina (1933). Directed by Rouben Mamoulian, with Greta Garbo and John Gilbert.

Random Harvest (1942). Directed by Mervyn LeRoy, with Ronald Colman and Greer Garson.

Rich and Famous (1981). Directed by George Cukor, with Jacqueline Bisset and Candice Bergen.

Show Boat (1936). Directed by James Whale, with Irene Dunne, Allen Jones, Helen Morgan, Charles Winninger, Hattie McDanial, and Paul Robeson.

Stagecoach (1939). Directed by John Ford, with John Wayne, Claire Trevor, and Thomas Mitchell.

Stella Dallas (1937). Directed by King Vidor, with Barbara Stanwyck and John Boles.

Woman's Face, A (1941). Directed by George Cukor, with Joan Crawford, Conrad Veidt, Melvyn Douglas.

Index

NOTE. Index prepared by Steven Affeldt and Katalin Makkai.

film (*continued*)
  relation to death, 171
  response to, 81
  uncanny power of, 58
  victimization in viewing, 69
  world of, 68
Filmer, Robert
  Patriarcha, 147
film screen
  and mother's gaze, 210 (*see also* gaze*)
  and Stella's gaze, 219
  as field of communication between women, 213–215
  Stella's walking away from, 212
  window as figure for in *Stella*, 206
Fischer, Kurt, 225n.11
Foucault, Michel
  Madness and Civilization, 48
freedom
  (woman's) turn to, 48, 70
  birth of, 141
  democratic demand for, 128
Freud, Sigmund, 20, 22, 90–91, 129
  "A Child Is Being Beaten," 113
  "Analysis Terminable and "Interminable," 111–113
  "Female Sexuality," 75
  "Preliminary Communication," 105
  "Project for a Scientific Psychology," 92
  "Rat Man" case, 105
  "The Dissolution of the Oedipus Complex," 167, 179–180
  and deferred action, 120
  and Dora case, 51–54, 103–104
  and German Idealism, 95
  and Kant, 95–97
  and narcissism, 160
  and the gift of a child, 144
  and the inherent sadistic component of erotic relationships, 133
  Beyond the Pleasure Principle, 83, 93
  Gradiva, 171
  Studies on Hysteria, 52, 103, 105, 127

The Interpretation of Dreams, 91, 94–95, 119
theory of fetishism in feminist film theory, 207
theory of human instinct, 20
friendship
  remarriage comedy's basis in, 11
  writing as a demand for, 12
Frye, Northrop, 87

Gallafent, Edward, xv
Garbo, Greta, 7, 17, 85, 106, 128, 184, 185
  capacity for radical shifts of mood, 19
  isolation registered in her temperament, 19
gaslight
  allegory of social organism, 75
  as allegory of spirit in *Gaslight*, 73–75
  as light of film, 68
Gaslight, xi, 3, 4, 6, 7, 14, 20, 30, 31, 37, 47–78, 103, 107, 123, 126, 132, 146, 168, 169, 184, 198, 209
gaze
  differences in (men's), 123–124
  film screen becoming Stella's, 219
  film's at audience, 210
  of the camera, 123–125
  search for mother's and infantalization in film viewing, 210 (*see also* film, infantalization in viewing)
  search for mothers, 215–216, 222
  Stella's, 216
gender
  issue of, 30, 98
  women in melodrama of unknown woman understood as struggling over, 30
Genesis, 5, 20, 21, 86
  Adam's discovery of language in, 28
  and *Adam's Rib*, 27–29
  and *The Awful Truth*, 24
  and *The Philadelphia Story*, 27–28